VIKING SOCIETY FOR NORTHERN RESEARCH
TEXT SERIES

GENERAL EDITORS
Peter Foote and Anthony Faulkes

VOLUME VIII

HEIMSKRINGLA
AN INTRODUCTION

BY
DIANA WHALEY

HEIMSKRINGLA
AN INTRODUCTION

BY
DIANA WHALEY

VIKING SOCIETY FOR NORTHERN RESEARCH
UNIVERSITY COLLEGE LONDON
1991

© Diana Whaley 1991

Reprinted by Short Run Press Limited, Exeter 2018

ISBN: 978-0-903521-23-9

Cover image: Chapter 15 of *Haralds saga hárfagra* in Fríssbók (Codex Frisianus), a manuscript from c. 1325 that includes *Heimskringla*. Arnamagnæan Collection, AM 45 fol., f. 10v.

CONTENTS

PREFACE	7
THE SAGAS OF *HEIMSKRINGLA* — ABBREVIATIONS AND CONVENTIONS, together with nicknames and approximate regnal dates of kings	8
INTRODUCTION. SNORRI AND *HEIMSKRINGLA* THROUGH THE CENTURIES	9
CHAPTER ONE. AUTHORSHIP	13
Snorri Sturluson as author	13
Medieval authorship	17
CHAPTER TWO. SNORRI AND THE AGE OF THE STURLUNGS	20
Sources	20
The Age of the Sturlungs	21
— Secular power in Iceland	21
— Christianity in Iceland	24
— Norwegian-Icelandic relations	26
Biographical sketch	29
Influence of Snorri's life on his writing	37
CHAPTER THREE. THE TEXT	41
The text in manuscript and print	41
— Manuscripts	41
— Editions	47
— Translations	49
Some major issues in the text	52
— The Separate and *Heimskringla* sagas of Óláfr helgi	52
— The Prologue(s)	55
— Saga-divisions, chapter-divisions, and their titles	57
CHAPTER FOUR. SOURCES AND INFLUENCES	63
Introduction	63
Individual lives of kings	66
Historical surveys	69
Other prose works known to Snorri	74
Skaldic verse	75
Oral tradition	77
Other influences	80

— Folktale	80
— Clerical writings	81
— Poetic paradigms	81
CHAPTER FIVE. STYLE AND STRUCTURE	83
Heimskringla and saga-style	83
Details of style	84
— Economy	84
— Unobtrusiveness	86
— Rhetoric	88
— Variety	89
Broader features of style	92
— The narrator	92
— Character	94
— Events	96
— Themes and opinions	99
Structure	102
— Ordering of material	102
— Formal units: chapter, saga, and saga-cycle	104
CHAPTER SIX. FROM HISTORY TO LITERATURE?	112
Introduction	112
How historically reliable?	115
— Factual accuracy	115
— Use of sources	119
— Author's standpoint	123
What kind of historical writing?	127
— Narrative	127
— Medieval historiography	128
— Saga	135
Literature?	138
Conclusion	143
FURTHER READING	144
BIBLIOGRAPHY	147
Editions and translations	147
Secondary literature	150
INDEX	160

PREFACE

This book is designed for students, scholars or interested laymen who have a keen interest in medieval Icelandic writings but not necessarily profound knowledge. My aim has been to give a fairly self-contained survey, based on previous scholarship and personal observation, of the information necessary to the understanding and appreciation of Snorri Sturluson's *Heimskringla*. The work is often regarded as the highest peak in the range of sagas about Norwegian kings, and this book will serve its purpose if it acts as a kind of base camp, a starting-point from which others can open up new routes and see the vista for themselves, for there is still a great deal to be explored and enjoyed.

Although the principal concern of the book is *Heimskringla* itself, the saga of Óláfr Haraldsson inn helgi (St Olaf), which forms the central third of the *Heimskringla* cycle, also survives in a different redaction as the *Separate Saga of Óláfr helgi* (also known as the 'Great' or 'Historical' saga), and hence that too falls within the scope of the book.

Throughout the writing of the book I have received benign and learned counsel from Professor Peter Foote and Dr Anthony Faulkes, and I thank them heartily for it. I am grateful for the interest and encouragement of friends and colleagues in the Viking Society and in the University of Newcastle upon Tyne. In particular I am pleased to express my gratitude to Mr John Frankis and Professor Jack Watt for so generously sparing time to cast fresh, and discerning, eyes over a pre-final draft. I am also indebted to Dr Lesley Johnson of Leeds University for thoughts (more subtle than those found herein) on medieval historiography. Closer to home, I would like to thank my family, especially my two sons for joyful diversions, my mother-in-law for unfailingly cheerful child-minding, and above all my husband for loving support at all times.

THE SAGAS OF *HEIMSKRINGLA*
ABBREVIATIONS AND CONVENTIONS
together with nicknames and approximate regnal dates of kings

I Prologus
- *Yng*   *Ynglinga saga*
- *Hálfdsv*   *Hálfdanar saga svarta* ('the Black')
- *Hhárf*   *Haralds saga hárfagra* ('Fine-hair', 868–931)
- *Hákgóð*   *Hákonar saga góða* ('the Good', 933–960)
- *Hgráf*   *Haralds saga gráfeldar* ('Greycloak', 961–970)
- *ÓlTrygg*   *Óláfs saga Tryggvasonar* (995–1000)

II *Ólhelg*   *Óláfs saga helga [Haraldssonar]* ('the Saint', 1015–30)

III *Mgóð*   *Magnúss saga góða* ('the Good', 1035–47)
- *HSig*   *Haralds saga Sigurðarsonar* (1046–66)
- *Ólkyrr*   *Óláfs saga kyrra* ('the Peaceful', 1067–93)
- *Mberf*   *Magnúss saga berfœtts* ('Barelegs', 1093–1103)
- *Msona*   *Magnússona saga* (1103–1130)
- *MblokHg*   *Magnúss saga blinda ok Haralds gilla* (1130–1136)
- *Hsona*   *Haraldssona saga* (1136–1161)
- *Hákherð*   *Hákonar saga herðibreiðs* ('the Broadshouldered', 1157–62)
- *MErl*   *Magnúss saga Erlingssonar* (1161–1184; saga ends 1177)

The regnal dates of Norwegian monarchs, especially the earlier ones, are disputed, and those given above are intended as no more than a rough guide.

Throughout the book, *Ólhelg* refers to the saga of Óláfr Haraldsson in *Heimskringla*. The style *Ólhelg(Hkr)* is used where confusion with the *Separate Saga of Óláfr helgi (Ólhelg(Sep))* is possible. The terms *Heimskringla* I, *Heimskringla* II and *Heimskringla* III refer to the divisions of the work, common in printed editions, whose contents are shown above.

Quotations from *Heimskringla* are taken from the edition of Bjarni Aðalbjarnarson, *Íslenzk fornrit* 26–28 (Reykjavík 1941–51). Other Old Icelandic texts are cited from the editions listed in the Bibliography but normalised according to the conventions of the *Íslenzk fornrit* series. Reference to standard texts is made by chapter, unless otherwise specified.

All translations, both from medieval texts and from modern writings in languages other than English are, unless otherwise stated, my own.

INTRODUCTION
SNORRI AND *HEIMSKRINGLA* THROUGH THE CENTURIES

THE great cycle of sixteen sagas known to posterity as *Heimskringla* 'The Circle of the World' is one of the outstanding products of medieval Iceland, and of the tradition of writings about Norwegian kings which flourished there and in Norway from the later twelfth century onwards. It is to some extent a compilation, from sources which are examined in Chapter Four, rather than an entirely new work. Yet so strong is the impression of integrity and artistry which *Heimskringla* gives that it is reasonable to speak of an author, and, for reasons explained in Chapter One, that author must be Snorri Sturluson (1178/9–1241).

Snorri was, in worldly terms, undoubtedly a great man. He was counted by his contemporaries *c.* 1200 among a handful of the most powerful laymen in Iceland, and was twice elected law-speaker or president of the Icelandic national assembly (*Alþingi* or Althing). At various times in his life he secured power and property widely throughout Iceland: around and inland from Borgarfjǫrðr in the west, in Eyjafjǫrðr and Skagafjǫrðr in the north, and in the south-west at Bersastaðir (nowadays Bessastaðir, site of the Icelandic President's residence). He became the richest man in Iceland, held lavish feasts at which many distinguished men were present, and could muster a thousand-strong show of force at the Althing. At the Norwegian court Snorri not only became a royal retainer (*hirðmaðr*) but a high-ranking one (*skutilsveinn*), and then a *lendr maðr* and possibly even a *jarl*. His poetic tributes to the rulers of Norway earned him a ship and fifteen other fine gifts which he commemorates in his *Háttatal*, vv. 28 and 95. He had the honour of meeting his death ultimately at the behest of the king of Norway, and his death is used as a chronological milestone in several sagas concerning the period. Snorri's life and its influence on his writing are examined in more detail in Chapter Two of this book.

Outstanding though Snorri was, his career in many ways typifies his age, an age which has been named from his own family, the Sturlungar. Not least, it vividly enacts the central paradox of the time. To judge from the eye-witness accounts of contemporary sagas, it was an era of brutal greed, of complex and relentless power-struggles. But it is remembered by us more as the coming-of-age of Icelandic saga-writing, in *Hallfreðar saga* and other sagas of poets, in *Orkneyinga saga* and *Færeyinga saga*, in *Sverris saga*, *Morkinskinna* and of course in the works of Snorri Sturluson himself: his great treatise on myth and poetry called *Snorra Edda* or the *Prose Edda*, the kings' sagas which are the subject of this book, and probably *Egils saga*. The contrast between political chaos and intellectual achievement might seem huge, but it is arguable that Snorri could not have shown such political and historical understanding in *Heimskringla* without the worldly experience he possessed, and it is because the political situation in thirteenth-century Iceland is a necessary background to the reading of Snorri's life and writings that a brief synopsis of it is also given in Chapter Two.

In the centuries since his death, Snorri has been remembered more as a writer than as a politician, and tributes of many kinds have been paid to him and his sagas of kings. The most direct kind is the circulation of the text in manuscript or print (discussed in Chapter Three) and its study as a work of great literary and historical interest (Chapters Five and Six). In Norway *Heimskringla* came to be regarded as a second bible, many Norwegians unaware that the author was actually an Icelander rather than a Norwegian. Around 1900 no fewer than one hundred thousand copies of *Heimskringla*, in translations into *riksmål* (*bokmål*) by Gustav Storm and into *landsmål* (*nynorsk*) by Steinar Schjøtt, were printed with support from the Norwegian government. In Iceland up to the present century *Heimskringla* inspired less fervent interest than the Sagas of Icelanders (*Íslendingasögur*), but there too it now takes its place among the greatest monuments of early Scandinavian literature.

In 1947 the two nations joined in a salute to Snorri which had been planned for 1941, the seven-hundredth anniversary of Snorri's death, but delayed by war. On 20 July fifteen thousand people, among them Crown Prince Olav of Norway and the premiers of both countries, met at Snorri's estate of Reykjaholt (now Reykholt). The many speakers on that occasion recalled what Snorri had given to Scandinavia, not only by recording its history, enriching its literature and immortalising its ancient language, but also by providing inspiration in the dark days of political oppression. When the words of Jónas Jónsson frá Hriflu rang out, 'Today two nations thank the author of *Heimskringla* for his help in their past battle for freedom,' they voiced the common opinion that the models of Nordic strength and spirit offered by Snorri's narrative had lent inspiration to the struggles for national independence fought in the nineteenth and earlier twentieth centuries, and to Scandinavian morale in the Second World War (*Snorrahátíð* 1950, 99; my translation). The celebration of Snorri's eight-hundredth birthday in 1979 was less euphoric, but it was marked by a number of publications, popular and scholarly, including the collection of essays in *Snorri: Átta Alda Minning*.

Like all great works of art, *Heimskringla* has been able to speak in different ways to different ages and peoples, rewarding their search for roots, heroes and ideologies. Although it has always belonged above all to Norway and Iceland, it provided the Swedes with a legendary history of their royal ancestors, and, at least up to the beginning of the present century, it was treasured by Danish, German and English scholars as a monument to a kind of pan-Scandinavian or even pan-Germanic heroic age. But the appeal of *Heimskringla* is more than national or 'northern', and there is always room for a personal element in any response to it, as may be seen by comparing the attitudes of two Victorian translators of Snorri. Mrs Joseph Reed published extracts from *Óláfs saga Tryggvasonar* so that:

> the rising generation may be made more sensible of the great blessings they enjoy, living as they do in the full light of Christianity, surrounded by Christian institutions and friends, when they compare their condition with that of the poor, benighted, and half-savage population of England and of Norway in the tenth century of the Christian Era ([*Heimskringla*] 1865, 6).

William Morris's view was quite different, and was nicely epitomised by a reviewer of his *Heimskringla* translation in the *Times Literary Supplement* for 23 March 1906:

> In the Sagas he found men walking free, not hampered with a complex civilization, but making 'the pomp of emperors ridiculous' by their native courage, their high spirit, their honour, their lively knowledge of real things, such as horses and boats. His political theories were mostly the result of his Icelandic reading; the Sagas were the touchstone that refuted the vanity of modern life. He could not get over the difference between modern England and the open life of the Sagas, where individual men are not lost in averages and statistics (p. 97).

Finally, tribute has been paid to Snorri and his kings' sagas by creative artists of modern times who have, however indirectly, drawn inspiration from them. Grieg's vivid unfinished opera *Olav Trygvason*, his cantata *Landkjenning*, melodrama *Bergliot* and music for the drama *Sigurd*

Jorsalfar are all products of collaboration with Bjørnstjerne Bjørnson and through him ultimately with Snorri. The same is true of Elgar's once-popular cantata *Scenes from the Saga of King Olaf*, to text mainly by Longfellow. Scenes and characters from *Heimskringla* are captured in paintings, mosaics, sculptures and tapestries, and Snorri himself stands proud and serene in a statue by Gustav Vigeland. The four figures of dragon, great bird, ox and giant which appear as supporters in the armorial bearings of Iceland (adopted in 1919) are the guardian creatures or *landvættir* depicted in ch. 33 of the *Heimskringla Óláfs saga Tryggvasonar*. Writers influenced by the spirit of the kings' sagas, if not always the letter, include Ibsen and Carlyle, as well as Bjørnson and Longfellow, already mentioned. The laurels for the strangest literary compliments to Snorri, however, must be shared by the spoof edition *Heimskringlam: edidit et emendavit Sibjørnus*, Christianiae 1889, and the saga to end all sagas, *Snorro Sturlesøns sidste saga* by 'Sørensen, studiosus' ('Sjællands stiftshovedstad' 1885), which is a seventeen-page Danish romance about 'Sigrid Strangedatter Sigurd Slembes Søster' in which every single word begins with *s*. Finally, the energies of the world of the sagas, the Off-Off Broadway Theatre Movement, and the playwright's imagination are brought together in defiant creativity in Paul Foster's *!Heimskringla! or The Stoned Angels* (1969).

CHAPTER ONE
AUTHORSHIP

SNORRI STURLUSON AS AUTHOR

SNORRI Sturluson is taken throughout this book to be the author of *Heimskringla* (and of the *Separate Saga of Óláfr helgi*, discussed in Chapter Three). This attribution rests on solid, though indirect, evidence. The author is not named in any surviving vellum manuscript of these works, but it is known that Snorri compiled books and was an authority on the Norwegian kings, and most scholars would agree that it was *Heimskringla* that he wrote. The nearest thing to a contemporary reference is the report in *Íslendinga saga* ch. 79 (84) that Snorri's nephew Sturla [Sigvatsson] stayed a long time with him at Reykjaholt 'and set great store by having *sǫgubœkr* copied out from the books which Snorri had put together.' The word *sǫgubœkr* could be translated 'saga-books', 'story-books' or 'history-books', but in any case it could well refer to *Heimskringla*. Sturla's stay, according to the saga's chronology, began in summer 1230, a decade since Snorri had visited Norway and, we might surmise, conceived the idea of writing sagas of kings.

Other thirteenth- and fourteenth-century sources mention Snorri Sturluson as an authority for facts relating to Norwegian kings. He is named in narratives of the battle of Svǫlð (AD 1000; *Óláfs saga Tryggvasonar in mesta* I 263, 264, 286 and 290; *Flateyjarbók* I 481, 483 and 492-94), and in connection with the battle of Ulster in which Magnús berfœttr fell (AD 1103; *Orkneyinga saga* ch. 42, *Magnúss saga skemmri* ch. 5, *Magnúss saga lengri* ch. 10). The formulas used are *nú / svá segir Snorri Sturluson, þessi er sǫgn Snorra*, and variants. The compiler of *Flateyjarbók* also has a chapter heading *Frásagnir Snorra um brotthvarf Óláfs konungs* (I 492) and mentions the fact that Snorri bears witness to the existence of narratives (again *frásagnir*) about Óláfr Tryggvason's possible survival and adventures after the battle of Svǫlð (I 494). The authors or redactors of the works named here all certainly knew and used *Heimskringla*.

There are *other* medieval references *to* sagas of Norwegian kings, in *Orkneyinga saga* ch. 21, *Knýtlinga saga* chs 1, 21, 22 and 124, *Þórðar saga hreðu* ch. 1 and *Flateyjarbók* I 152, 217 and III 469. The precise wording of the references varies. *Í ævi Nóregskonunga* is commonest, but *í ævisǫgu / ævisǫgum / sǫgum / bók Nóregskonunga* and, in *Knýtlinga saga* ch. 22, *í sǫgu Magnúss konungs ins góða*, are also found, and although they do not name Snorri they are usually taken to mean *Heimskringla*. The events concerned span the mid-tenth century (reigns of Haraldr gráfeldr, Hákon jarl Sigurðarson and the Danish Haraldr Gormsson) to the third quarter of the twelfth century (reigns of Magnús Erlingsson and the Danish Valdimarr Knútsson).

The next references to Snorri as a historical writer appear two centuries later. The *Oddverja annáll* (sixteenth century but based on earlier materials) states *s. a.* 1241 that Snorri 'compiled the Edda and many other learned books, Icelandic sagas' (*Islandske Annaler* 1888, 481). Two sixteenth-century translators of *Heimskringla*, Laurents Hanssøn and Peder Claussøn Friis, also name Snorri as its author. Hanssøn quite explicitly labels the Prologue as *Fortalen Snorris Sturllis historiographi Noru[egiae]* and *Fortalenn Snorris Sturlesenn vdi konninge Boghen*, and Friis, working independently, referred to the work in a note as *Snore Sturlesøns gamle Norske Chrønicke* (these are quoted in *Heimskringla* 1941–51, I, vii and n. 2). Not all the authorities of this period agreed, however. Christiern Pedersen (d. 1554), when gathering materials bearing on early Danish history, used a '*norsk krønicke*' compiled from a manuscript of *Heimskringla*, Bergsbók, and a manuscript of *Fagrskinna*. He thought that this 'chronicle' was by Bishop Ísleifr or Ari the Priest. No author was named by Mattis Størssøn (d. 1569) in his translation of *Heimskringla*, nor by Arngrímur Jónsson 'the Learned' when he cited *Heimskringla*'s Prologue in his geographical and historical treatise about Iceland, the *Crymogaea* of 1609. By 1632, though, Arngrímur, writing to the antiquarian Ole Worm, was able to credit him with bringing 'our, or rather your, Snorri ... out of the deep night of oblivion' (*profunda oblivionis nocte*, Worm, ed. Jakob Benediktsson, 1948, 30). Worm was in process of publishing Friis's translation of *Heimskringla*, and this appeared under the title *Snorre Sturlesøns Norske Kongers Chronica* the following year (ed. Storm 1881). It has been argued by Jakob Benediktsson, refining earlier work by Guðbrandur Vigfússon, Gustav Storm and others, that a medieval manuscript which was not Kringla or any of its near relatives (discussed in Chapter Three below) named Snorri as author of *Heimskringla*, and that this manuscript, now lost, was the source of Hanssøn and Friis's information (1955; see also Louis-Jensen 1977, 49–51 and 192–3, and Ólafur Halldórsson 1979).

Other kinds of evidence suggest that *Heimskringla* is Snorri's work. The *Separate Saga of Óláfr helgi* and *Heimskringla* exhibit many of the same literary features as *Snorra Edda*, which is again generally agreed to be his work: epic scope, an organising and rationalising intelligence, narrative verve, and resourceful use of skaldic verse. Hence Guðbrandur Vigfússon, for instance, found it 'impossible not to be struck with the similarity of mind and conception displayed in works of such different character' (1878, I lxxvii). There is also narrative material in common, such as the story of Gefjun and Gylfi (see Clunies Ross 1978).

Further, Snorri's education and experience would have equipped him well, probably better than any of his contemporaries, for the task of producing such a work as *Heimskringla*, and his great wealth would have allowed him the luxury of procuring source-books and of delegating management of his estates to others when he desired. All of these factors are far too vague actually to prove the theory of Snorri's authorship, but they are all compatible with it.

These and other reasons have persuaded most, if not all, scholars of the past century that Snorri is the author of *Heimskringla*, and indeed the giants of *Heimskringla* scholarship have all readily accepted it, among them Bjarni Aðalbjarnarson (*Heimskringla* 1941-51, I, viii and nn. 4-6 for his opinion and references to Gustav Storm, Finnur Jónsson and Sigurður Nordal) and Hallvard Lie (1961, 299).

For some scholars, however, acceptance of Snorri's authorship was qualified. They thought *Heimskringla* was his work, but not in the form in which it now survives. Konrad Maurer disputed Snorri's authorship of the complete *Heimskringla*, believing him rather to have composed a number of individual sagas which were later assembled with others to make the whole cycle (1867, esp. 490 and 588-619). Like others at that time and since, he felt the impress of Snorri's authorship to be weakest in the final sagas of the cycle, maintaining that the four sagas following the death of Sigurðr Jórsalafari in 1130 were not the work of Snorri at all.

There are indeed points in favour of this general theory. For example, Snorri is not cited by other writers as an authority for the later reigns in the way that he is for the earlier, and the later sagas do not so clearly bear the hallmarks of his language and style. But Snorri's sources for the twelfth-century reigns were often written close to events and needed little alteration by him, so that it would have been perverse of later generations to regard him, in preference say to his source Eiríkr Oddsson (see Chapter Four: Historical Surveys), as an authority for the 1130s. Further, the 'Snorri hallmarks' do not vanish entirely in the last part of *Heimskringla* but are only gradually reduced (see Boesen 1879, 141). It may be true that some linguistic features of the later sagas, such as f. pl.

páskir replacing *páskar* 'Easter' or the relative *þar sem* replacing *þar er* in the sense 'where', are characteristic of Old Icelandic after 1240 (Widding 1976), but such features are notoriously difficult to date, and scribal interference is impossible to rule out. Moreover, the evidence of vocabulary favours the unity of *Heimskringla*. Peter Hallberg, investigating Snorri's putative authorship of *Egils saga*, made a systematic comparative study of the rare vocabulary in *Heimskringla*, *Egils saga* and four other major *Íslendinga sögur* (1962b). For this purpose he divided *Heimskringla* into 'Snorri A' (the long sagas of Óláfr Tryggvason and Óláfr Haraldsson which occupy part of *Heimskringla* I and all of *Heimskringla* II) and 'Snorri B' (the remainder of *Heimskringla*, including the last four sagas which are under discussion here). Hallberg's figures for *Heimskringla* as a whole and for *Egils saga* show an affinity between the two which is strikingly closer than that between *Heimskringla* and any of the other *Íslendinga sögur*, and this supports the case for Snorri's authorship of *Egils saga*. But incidentally the figures also show a very strong affinity between 'Snorri A' and 'Snorri B', which supports the case for Snorri's authorship of the whole of *Heimskringla*. Moreover, an examination of Hallberg's data for 'Snorri B' shows a very close match between the last four *Heimskringla* sagas and the rest of 'Snorri B'. In all, therefore, it seems reasonable to see the closing sagas of *Heimskringla* as being Snorri's work, albeit less thoroughly worked over by him.

Konrad Maurer was working at the same time as Guðbrandur Vigfússon and to some extent in consultation with him. Guðbrandur thought that the *Heimskringla* sagas as preserved in the Kringla manuscript were a mutilated version of fuller originals whose nature is better represented by compilations such as *Óláfs saga Tryggvasonar in mesta* and *Hulda-Hrokkinskinna* (see Chapter Three: Manuscripts, below). Only *Óláfs saga helga*, he maintained, had escaped the hand of an abridger whose hallmarks were omission of some of the best episodes, 'clumsy arrangement' and diction which was 'poor and meagre beside the rich full style of the rightful text'. He suggested that Icelanders working in Norway and to a Norwegian commission in the 1260s were the likely makers of such an abridgement (1878, I lxxxii–lxxxvii).

The most recent, and most iconoclastic, contribution to the authorship question came in a paper by Alan Berger in 1979, the year which was celebrated as Snorri's eight-hundredth anniversary year. Reviving and developing Guðbrandur Vigfússon's theory, Berger agrees with him that the *Heimskringla* sagas derive from the compilations and hence are much later works than usually thought. Among the important ramifications of the theory are the ideas that what Snorri wrote could have been *Fagrskinna* rather than *Heimskringla*, that 'Jöfraskinna is the *Heimskringla* manuscript closest to the original, or is the original,' and hence, 'since Jöfraskinna was written by a Norwegian, perhaps *Heimskringla* is a Norwegian work' (p. 11). If correct, the theory would profoundly rock established views not only about *Heimskringla* but also about the development of historical saga-writing and saga-style generally. However, the paper has remained unpublished and hence not generated further public debate; and it is noticeable that the remaining scholarly writings of the anniversary year of 1979 repeatedly hailed Snorri as author, beyond reasonable doubt, of *Heimskringla*.

MEDIEVAL AUTHORSHIP

Few nowadays, then, would question that Snorri, more than anyone else, is the author of *Heimskringla*. What needs further thought, though, is the nature of authorship in the Middle Ages, which was altogether less individual, more corporate than post-medieval and especially post-Romantic authorship. Two crucial ways in which this is so will be examined here. The first concerns the medieval author and those immediately around him. The opening sentence of Snorri's Prologue to *Heimskringla* contains the idiom *lét ek skrifa*, literally 'I caused to be written', and in *ÓlTrygg* 80 he uses *rita* and *rita láta* apparently interchangeably within a few lines. (He also applies the phrase *lét rita* to King Sverrir in *Hsona* 32.) These phrases suggest that Snorri's method of composing saga-works was to make use of at least one scribe, sometimes dictating to him, and sometimes instructing him to incorporate a passage from a pre-existing source, possibly with some prescribed alteration. Such a scribe would presumably be a man in holy orders, for there were several in Snorri's entourage. Collaboration between lay patrons and clergy in the production of secular vernacular literature would find plentiful parallels in Europe from the twelfth century onwards (Lönnroth 1965, 15), and the scriptorium was a perfectly normal phenomenon, especially within monasteries. Vincent of Beauvais's *Speculum Historiale*, to name just one example, has been called 'a monument of team-work', a number of friar assistants being involved in assembling and arranging the material (Smalley 1974, 179).

Other kinds of cooperation could also have a shaping influence. Ari Þorgilsson explicitly says in his *Íslendingabók* (p. 3) that he wrote the first version of the book for Bishops Þorlákr and Ketill and showed it to them and to Sæmundr the priest—Sæmundr Sigfússon 'the Learned'. Similarly, a remark in the final chapter (ch. 14) of *Yngvars saga víðfǫrla* seems to suggest that Oddr Snorrason corresponded with Jón Loptsson and Gizurr Hallsson about the writing of his (now lost) Latin life of Yngvarr. Gizurr is also said to have been consulted by Gunnlaugr Leifsson over his *Óláfs saga Tryggvasonar*—in fact he kept the draft for two years before returning it for revision (*Flateyjarbók* I 517). In the light of this and other evidence it seems likely that Snorri discussed his writing with men such as Styrmir Kárason, who was a member of his household and a trusted friend, a priest and the writer of a saga of Óláfr helgi and a version of *Landnámabók*. It is, further, known from the *Íslendinga saga* passage mentioned at the start of this chapter that Sturla Sigvatsson read and copied Snorri's 'saga-books'; and another nephew of Snorri's, Óláfr Þórðarson hvítaskáld, was probably old enough to take an active interest. Certainly the later literary distinction of Óláfr and his younger brother Sturla suggests a vigorous intellectual life within the Sturlung clan at this time.

The interests and tastes of Snorri's wider audience doubtless also helped to shape his writing, but the nature of that audience can only be surmised from the sagas themselves and from what is known of Snorri's life. The Prologue to the *Separate Saga of Óláfr helgi* intimates that the work was intended for Norwegian as well as Icelandic consumption, and we can envisage that within Iceland those most deeply interested were distinguished men who themselves had visited the Norwegian court, and perhaps especially members of the Oddaverjar, to whom Jón Loptsson had passed royal Norwegian blood (see Chapter Two: Influence of Snorri's life on his writing).

The second major characteristic of the medieval author is that he is unlikely to hold originality or personal expression as priorities. As Émile Mâle said of medieval art and literature: 'Its value lies less in conscious talent than in diffused genius. The personality of the artist does not always emerge, but countless generations of men speak through his mouth' (1925, 4). Rather, if he has a conscious view of his rôle at all, it will be as part of a communal endeavour to preserve and improve on traditional materials. In an age without copyright laws, a writer of the stature of Bede has no qualms about producing a life of St Cuthbert which is a re-casting of an existing one, and the author of *Hungrvaka* compares his work with a spoon made of horn, respectable in its raw materials but in need of further refining by himself and others (*Biskupa sögur* I 59–60). The individual text is not so much a fixed entity as a stage in a process, for in an age before printing every manuscript can be anything from a near-exact copy to a brand-new work, with all kinds of revised editions in between. Indeed brand-new works are rare, and the medieval writer's reliance on traditional materials, his blending of the rôles of scribe, editor and creative author, make it entirely appropriate to describe his activity as compilation—*saman setja* (possibly a calque on Latin *componere* 'to put together, compose'). The phrase is used of Snorri in the passage from *Íslendinga saga* above, and elsewhere of other writers such as Styrmir Kárason, Óláfr hvítaskáld and the authors of *Hungrvaka* and *Maríu saga*. The notion of compilation is twinned with that of collaborative work in a rubric which follows the Prologue to the *Separate Saga of Óláfr helgi* in the fragmentary manuscript AM 921 4to: *Þessa sǫgu hafa þeir spǫku saman setta, fyrst um Harald hinn hárfagra.* 'Wise men have compiled this saga; it begins with Haraldr hárfagri.'

To conclude, to call Snorri the author of *Heimskringla* is in my view fully justified, so long as the nature of that authorship is borne in mind. As is demonstrated elsewhere in this book, *Heimskringla* is both a unique work and a compilation of extracts, a masterpiece and a stage in a process, and in the same way Snorri has distinct attributes as an author but sometimes appears more as a compiler and editor. I would therefore dissent from Finnur Jónsson's claim that 'the work is from first to last the expression of one man's individuality' (*en mands personligheds-udtryk*, 1923, 706), but at the same time would see Snorri in a more creative rôle than Lars Lönnroth allows him in calling him 'primarily a patron of literature and the centre of a large network of scribes, informants and collectors of traditional material' (1965, 14).

CHAPTER TWO

SNORRI AND THE AGE OF THE STURLUNGS

SOURCES

BY far the most important portrayal of Snorri Sturluson and his age is found in *Íslendinga saga*, the main item in the *Sturlunga saga* collection and the work of Snorri's nephew Sturla Þórðarson (1214–84). Its narrative spans virtually all of Snorri's life and is particularly full for the last decade. Snorri also figures, more sporadically, in other sagas in the *Sturlunga* compilation, in Sturla Þórðarson's *Hákonar saga Hákonarsonar* and in sagas of contemporary Icelandic bishops, especially the various sagas of Guðmundr Arason (although these are partially dependent on *Íslendinga saga*). The Icelandic annals are useful for assigning dates to major events in Snorri's life, and further biographical scraps can be gleaned from genealogical lists, from letters and from verses, especially Snorri's own (*Skjaldedigtning*, A II 52–79, B II 60–90). The *Reykjaholtsmáldagi* 'Inventory of Reykjaholt' mentions Snorri, and the third hand in it may conceivably be his own (see Turville-Petre 1937–45 for discussion and Jónas Kristjánsson 1988, 171 for photograph).

Like any other character in a saga, Snorri is portrayed in the narrative sources through the words and actions ascribed to him, the views of other characters, and, less frequently, direct authorial statement. How far the saga-character corresponds with the historical Snorri we cannot judge. The—not especially sympathetic—picture of Snorri in *Sturlunga saga* can rarely be checked against other sources, and it is difficult to gauge how partisan the apparently even-handed narrative might actually be. Moreover, Sturla Þórðarson was only in his twenties at the time of Snorri's death in 1241, and his *Íslendinga saga* is thought to date from the 1270s. On the other hand, there is no particular reason to suspect that Sturla knowingly falsified salient facts, and indeed the sheer incoherence of his portrait of Snorri inspires trust: an author's fiction might have been tidier. The brief account of Snorri and his times which follows is undoubtedly too tidy, and the best antidote is a reading of the sources themselves.

THE AGE OF THE STURLUNGS

Secular power in Iceland

The term *Sturlungaöld* has been applied, at least since the beginning of the fifteenth century (*Sturlunga saga* 1946, II vii), to the closing decades of the Icelandic Commonwealth, leading up to Iceland's submission to Norwegian rule in 1262–4. The beginning of the age is difficult to date, and has been variously set in the middle, the last quarter, or the end of the twelfth century, or as late as c. 1220. The age is aptly named from the Sturlungar, for although Sturla Þórðarson (Hvamm- or Hvamms-Sturla, d. 1183) held only one chieftainship (*goðorð*), he was commemorated in a saga bearing his name (*Sturlu saga*), and his gifted and ambitious descendants achieved ascendancy over older chieftainly families, playing a central rôle in thirteenth-century events, as well as recording them for posterity.

The population of medieval Iceland cannot be estimated with any great confidence, but a credible guess for the thirteenth century is 70,000–80,000 (Einar Ól. Sveinsson 1953, 72), compared with an estimated third or half of a million in Norway at the same time (Helle 1974, 147). This was probably not a great increase over the close of the settlement period, around 930, and the superficial patterning of society was not much changed. Iceland was a republic, in which a relatively small number of chieftains (*goðar*) dominated a few thousand freeholding farmers who let out land to tenants on annual contracts. There were also labourers employed by others, and at the bottom of the scale were slaves (at least until the twelfth century), freedmen and the vagrant population whose gossip-mongering so well serves the plot mechanisms of the *Íslendinga sögur*.

The machinery for making and administering law in thirteenth-century Iceland had its roots in the so-called Saga Age, having been established in the constitution of 930, revised c. 962. The land was divided into four Quarters (*fjórðungar*), each of which had three *þing* or judicial assemblies, except that the northern Quarter had four. Little is known about the detailed working of the district assemblies, but it is known that three *goðar* were attached to each one, so that the northern Quarter was represented by twelve *goðar* and the other three Quarters by nine *goðar*. As a secondary, compensatory, development the three other Quarters were allocated three additional chieftainships each, bringing the total to forty-eight. The *goðorð* or chieftainship as originally constituted embraced sacral duties as well as secular authority. It was not necessarily tied to geographical areas, except that it could not straddle two Quarters, and farmers were at least nominally free to give allegiance to whichever *goði* they pleased within their own Quarter.

The *Alþingi* (Althing or national assembly) met at Þingvǫllr, now Þingvellir, each year for two weeks around midsummer. There, the *goðar* wielded their power, directly in the Court of Legislature (*lǫgrétta*) and through nominees in the judiciary, which consisted of the Quarter courts (*fjórðungsdómar*) and, from the early eleventh century, the Fifth court (*fimmtardómr*). The membership of the *lǫgrétta* was importantly modified by the addition of the bishops of Skálaholt and Hólar after the consecration of the first of them in 1056 and 1106 respectively. Its function was to pass and amend laws, elucidate existing laws and grant or deny exemptions, and, as appropriate, to elect or re-elect a lawspeaker (*lǫgsǫgumaðr*) who, in a kingless country, was the nearest approximation to a national figurehead. Part of the *lǫgsǫgumaðr*'s original brief had been to recite the laws, one third each year, although since the law had been committed to writing, beginning in 1117, this function is presumed to have changed. The *lǫgsǫgumaðr* retained his presidential rôle at the Althing and frequently advised on points of law or arbitrated in lawsuits which had reached deadlock.

Despite the apparent stability of this system, social, economic and political realities had changed by the early thirteenth century, notably in the form of a massive concentration of wealth and chieftainly authority which accelerated during Snorri's lifetime. The country came to be dominated by a handful of powerful families: the Haukdœlir and Oddaverjar in the south (jointly referred to as the Sunnlendingar); the Sturlungar in the western Quarter and parts of the northern Quarter, especially in Eyjafjǫrðr; the Ásbirningar in the rest of the northern Quarter centring on Skagafjǫrðr; the Vatnsfirðingar jostling, with waning success, for hold over the west against the Sturlungar and Ásbirningar; and the Svínfellingar more or less unchallenged in the eastern Quarter. Thus, by the end of Snorri's lifetime, power came to be shared not between forty-eight free and roughly equal *goðar* but between a small number of magnates (*hǫfðingjar*) from these great families who enjoyed ownership of multiple chieftainships, nominating puppet *goðar* and dictating policy at the Althing. As the leading chieftains acquired yet more farms, the number of freeholders decreased correspondingly. The districts dominated by the new *hǫfðingjar* were geographically more clearly defined than those of the old *goðar*, and could be very large, extending over whole Quarters and even beyond. The sons of Hvamm-

Sturla are prime examples. The family chieftaincy which Sigvatr maintained (and in 1223 passed to his son Sturla) was in Dalir in the western Quarter, between the hand-shaped peninsula of the Vestfirðir and Snæfellsnes, but the Sturlungar also cast their shadows over the northern and southern Quarters, Sigvatr establishing himself in Eyjafjǫrðr, Snorri in Borgarfjǫrðr and Álptanes, and Þórðr on Snæfellsnes.

Wealth, no less than power, accumulated steadily in the hands of the leading families. To gauge just how lucrative the possession of a *goðorð* had been in the early days of the Commonwealth is a difficult problem (addressed by Byock, 1988, especially ch. 5), but certainly the leading families now benefited greatly not merely from ancient secular dues such as thing-tax but also from ecclesiastical ones, for the churches on great estates such as Skálaholt, Oddi, Reykjaholt or Svínafell brought in considerable income in the form of gifts, tithes and other revenues.

Thus the 'super-powers' of the time, the great chieftainly families, had empires to defend, and they defended them with neurotic zeal. Family bonds, however, could be strained by rival loyalties—to friends, kinsmen-in-law or personal ambition—and individual incidents could disturb the whole mesh of taut and shifting allegiances, stirring men to intervene in events which did not immediately concern them. All this was tragically exemplified by the history of the Sturlungar and of Snorri Sturluson himself. Snorri's three main sources of support—his brothers, his foster-kin the Oddaverjar and his kinsmen-in-law—were often rocked by internal disputes and Snorri's relations with them were in constant flux throughout his life, bringing him close to many of the appalling events of the time, if not being himself directly responsible for them. His son-in-law Þorvaldr, for instance, was attacked and burned to death in 1228 while staying at the farm of a friend. The venture was led by the sons of Hrafn á Eyri but instigated by Snorri's nephew Sturla Sigvatsson (*Íslendinga saga* ch. 67 (72)). When an over-zealous revenge party led by Þorvaldr's son Þórðr broke into Sturla's home at Sauðafell he was not there, but many others were injured, including a woman who lost both breasts (ch. 71 (76)). Sturla and others thought Snorri was behind this raid (chs 72–73 (77–78)), but they won no support for an attack on him. Snorri lived to hear more evil news—of his son Órœkja mutilated at Sturla's command and Sturla himself and his father Sigvatr killed in the battle of Qrlygsstaðir, the largest ever to take place in Iceland—and to meet death from a party of attackers which included several of his kinsmen-in-law. (See further the Biographical sketch below.)

The age was vicious indeed, but it also nourished minds sophisticated and thoughtful, whose quality can be judged from an abundance of saga-writings including *Heimskringla* itself. A few other points, moreover, may put its barbarity in perspective. First, the sagas of the *Sturlunga* collection, like any journalistic reporting, highlight the shockingly memorable at the expense of the peacefully mundane. Second, our impression of the age is partly coloured by comparison with the earlier Icelandic world portrayed in the *Íslendingasögur*, where violence is also rife but appears somehow cleaner, more stylised, more ethically motivated. Third, turbulent though events in Iceland are at this time, the picture elsewhere is hardly prettier, and as a near-random illustration of this we may take the Icelandic annals for 1222 (often regarded as a likely date for the completion of Snorri's *Edda*). Here, alongside routine obits and reports of an eruption of Hekla, a comet and the sun turning red, we gain glimpses of tumult in Iceland: the killing of Tumi Sigvatsson, a fracas on Grímsey leading to the capture of Bishop Guðmundr and his departure overseas, and the castration of two priests. But in Caithness Bishop Adam is burned to death, and in retribution for this the Scottish king has fifty (or eighty) men mutilated by amputation of limbs; a battle is fought in Oslo on St Hallvard's day by the pretender king Sigurðr; and Andrés skjaldarband and Ívarr af Útvíkum raid Bjarmaland (Permia, by the White Sea; *Islandske Annaler* 1888, 63 (*Henrik Høyers annaler*) and 126 (*Annales regii*)). Still further afield, violence of a more massive and organised kind could be found. The Crusades were in abeyance, the Fifth having come to nothing in Egypt in 1220, but Ghengiz Khan completed his conquest of Afghanistan with a massacre in Herat.

Christianity in Iceland

The early days of Icelandic Christianity after the Conversion *c.* 1000 were characterised by tolerance and compromise. The *goðar*, who in pre-Christian days had fused priestly and chieftainly functions, continued to do so. They frequently took clerical training to the level of deacon or even of priest, and still in the early thirteenth century the office of lawspeaker was often filled by a cleric, so that lay and ecclesiastical interests rarely clashed. The corollary was, however, that the rights of the church were severely circumscribed. Ecclesiastical affairs were almost all arbitrated at the otherwise secular Althing, the bishops of Skálaholt and Hólar were elected by lay and clerical chieftains, then approved by the people at large, and priests had no legal immunity and were not generally celibate.

The ease and moderation of Icelandic Christianity in the eleventh and early twelfth centuries were superficial and temporary. The number of clergy grew. Páll Jónsson, bishop of Skálaholt 1195–1211, calculated that 290 priests were needed to man the 220 main churches of his diocese (*Biskupa sögur* I 136). In addition to priests, there were clerics in lesser orders. Monasteries proliferated, beginning with Þingeyrar in 1133 and followed by six more foundations, including one convent, over the next century. (Others were shortlived.) The monastic life only called a tiny minority, yet as well as suggesting alternatives to the materialism and turbulence of the world outside, it nourished much intellectual, especially literary, activity.

As the presence of the church grew, so its demands, moral and economic, became more defined, especially when external ecclesiastical authority moved from the distant Lund to the newly-created archdiocese of Niðaróss (Trondheim) in 1152–53. Soon after this, a movement initiated by Pope Gregory VII a century before to make the church more independent of secular power, law and society finally penetrated to Iceland. Þorlákr Þórhallsson, bishop of Skálaholt 1178–93, promoted this cause with zeal, insisting especially on the church's authority over its own property and revenues; and the resistance to it offered by Snorri Sturluson's foster-father Jón Loptsson, chieftain and deacon, well epitomises the old order in its struggle against the new demands of the church.

During the adulthood of Snorri Sturluson the storms over ecclesiastical autonomy centred on the person of Guðmundr Arason 'the Good', who was bishop of the northern diocese of Hólar 1203–37, a zealot and miracle-worker. (Guðmundr was a friend of Snorri Sturluson, but it is doubtful whether Snorri had much sympathy for his particular kind of religion.) The extravagant brand of Christianity offered by Guðmundr Arason doubtless helped to give definition to its opposite: a staunch scepticism of which *Sturlunga saga* gives several examples, in jibes about relics and miracles or in outright sacrilege when church buildings became theatres for bloody encounters. General disrespect for episcopal dignity came to a head in 1209 when Guðmundr, who proved less malleable than his chieftainly supporters had expected, was ejected from his see at Hólar by a massed attack. Much of his episcopate was then spent wandering the countryside, and after another attack in 1222 in which Sigvatr Sturluson and Sturla Sigvatsson led 360 men against him on the island Grímsey, the bishop was forced, not for the first time, to seek refuge and support in Norway.

The decades around 1200 saw an increasing tendency for the archdiocese of Niðaróss to intervene in Icelandic affairs. Many of the archiepiscopal messages concerned ecclesiastical or moral issues such as marital customs, the conduct of clerics, and ownership of church property, but the opposition that the Icelandic bishops met when they tried to implement directives on these matters, as well as other kinds of strife, often opened the way for the Norwegian church hierarchy to assert its authority more widely. Further, since the Norwegian church and state were closely interdependent, the authority of the church could be used by the crown to secure a foothold in Iceland. A few examples will suffice. In the 1170s violent quarrels between Icelanders and Norwegians led Eysteinn Erlendsson, archbishop of Niðaróss (1161–88), to write to the Icelanders involved, bidding them make amends for what had been done against the king and his people. One possibility mentioned is that those addressed should come to Norway to meet the king and the archbishop (*Diplomatarium Islandicum* I 223, no. 38). In 1211 Archbishop Þórir put the weight of his authority on the side of the oppressed Bishop Guðmundr by addressing a reproachful letter to magnates who included Snorri Sturluson (quoted in *Íslendinga saga* ch. 26 (31) and in the sagas of Guðmundr, *Biskupa sögur* I 571–3, II 90–92). This had a certain quietening effect, although the magnates characteristically ignored the archbishop's request that they should submit themselves to his arbitration in Norway. Again in 1232 Sigvatr Sturluson and Sturla Sigvatsson were summoned to Norway by Archbishop Sigurðr on account of their part in the Grímsey expedition of 1222 and further harrassment of Bishop Guðmundr (*Íslendinga saga* ch. 88 (93), *Biskupa sögur* I 554, II 149). This time Sturla not only sailed out to Norway, but also made a pilgrimage to Rome, where he did cruel penance for his various acts of violence. In 1238 Norwegian influence over the Icelandic church reached a new level when a combination of circumstances enabled the archbishop of Niðaróss to appoint Norwegian bishops to both Icelandic sees.

Norwegian-Icelandic relations

At the beginning of the thirteenth century it might have appeared unlikely that Icelanders would ever bow to Norwegian rule. Icelandic tradition as embodied in *Landnámabók* and sagas, including *Laxdæla* (ch. 2) and *Egils saga* (ch. 5), held that the land had been settled especially by Norwegian landowners whose independent spirit had rebelled against the efforts of King Haraldr hárfagri to extend his rule over the whole of

Norway. The republican constitution created in the new land was therefore highly prized by succeeding generations of Icelanders.

Further, bad as things were in Iceland at the time, the Norwegian (and general European) model of a centralised monarchy buttressed by the church offered no guarantee of stability. Norway throughout most of Snorri's lifetime was in a state of intermittent civil war, with clashes both between individuals and between church and state. Even the remarkable Sverrir Sigurðsson, who ruled in rivalry with Magnús Erlingsson 1177–84 and alone 1184–1202, was not unchallenged by pretenders, and it was in his reign that the 'crozier' or *baglar* movement led by Bishop Nikulás Árnason of Oslo established a rival kingdom in eastern Norway which enjoyed a more or less independent existence until 1217. Undeterred by this, and by papal censure ending in excommunication, Sverrir affirmed the divine right of kingship and the mutual obligations of church and monarchy so strongly that the ideal survived both the two years of confused succession which followed his death and the reign of the feeble Ingi Bárðarson (1204–17). In 1217 Hákon Hákonarson, aged thirteen, came to the throne with Skúli jarl Bárðarson, half-brother to Ingi, acting as regent. A princely figure, Skúli quelled a series of uprisings by vigorous military campaigns, and by 1228 had secured some stability in the realm. Meanwhile, Skúli's political rôle shrank as Hákon grew increasingly mature and determined, and relations between the two grew more tense. Skúli's attempted uprising of 1239–40 came too late and resulted in his defeat and death.

From *c.* 1228 the Norwegian state in many ways came of age. Hákon lived on until 1263, having secured the succession for his son Magnús. Building on the legacy of Sverrir, he established the principle that Norway should be ruled by a single, legitimate heir to the dynasty ordained by God and supported by the church, and ceremonially enacted the principle in his brilliant coronation at the hand of the papal legate Cardinal William of Sabina in 1247. His strong, centralised administration, headed by a largely new landed aristocracy, drained power over lawmaking and king-making away from the local assemblies (*þing*).

The relative stability of the Norwegian realm under Hákon Hákonarson must have made Norwegian overlordship a much more attractive option to the Icelanders in their worst moments of anarchy and violence. Iceland's troubles supplied a pretext for Norwegian intervention and, as seen above, ecclesiastical authority provided a convenient analogue and channel by which royal rights could be established there. Hákon, maintaining that peace would come to Iceland only by single rule (*Hákonar saga Hákonarsonar* ch. 180), nurtured the ambition of bringing the Icelanders back under the control of their former homeland, and he received ecclesiastical sanction for this when Cardinal William voiced the opinion that Iceland's position outside kingly rule was anomalous (ch. 257).

Hákon's pursuit of his ambition was favoured by various circumstances, among them the bond of shared language and history between the two countries to which the kings' sagas themselves bear witness. There was also a tangible Norwegian presence in Iceland, in the picturesque person of King Hákon's falcon-catcher, but also and more importantly in quite large numbers of merchants, some of them courtiers, who wintered in Iceland as guests of such men as Snorri. Disputes over trade provided another pretext for Norwegian intervention in Iceland. In 1215 and succeeding years troubles broke out between Norwegian merchants and members of the Haukdœlir and Oddaverjar, which convinced Skúli jarl of the need to launch a military expedition to secure traditional Norwegian rights in Iceland (see p. 33 below). The Icelanders, for their part, needed the trade link as a life-line, but, lacking adequate shipbuilding resources, depended on the Norwegians to maintain it. In particular, they needed imported goods—not just fine cloth, ale or wine, but also basics such as grain (especially when poor weather or strife threatened the always marginal Icelandic harvests), timber, tar and wax. They also needed outlets for their own sheepskins, hides and homespun cloth.

Whatever the general factors which propelled Iceland towards resigning its independence, a particular impetus was given by the machinations of individuals who saw royal support as a means of promoting their own interests and thwarting their rivals. In larger numbers than previously, distinguished Icelanders in the early thirteenth century became sworn liegemen of the Norwegian king (*hirðmenn, handgengnir menn*), and this was naturally encouraged by the crown, which stood to gain influence, and later lands and *goðorð*, in Iceland. Snorri himself was prominent among those who took this traditional path to prestige, and he was manifestly attracted by the cultivated splendour of the Norwegian court and the status afforded him there. Back in Iceland he gave Norwegian-style feasts (*Íslendinga saga* ch. 60 (65)) and had his supporters drawn up in the Norwegian way (ch. 99 (104)). One summer at the Althing eighty of his following of six hundred were Norwegians (ch. 34 (39)). His attempts to secure royal favour, however, fatally misfired and in the end he sided with the wrong Norwegian faction—that of Skúli jarl—and met his death at the command of Hákon and his new favourite Gizurr Þorvaldsson. Gizurr was in 1258 created *jarl* and assigned authority over great tracts of Icelandic territory. It was he who in 1261 proposed that tribute should be paid to the crown, and in 1262–4 the Icelandic nation, region by region, pledged loyalty to Hákon.

BIOGRAPHICAL SKETCH

Snorri was born in Hvammr, western Iceland, in the late 1170s. The exact date is uncertain. The evidence of *Íslendinga saga* mainly favours 1178, but the Icelandic annals point to 1179 (see *Sturlunga saga* 1946, I 555 n. 1). Snorri's father was Sturla Þórðarson, or Hvamm-Sturla, shrewd, ambitious and eloquent; his mother was Guðný Bǫðvarsdóttir. Sturla held the *Snorrungagoðorð*, the chieftainship of the descendants of Snorri goði, the central figure of *Eyrbyggja saga*. Snorri's brothers Þórðr and Sigvatr were older, by thirteen and eight years respectively, and both became distinguished men. Þórðr turned out a devout, benevolent, self-controlled character, Sigvatr a man of fine words and ironic humour whose rationality was not hampered by religious zeal and whose often rnthless efforts were concentrated on the good of his gifted but relentlessly ambitious son Sturla. When Abbot Arngrímr, writing in the fourteenth century, said that of the sons of Hvamm-Sturla Þórðr was the best, Sigvatr the worst, and Snorri in the middle he was talking principally about their relations with Bishop Guðmundr Arason, but his words perhaps have a wider application (*Biskupa sögur* II 71–2). Two daughters of Hvamm-Sturla and Guðný are also named in genealogical lists, Helga and Vigdís, and Sturla had nine other children by his first wife Ingibjǫrg and other women.

From the age of two or three Snorri was fostered at Oddi in southern Iceland (*Sturlu saga* ch. 34, *Íslendinga saga* ch. 1), which was a great centre of learning and of ecclesiastical and secular prestige. His foster-father was Jón Loptsson (d. 1197), who was a deacon—the rank of holy orders next below priest—and the greatest chieftain of his day. In 1199, by the arrangement of his foster-brother Sæmundr and brother Þórðr, Snorri married Herdís, daughter of Bersi inn auðgi 'the Wealthy'. Bersi was priest at Borg, and is thought to have held the *goðorð* of the Mýramenn (Nordal 1920, 13). His nickname refers to riches amounting to eight hundred hundreds (a hundred being roughly equivalent to the value of a cow). The *Snorrungagoðorð* was held at this time by Snorri's brother Sigvatr, and most of Snorri's own inheritance of forty hundreds had been used up by his mother Guðný. She did, however, give him Hvammr as part of his marriage settlement (*Íslendinga saga* ch. 10). Two or three years later Snorri inherited his father-in-law's estate (ch. 15 (20)), from which he was able to extend his power more widely in Borgarfjǫrðr. Soon afterwards he was given a half share in the nearby *Lundarmannagoðorð* by his uncle Þórðr Bǫðvarsson í Gǫrðum, who regretted his decision when he discovered how high-handed Snorri could be (ch. 15 (20)). About 1206 Snorri moved to Reykjaholt (*Íslendinga saga* ch. 16 (21)), again with Þórðr's help and by agreement with the priest Magnús Pálsson, who continued to live there with his wife Hallfríðr, a granddaughter of Ari 'the Learned'. Reykjaholt was the centre of a *goðorð*, and it was to be Snorri's main residence and power-base for the rest of his life. As *Íslendinga saga* ch. 16 (21) puts it, 'He then became a great chieftain, for he was not short of money.'

Herdís remained behind in Borg until her death in 1233. She had borne two children to Snorri who lived to adulthood, Hallbera and Jón murtr. Snorri also had three surviving children by other women: Órœkja, Ingibjǫrg and Þórdís (*Íslendinga saga* ch. 16 (21), *Ættartölur* ch. 2). Sturla Þórðarson, apparently referring to these offspring, describes Snorri as *fjǫllyndr*, 'inconstant' or 'loose-living' (ch. 16 (21)), although children by mistresses were not unusual among the chieftainly class in Snorri's day. Certainly, a verse fragment attributed to Snorri celebrates his appreciation of 'a woman, finest of women' *(svanni I svanna vænstr)* whom he saw letting her hair fall loose as he entered a house (*Skjaldedigtning* A II 79, B II 90, v. 7).

Not long after his move to Reykjaholt, Snorri gained a foothold in the northern Quarter when he was given a share in the *Eyvellingagoðorð* in Húnavatnsþing by Þorsteinn Ívarsson (*Íslendinga saga* ch. 18 (23)), and his involvement with northern affairs deepened when he joined the armed force which in 1209 removed Guðmundr Arason from his episcopal seat at Hólar. It seems that he did so in support of his brother Sigvatr, a firm enemy of Guðmundr, but by mediating with the bishop he helped prevent events taking a nastier turn than they did, and he took him home to Reykjaholt with him and gave him honourable hospitality for the winter (*Biskupa sögur* II 74 and 76; *Íslendinga saga* ch. 24 (29)). Snorri may also have extended his influence into Skagafjǫrðr, also in the north, by having a *goðorð* entrusted to him by Arnórr Tumason when he went abroad (*Íslendinga saga* ch. 74 (79), though cf. chs 29 (34) and 40 (45)). Added to all of this, Snorri's abilities, in particular his legal knowledge, gained national recognition when he was chosen as law-speaker (lǫgsǫgumaðr) at the Althing for the term 1215–18, and he held the post again in 1222–31 (or longer; he is said to hold the lǫgsǫgn in Íslendinga saga ch. 90 (95), i.e. in 1233).

Snorri's hold on his far-flung empire of farmsteads was somewhat tenuous. His ambition was huge but, because of his own temperament and the times in which he lived, he was often forced onto the defensive. In the pages of Íslendinga saga we find him building fortifications at Víðimýrr (ch. 74(79)), galloping away in fright from a party of peacemakers at Hítará (ch. 109 (114)), and frequently sending out spies and assassins. Rather than acting directly he is more often seen mediating, equivocating, shifting allegiances, inciting others or deploying his legal expertise to his own ends.

Snorri's activities as chieftain were many and complex, and here only a few incidents will be mentioned to illustrate the traits mentioned above. During his days at Borg in the early 1200s, Snorri attempted to worst Orcadian merchants who were his guests, and when this provoked them to kill one of his household, Snorri chose to egg his brothers against them, and to send assassins, rather than striking himself. Even so he failed to get his revenge (Íslendinga saga ch. 15 (20)). Malice again turned to violence c. 1214 at Melr in the northern Quarter between men of Víðidalr and Miðfjǫrðr. Many of them were nominally Snorri's þingmenn, but his attempts to assert his authority and stop them coming to blows were unheeded, and one Þorljótr frá Bretalœk had to part them by driving horses between them (ch. 33 (38)). Snorri did, however, subsequently manage to arbitrate between the parties by legal means.

Shortly afterwards, during Snorri's first term as lǫgsǫgumaðr (c. 1216), he became involved in a dispute with Magnús allsherjargoði, grandson of Jón Loptsson, which grew out of a brawl between their henchmen. Snorri fabricated a charge against Magnús, manoeuvring him out of an inheritance on a technicality and securing his outlawry. Sturla Þórðarson comments that Snorri's prestige was greatly enhanced by this and other cases (Íslendinga saga ch. 34 (39)).

The more personal and everyday side of Snorri's life is harder to reconstruct, despite his prominence in Sturlunga saga. There is no description of his appearance, next to no direct quotation of his words, and little mention of his daily life as manager of his estates and as a private individual, aside from scraps of information such as that he lost a hundred (i.e. 120) cattle at Svignaskarð in the dire 'Sand-Winter' which followed the volcanic eruption off Reykjanes in 1226 (Íslendinga saga ch. 60 (65)), or that during the Althing one year he suffered from the skin disease erysipelas (ch. 75 (80)). The nearest that Sturla Þórðarson comes to a general portrait of his uncle is his comment that he was a practical man, skilled in all he turned his hand to and a giver of sound advice to others (ch. 34 (39)). Snorri sent greetings in a *lausavísa* to a cherished friend Eyjólfr (*Skjaldedigtning* A II 79, B II 90, v. 6), and we know from elsewhere that he showed friendship to many, most notably perhaps to Bishop Guðmundr Arason. The *Prestssaga Guðmundar góða* ch. 18 shows Guðmundr present at Snorri's wedding; see also *Íslendinga saga* chs 81 and 98 and, for other friendships, chs 51, 52 and 69. At various times Snorri's household included the poet Sturla Bárðarson and the saga-writer Styrmir Kárason, two men, Tafl-Bergr and Dansa-Bergr, whose nicknames suggest expertise in chess and dancing, and a man called Jón who was considered the strongest in Iceland. A German called Herburt, who was very accomplished with his shield, is named among Snorri's supporters at the Althing one summer (ch. 34), and a Norwegian named Sigurðr was sufficiently attached to his master Snorri to welcome a chance to avenge his slaying (*Þórðar saga kakala* ch. 16 (179)).

There is little direct evidence about the nature or depth of Snorri's religious commitment. *Íslendinga saga* ch. 52 (57) seems to suggest that Snorri contributed to the endowment of the monastery at Viðey. We also know from the *Reykjaholtsmáldagi* that he made gifts to the church at Reykjaholt: a reliquary jointly with the priest Magnús and bells jointly with his partner Hallveig. On one occasion he is said to have been reluctant to attack his brother Sigvatr during a holy season (probably Lent, *Íslendinga saga* ch. 112 (117)).

Having paused to review some general features of Snorri's life, public and private, we resume the chronological account with his visit to mainland Scandinavia in 1218–20 (*Íslendinga saga* ch. 35 (40)). Snorri had begun to cultivate the ruling powers of Norway long before, sending panegyrics to King Sverrir, the young King Ingi Bárðarson, and Hákon jarl galinn, half-brother and regent to Ingi, but all three had died (respectively in 1202, 1217 and 1214) before he could visit them, and the poem for Sverrir may have been a memorial lay (so Nordal 1920, 73). Hákon's gifts to Snorri in reward for his poem—a sword, shield and corselet—are commemorated in a verse by the skald Máni (*Skjaldedigtning* A I 539, B I 520, v. 4, quoted *Íslendinga saga* ch. 34 (39)).

The two winters were spent with Skúli jarl Bárðarson, regent to King Hákon Hákonarson, presumably in Tønsberg, Trondheim and Bergen (*Hákonar saga Hákonarsonar* chs 55, 56, 59), and in the intervening summer of 1219 Snorri went farther south-east to 'Gautland' (Västergötland, Sweden). There he visited Frú Kristín Nikulássdóttir, widow of Hákon jarl galinn and now wife of the Swedish lawman Áskell or Æskil. He had sent a praise-poem, *Andvaka* 'Wakefulness', to her some time before. She received him with great honour and sent him away with gifts including a standard which had belonged to King Eiríkr Knútsson of Sweden (*Íslendinga saga* ch. 35 (40)).

On his return to Norway, Snorri was granted the title of *skutilsveinn*, literally 'plate-boy' but actually a high-ranking office in the court, by Skúli jarl and King Hákon (*Íslendinga saga* ch. 38(43)), and then of *lendr maðr* 'landed man' or 'baron'. Snorri was the first Icelander so honoured. He also received a ship and fifteen other gifts, apparently as a reward for his poetic flattery of Skúli (so *Háttatal* 95 and *Íslendinga saga* ch. 38 (43)). Before leaving for Iceland Snorri took a leading part in deflecting Skúli from his intention to harry Iceland because of a bitter dispute which had arisen between Icelanders (Snorri's foster-kindred the Oddaverjar) and Norwegian merchants. Snorri promised to work, with his brothers, for Icelandic submission to Norwegian rule, but after he arrived home in the summer of 1220 he made little progress, and apparently little effort, in this direction. This may have been partly because of strife between the Oddaverjar (especially Loptr, son of Bishop Páll) and the Haukdœlir (especially Bjǫrn Þorvaldsson), into which Snorri was drawn (ch. 39 (44)), but also because of the mistrust and even scorn which greeted his dealings with the Norwegian crown and his showy return home. However, he did keep his promise to send his son Jón murtr to Norway as a hostage, and secured the safety of Norwegian merchants in Iceland for some time. (For this whole matter, see *Hákonar saga Hákonarsonar* ch. 59 and *Íslendinga saga* chs 38 (43) and 41 (46).)

The 1220s were a time of success and relative peace for Snorri. It was probably in the early part of the decade that he produced his great treatise on myth and poetry, the so-called *Snorra Edda*, and for the rest of the decade the *Separate Saga of Óláfr helgi* and *Heimskringla* must have been his main literary preoccupations.

It was at this time that Snorri made a second union (probably not technically a marriage), which was to be more successful, personally and financially, than his first, although it began strangely, to judge from Sturla Þórðarson's rather sneering report. In Snorri's circle of acquaintance were the two sisters Hallveig and Solveig, daughters of Ormr Jónsson and granddaughters of Jón Loptsson. Snorri, we learn, took great pleasure in Solveig's conversation, and manipulated a division of property with her brothers in her favour (*Íslendinga saga* ch. 49 (54)). He was much put out when she married Sturla Sigvatsson (ch. 50 (55)). Hallveig he thought ridiculous when he saw her riding with her capeflaps sewn over her head like a hat (ch. 49 (54)). Nevertheless, he formed a partnership with her which lasted from 1224 until her death in 1241, which he mourned deeply (chs 53 (58) and 149 (153)). Hallveig was the widow of Snorri's old enemy Bjǫrn Þorvaldsson. Already the richest woman in Iceland (ch. 49 (54)), she had recently inherited Kolskeggr auðgi's fortune (ch. 52 (57)), and she brought Snorri a fortune of eight hundred hundreds, technically held in custody for her young sons Klœngr and Ormr, and territory in and around Fljótshlíð. Snorri's brother Þórðr felt foreboding at this situation (ch. 53 (58)). As he saw, Snorri's desire for peace and harmony, fulsomely voiced on occasion, could all too easily come into collision with his greed for power and property and with the ill-will of others.

Snorri and Hallveig had no children who survived to adulthood, though, as already seen, he had two by his first wife Herdís and others by other women. Sturla Þórðarson's account shows Snorri displaying the same kind of meanness towards his own children as to his stepsons and kinsmen-in-law. He denied his son Jón the marriage-portion of Stafaholt which he requested, offering a poorer alternative. He relented too late to stop Jón sailing to Norway, where he subsequently died from wounds sustained in a scuffle (*Íslendinga saga* chs 75 (80) and 79 (84)). Later Snorri resisted the same request from his illegitimate son Órœkja (ch. 90 (95)).

Also in the 1220s Snorri made various, seemingly astute, alliances by marrying his daughters to distinguished members of chieftainly families: Þórdís to Þorvaldr Vatnsfirðingr Snorrason in settlement of a dispute (*Íslendinga saga* ch. 51 (56)), Ingibjǫrg to Gizurr Þorvaldsson of the Haukdœlir (ch. 53 (58) and *Guðmundar saga* 1983, ch. 100), and Hallbera, her first marriage to Árni Magnússon óreiða having failed, to Kolbeinn ungi Arnórsson of the Ásbirningar (ch. 63 and *Guðmundar saga* ch. 96). Reinforced by these alliances, Snorri's empire seemed secure, yet even at the time there were doubts about its stability, which were voiced during a *mannjafnaðr* (conversation about the merits of different men) which took place when Snorri was sitting in his bath (the now famous and well-restored Snorralaug, an outdoor pool fed by geothermal water). One of the men present remarked that Snorri was unequalled among chieftains because of his connexions by marriage.

Snorri conceded their importance, but his bodyguard Sturla Bárðarson uttered a four-line verse comparing Snorri's endowment of kinsmen-in-law with those of the legendary Danish king Hrólfr kraki (*Hleiðrar stillir* 'prince of Lejre', emended from *leiðar stillir, Skjaldedigtning* A II 45, B II 54, v. 3, and *Íslendinga saga* ch. 64 (69)). The comparison is a dark one, for Hrólfr met his death at the hands of a brother-in-law, Hjǫrvarðr, and the whole verse, with its intercalated *ójafnaðr gefsk jafnan illa* 'injustice always turns out badly', was—if genuine—pointedly prophetic. Snorri was to provoke enmity in his kinsmen-in-law and meet his death only yards from the scene of the conversation. Snorri's brother Þórðr also felt foreboding when Snorri turned away from Sigvatr and Sturla and took up with Kolbeinn (*Íslendinga saga* ch. 87 (92)).

Relations between the Sturlung brothers Þórðr, Sigvatr and Snorri, and their sons, had always been precarious, but were particularly unwholesome about this time. From the mid-1220s Snorri, seemingly ever more invincible because of his powerful allies, joined with his brother Þórðr in moves to oust their nephew Sturla Sigvatsson from the *Snorrungagoðorð* (*Íslendinga saga* chs 52 (57) and 56–57 (61–62)). At the Þórsnessþing in 1227 the *goðorð* was shared out, two thirds to Snorri's son Jón murtr and one third to Þórðr (ch. 61 (66)). Sturla responded by leading a party of men to Þórðr's farmstead at Hvammr and inflicting some token wounds on his men, though not on Þórðr himself (ch. 61 (66)). There were some periods of remission, but in 1235 a clash of interests in the Vestfirðir between the younger men came to a head when Órœkja Snorrason raided lands around Vatnsfjǫrðr controlled by Sturla Sigvatsson, and the following year Sturla came into Borgarfjǫrðr with a thousand men, attacked Órœkja and took over Snorri's farmstead at Reykjaholt. Snorri had retreated south to Bersastaðir. Sturla's orders to blind and castrate Órœkja were only partly fulfilled, and Órœkja fled to Norway (chs 113–15 (118–20)).

Meanwhile, the strength Snorri had obtained through his daughters' marriages proved, as prophesied, to be short-lived. Hallbera's second marriage, to Kolbeinn ungi, lasted officially until her death in 1231 (*Íslendinga saga* ch. 81 (86)), but had actually failed before (ch. 75 (80)), as did Ingibjǫrg's to Gizurr, despite the efforts of their fathers to reconcile them (ch. 82 (87)). Þorvaldr Vatnsfirðingr was burned to death in 1228 (as noted above, p. 23). Snorri's relations with his former sons-in-law, like all his other connexions, were variable, but these men shared a general suspicion of Sturlung ambitions, and Snorri's acquisitiveness fuelled their hostility. After some wrangling with Kolbeinn ungi, Snorri successfully laid claim to a half-share in his chieftainships at the Althing of 1232. He had eight hundred men with him at the time (chs 83 (88), 86 (91), 87 (92)). Árni óreiða, the first husband of Hallbera Snorradóttir, had also been cheated of property (ch. 53 (58)); and Gizurr had his grievances, though general fear of Sturlung power was probably his strongest motive (see ch. 121 (126) on his rivalry with Sturla Sigvatsson and good relations with Snorri).

With his nephew Sturla Sigvatsson Snorri could reach no satisfactory resolution after the violent events of 1236, and his ally Þorleifr í Gǫrðum was crushed by Sturla (*Íslendinga saga* ch. 124 (129)), so the following year Snorri, with Þorleifr and others, made his second voyage to Norway (ch. 126 (131)). A rift had developed between Skúli jarl, who was planning an uprising, and the now adult King Hákon Hákonarson, although it seemed temporarily to be bridged, and Snorri sided with Skúli, staying initially with his son Pétr and then with the jarl himself. He did not seek out Hákon, and his earlier failure to promote Norwegian power in Iceland must have angered the king, who had by now passed that task to Sturla Sigvatsson. It was while Snorri was in Norway that Sigvatr Sturluson and Sturla Sigvatsson met Kolbeinn ungi and Gizurr Þorvaldsson in the massive battle of Qrlygsstaðir in Skagafjǫrðr (1238; ch. 138 (143)). The two Sturlungs were killed in the fighting, and three more of Sigvatr's sons, Þórðr krókr, Kolbeinn and Markús, were executed in the aftermath. Learning of this, Snorri prepared to sail from Niðarós and was not deterred by the king's ban on his leaving the country: *Út vil ek*, 'I am going.' It was later rumoured in Iceland that Snorri had secretly been given the title of *jarl* by Skúli, and Sturla Þórðarson quotes a phrase from Styrmir Kárason in which Snorri is referred to as *fólgsnarjarl* 'secret jarl'. There were said to have been four witnesses, including Snorri's own son Órœkja and nephew Óláfr Þórðarson, but of the four only a Norwegian, Arnfinnr Þjófsson, would vouch for the title (ch. 143 (147); see further Hallan 1972). On his return to Iceland in 1239 Snorri was entrusted with Sturla Sigvatsson's farm at Sauðafell by his widow Solveig. Snorri deputed this, as well as his share in the family *goðorð*, to Sturla Þórðarson, desiring his goodwill at this time (ch. 145 (149)).

In 1240 Gizurr Þorvaldsson received letters from Norway in which the king charged his sworn liegeman Snorri with the treasonous offence of leaving Norway in defiance of his ban, and commissioned Gizurr to bring Snorri to him or failing that to kill him (*Íslendinga saga* chs 146 (150) and 151 (155)). The next year, on the night of September 22nd,

Gizurr brought a force of seventy men to Reykjaholt. In the party was Kolbeinn ungi, who had not forgotten his loss of property to Snorri after the death of his wife Hallbera Snorradóttir, and Klœngr, Snorri's stepson and nephew of Gizurr Þorvaldsson, who had also been manoeuvred out of his inheritance, and who was later to be the main target for Órœkja's revenge (ch. 153 (158); *Þorgils saga skarða* ch. 1 (221)). Another disenchanted former son-in-law, Árni óreiða, had brought the king's message to Gizurr. At Reykjaholt, the priest Arnbjǫrn was duped into thinking that there was a chance of negotiating a peace and gave away Snorri's whereabouts. Five of Gizurr's men found Snorri in the cellar, and despite his repeated plea (or command?), *Eigi skal hǫggva*, 'Do not strike,' despatched him there (*Íslendinga saga* ch. 151 (156)).

King Hákon Hákonarson acknowledged responsibility for Snorri's death (*Þórðar saga kakala* ch. 45 (208)), but made it clear that Snorri would not have died if he had come to see him (*Hákonar saga Hákonarsonar* ch. 244). He claimed the whole of Snorri's property except for the ecclesiastical estate of Reykjaholt (*Þorgils saga skarða* ch. 10 (230)), and placed it—not without opposition—in the hands of Snorri's nephew Þórðr kakali (*Hákonar saga Hákonarsonar* ch. 257 and elsewhere). Snorri is said to have been the first Icelander whose property came under the Norwegian crown (*Oddverja annáll* s. a. 1241, *Islandske Annaler* 1888, 481, which specifies Bersastaðir and Eyvindarstaðir; there is some doubt as to whether this refers to ceding during Snorri's life or confiscation by the king after his death).

INFLUENCE OF SNORRI'S LIFE ON HIS WRITING

It is always intriguing, but hazardous, to look for parallels between the life of an author and the events he describes, and we cannot know whether Snorri at all consciously brought his own experience to bear on his study of the past. On the other hand it is evident in general terms that his upbringing and his political career equipped him well as a writer of saga-histories, and that there are specific points in his writing which are so close to his own experience that they may be more than coincidence. The more general matters are discussed first here.

The broad sweep of geographical description which opens *Heimskringla* is not an empty gesture. Snorri's intellect and experience fitted him to be truly a man of the known world. His own travels took him at least to Norway and to Västergötland in Sweden; and sometimes his references to burial mounds and other memorials of the past, including several in the Trondheim area (e.g. *ÓlTrygg* 88) and one south in Haugesund (*Hhárf* 42), sound as though they stem from personal visits. His countrymen, some of them still fired with Viking Age wanderlust, travelled to Europe, Russia, Byzantium and the Holy Land, whether as raiders, merchants, mercenaries, scholars, pilgrims or poets, and both in Iceland and mainland Scandinavia Snorri had ample opportunity to learn from these travellers. In Oddi, for instance, Jón Loptsson doubtless told tales of his grandfather Sæmundr Sigfússon's days as a student in 'Frakkland', as well as of his own exciting times in Norway (see below). Jón's son Páll stayed some time in Orkney as a guest of Haraldr jarl Maddaðarson, as well as studying in England. Gizurr Hallsson, a frequent visitor to Oddi and Skálaholt, had made a pilgrimage to Rome and wrote an account of his journey, the now lost *Flos Peregrinationis*. Several other men known to Snorri made their way to Rome to expiate their sins.

Just as Snorri's travels, conversations and reading gave him some sense of Scandinavia's place in the circle of the world, so his experience nurtured a sense of the past—an interest both in past deeds and in oral and written traditions about them. His ancestors included chieftains of the later tenth and early eleventh centuries such as Snorri goði and Guðmundr inn ríki, who figure prominently in *Eyrbyggja saga* and other *Íslendingasögur*. Another, Halldórr Snorrason, campaigned with King Haraldr Sigurðarson and brought back tales of his Mediterranean adventures to Iceland. Other ancestors were the skalds Egill Skalla-Grímsson (tenth century) and Markús Skeggjason (late eleventh to early twelfth century). The farmstead at Borg which Snorri gained by marriage also had connections with poets: not only Egill but also Gunnlaugr ormstunga and Einarr Skúlason, whose *Geisli* 'Sunbeam', declaimed in Trondheim cathedral *c.* 1153, was such a glittering contribution to the literature about Óláfr helgi.

Snorri's foster-home Oddi had once been the home of the historian Sæmundr Sigfússon inn fróði (the Learned), whose descendants by blood and by education played a central rôle in the intellectual life of medieval Iceland (see Einar Ól. Sveinsson 1937). Outstanding among these was Sæmundr's grandson Jón Loptsson, a deacon, the greatest chieftain of his day and the son of an illegitimate daughter of King Magnús berfœttr of Norway (d. 1103). Jón had been present at the coronation of Magnús Erlingsson in 1163 (or conceivably 1164, Helle 1974, 59), at which his mother's royal parentage had been acknowledged (*MErl* 21–22). Pride in his royal ancestry is neatly embodied in the anonymous *Nóregs konungatal* 'List of the Kings of Norway', a poem which serves as a reminder that Snorri must have received his grounding in genealogy and skaldic verse—both essential to his historical writing—at Oddi (on this poem see further Chapter Four, Historical surveys). Further, Oddi lies at the heart of what is now known to saga-readers as *Njáls saga* country, between the two Rang rivers, and perhaps the stories told in the region also encouraged Snorri's knowledge of and interest in the past.

Snorri presumably began to acquire his legal expertise in Oddi too, for Jón Loptsson's son Ormr was a fine lawyer, while another son, Bishop Páll of Skálaholt, was credited with a legal reform which combatted fraud in cloth-trading. The clarity of thought and power of memory which are evident in *Heimskringla*, as well as the prominence of law and justice as a theme, were doubtless encouraged by Snorri's legal studies, and it is striking that three of Snorri's contemporaries—Styrmir Kárason, Óláfr Þórðarson and Sturla Þórðarson—like him combined the rôles of law-speaker and scholar-author.

Snorri is the first of the major Icelandic prose-writers known to us by name who was not a cleric of any kind, and in its overall style—its rationalistic and non-judgmental viewpoint and almost total lack of Latinisms—*Heimskringla* is a fitting product of the Icelandic secular aristocracy of the thirteenth century.

There are also some narrative features which Snorri's kings' sagas share both with the *Íslendingasögur* and with the accounts of Snorri and his contemporaries as told in *Sturlunga saga*. Dreams, prophecies, omens, neat repartee and jokes and epigrams at the moment of death are part of the substance of life in all three kinds of saga, though their significance is difficult to assess. Doubtless we have to do with a literary shaping and polishing of a more random reality, but at the same time the real-life action in the Sturlung age could have modelled itself on patterns known from oral or written story.

The detached style of narrative which *Heimskringla* shares with other, mostly later, pieces of 'classical' saga-writing makes it difficult to draw firm conclusions about attitudes and values within the work (see further Chapter Five, Themes and opinions). However, it is hard not to see the attitude of conditional admiration towards the Norwegian monarchy in *Heimskringla* as reflecting the ambivalence of Snorri's career, in which the Norwegian court was both a glamorous magnet and a threat to Iceland's independence. In writing *Heimskringla* Snorri was providing a definitive national history not only for his Norwegian 'cousins' but also, insofar as their history was shared, for his fellow Icelanders. Yet at the same time the work insists on the separateness of Iceland and Norway. The large sections from *Færeyinga saga* and *Orkneyinga saga* which Snorri adapted for *Óláfs saga helga* are strongly preoccupied with questions of sovereignty, and the same saga uniquely contains the rousing speech by Einarr Þveræingr Eyjólfsson opposing Norwegian encroachment on Iceland, which must surely have voiced the view of many thirteenth-century Icelanders (*Ólhelg* ch. 125). Similarly, the internal affairs of Norway had the same ambivalence in Snorri's time as in many of the reigns covered in *Heimskringla*. Internal strife could be calamitous, but on the other hand, unity was often paid for by suffering tyranny and bloody suppression.

At a more detailed level, some of Snorri's own experiences chime with episodes in *Heimskringla*—whether by chance or design. His capricious treatment of his own children might be thought to be reflected in the similar behaviour of Haraldr hárfagri, and his succesful union with Hallveig, sister of Solveig, recalls Óláfr Haraldsson's with Ástríðr, after he had been disappointed in his bid to marry her lovely and intelligent sister Ingigerðr (*Ólhelg* chs 91–2). Again, Snorri has been seen as his own prototype for the Swedish law-speaker Þorgnýr (see Chapter Six, Author's standpoint).

A further kind of correspondence is between the characters in *Heimskringla* and people known to Snorri. Hákon jarl Sigurðarson, for instance, who on being ousted from Norway departs to Denmark and takes to his bed (*ÓlTrygg* 9), has been compared with Hvamm-Sturla, who used to brood in bed when in low spirits (*Sturlu saga* ch. 36), while more generally Hákon's ruthless duplicity resembles the shifting loyalties of the Sturlung age. Similarly, the career of Óláfr Haraldsson, with its dogged pursuit of a politico-religious ideal in the teeth of chieftainly opposition, has been compared with that of Bishop Guðmundr Arason (Ciklamini 1978, 41). Some of the comparisons which have been made, however, are rather far-fetched, and the convincing ones are not very numerous in a work so large. The whole subject might well repay further investigation, though it seems unlikely that Snorri would ever be shown to have written thirteenth-century history into *Heimskringla* in any systematic way.

CHAPTER THREE
THE TEXT

THE TEXT IN MANUSCRIPT AND PRINT

Manuscripts

THE manuscripts of Snorri's historical writings are, considering the expense of vellum and scribe-hours, quite abundant, whereas the survival of their antecedents, among them Ari Þorgilsson's lives of kings, the *Oldest saga of Óláfr helgi*, Oddr Snorrason's *Saga Óláfs Tryggvasonar* and *Morkinskinna*, is on the whole poor. The explanation for this may, at least in part, be that the early works were cherished less once superseded by Snorri's fuller and more sophisticated writings.

For the *Separate Saga of Óláfr helgi* the manuscripts are particularly numerous. In the edition completed by O. A. Johnsen and Jón Helgason in 1941 the main text is from Perg. 4: o nr 2, Royal Library Stockholm (henceforth Stockholm 2), and variant readings are printed from twelve manuscripts, with selective use of another ten interpolated manuscripts. Of this total, eighteen (denoted AM) are in the Arnamagnæan collection housed jointly in Copenhagen and Reykjavík, three in the Royal Library Stockholm (KBS), two in the 'Old Collection' of the Royal Library Copenhagen (GKS; one of these, Flateyjarbók, has now been transferred to Reykjavík) and one in the University Library, Copenhagen. Further, two of the catalogue numbers actually represent fragments originally belonging to several manuscripts (though conversely some groups of fragments with different shelfmarks may come from a single codex), and there are yet more manuscripts not used in the edition.

Heimskringla too was evidently quite popular, though its bulk may have discouraged very frequent copying. In Bjarni Aðalbjarnarson's edition for the *Íslenzk fornrit* series, apart from the main text from (transcripts of) Kringla, variants are printed from five major manuscripts, all of them to some extent incomplete, as well as from a handful of smaller fragments and secondary sources. Again the principal manuscripts are almost all in the Arnamagnæan collection. In the case of at least two, Fríssbók or Codex Frisianus (= AM 45 fol., henceforth F) and the original of Jöfraskinna (J), it seems that the scribe or his patron was already in possession of a copy of the *Separate Saga* and therefore omitted the saga of Óláfr helgi from *Heimskringla*. In the case of J, an abbreviated text of the *Separate Saga* was inserted later. Some other manuscripts, too, were evidently written by scribes who had access to complete or partial texts of both *Heimskringla* and the *Separate Saga*. Bergsbók (KBS Perg. fol. nr 1, henceforth Bb) contains a copy of *Óláfs saga helga* in which sixty chapters are textually close to the Kringla manuscript of *Heimskringla* while the remainder clearly belongs to the Separate redaction. The fragments AM 325 IX, 2 4to and 325 XI, 1 4to are also hybrids (see Louis-Jensen 1977, 32; Johnsen and Helgason, in their 1941 edition of the *Separate Saga*, p. 1119, regarded these as *Heimskringla* manuscripts).

Though numerous, the manuscripts of Snorri's kings' sagas were no less vulnerable than other medieval vellums to loss or damage from neglect, over-use or re-use (as bookbindings for instance), or from natural enemies such as damp, fire or shipwreck, and all of those which survive are removed from their archetype by at least one stage. Stockholm 2, the oldest manuscript of the *Separate Saga of Óláfr helgi* and the only complete one, is dated *c*. 1250–1300. (The *Registre / Indices* volume to *Ordbog over det norrøne prosasprog / A Dictionary of Old Norse Prose*, 1989, is the source for this, as for other datings in the present section.) The single surviving leaf of Kringla, from *c*. 1258–64, is the oldest remnant of any *Heimskringla* manuscript. This leaf, formerly KBS Perg. fol. nr 9, I, is now Lbs. fragm. 82 in the National Library of Iceland (see Stefán Karlsson 1976, 17–19, on its dating). Not only are the archetypes of the *Separate Saga* and *Heimskringla* lost, but also many manuscripts which must be postulated as intermediate stages between existing ones.

Copying seems to have been carried out largely or solely by Icelandic scribes, but their patrons were both Norwegians and Icelanders. Indeed, of the six main extant *Heimskringla* manuscripts only Kringla and AM 39 fol. (39) have no known early associations with Norway. The specific nature of the Norwegian connection in the remaining four is elusive. In the case of Jöfraskinna and Eirspennill (see below), for example, Bjarni Aðalbjarnarson's confident attribution to Norwegian scribes (*Heimskringla* 1941–51, III, lxxxix and xc) has given way to suggestions that these are Icelandic manuscripts produced for a Norwegian market; Fríssbók may also have been designed for export (Louis-Jensen 1977, 20–23 and references; Stefán Karlsson 1976, 7). Once written, *Heimskringla* manuscripts were preserved in Iceland, in Norway and Sweden, and in Denmark, which from the seventeenth century to the

1970s provided the main home for Icelandic manuscripts. Early Norwegian connections for the manuscripts of the *Separate Saga* are, by contrast, scarcely in evidence at all.

It is fortunate that the collection and preservation of vellums went hand in hand with copying onto paper. The thirteenth- and fourteenth-century manuscripts K, J and G (see below) were all but lost in the fire of 1728 which destroyed much of Árni Magnússon's collection in Copenhagen, and Scandinavian posterity owes much to men such as Ásgeir Jónsson who had earlier transcribed them, and to Þormóður Torfason or Torfæus, who commissioned this work (and gave a number of the manuscripts their elegant names).

The chief manuscripts of *Heimskringla* fall into two groups, usually designated the Kringla (K) and Jöfraskinna (J) groups, or, as by Louis-Jensen (1977), the x and y classes respectively. K is thought to be nearest to Snorri's original text, and is used as the main manuscript for most printed editions. Except for the one leaf mentioned above it is now only extant in the seventeenth-century paper transcripts AM 35, 36 and 63 fol., by Ásgeir Jónsson, which make up a complete text and are often collectively referred to as K, and the less careful KBS Papp. fol. nr 18 (18), mostly by Jón Eggertsson. The original vellum K must have been copied not from the archetype but from a copy of it, now lost (*x). 39 and F are also descended from *x, with an intermediate stage *x^1 in common. 39 (*c.* 1300) is considered a much closer copy of this common original than F (early fourteenth century), and is most useful for its text of the sagas from Magnús góði to Magnús blindi and Haraldr gilli. It is, however, in a very fragmentary state.

The text of the J group in general seems farther from the archetype than that of the K group. Eirspennill (E), Jöfraskinna (J) and Gullinskinna (G), together with the fragmentary AM 325 VIII, 1 4to and 325 X 4to, are the main manuscripts here. All date from the fourteenth century, mostly the early part of it, and all appear to descend from a lost *y, a manuscript which again was at least one copying away from Snorri's original. E (AM 47 fol.) is probably the best representative of this branch, but it contains little more of *Heimskringla* than the final third, the sagas of Magnús góði onwards. J is now represented by the copies J1 (AM 37 fol., incomplete), J2 (AM 38 fol.) and Sp (the copy of the Prologue and *Ynglinga saga* made by Sparfwenfelt in 1682, preserved in Uppsala University Library, Salanske Samling, R 685). The text of G only exists in AM 42 fol., a paper copy by Ásgeir Jónsson, which begins near the close of *Haralds saga Sigurðarsonar*.

The relations of the *Heimskringla* manuscripts may be summarised in the following stemma (which closely follows Bjarni Aðalbjarnarson's, *Heimskringla* 1941–51, III, xciv).

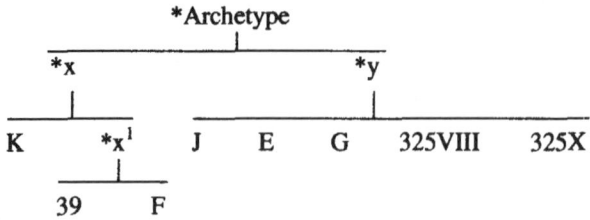

The implications of the presumed stemma are that the transcripts of K, especially those by Ásgeir, make a worthy main manuscript for *Heimskringla*, but not an infallible one, and where 39 and F have a common variant reading, especially one which finds support in manuscripts of the J group, this reading is probably nearer to Snorri's original.

Bjarni Aðalbjarnarson emphasised that the stemma can only be provisional until a new critical edition of the work is made (*Heimskringla* 1941–51, III, xciv and n. 1), and Jonna Louis-Jensen, while acknowledging the value of his work, draws attention to the limitations of a stemma which is designed to capture the manuscript relations for the work as a whole. In actuality, only K and 39 are known to have contained all three parts of *Heimskringla*, no J-group manuscript contains *Óláfs saga helga* and in that group only J itself has texts of both *Heimskringla* I and III. Accordingly, a separate study of the manuscript materials for each of the three parts would be more appropriate (1977, 36). Louis-Jensen's own immediate contribution—a substantial one—is to refine our knowledge of the relations of the J (or y) manuscripts for *Heimskringla* III. Using the evidence of the compilation *Hulda-Hrokkinskinna* and of early translations of *Heimskringla* in addition to the manuscripts shown above, she proposes a clearer and fuller model for the lost stages in the transmission (1977, 37–59).

The relations between the manuscripts of the *Separate Saga of Óláfr helgi* are complex, but Johnsen and Helgason distinguish three main classes, which they designate A, B and C. The best representatives of classes A and C are Stockholm 2 and Stockholm 4 respectively. For class B, 68 and 61 are almost the sole manuscripts, and 61 is in fact partly of the B class, partly of the C. Stockholm 2, the oldest and best manuscript, is naturally taken as the basis for their printed edition. However, one should not ignore the caution voiced by Nordal (1914, 170) that, since Stockholm 2 contains several readings apparently corrupted from the original ones, it should not be overrated as the definitive version of the saga. Where there is disagreement among the manuscripts of the *Separate Saga of Óláfr helgi*, the original reading can often be recovered by reference to the *Heimskringla* manuscripts. (For relevant stemmata, see the 1941 edition, pp. 1103 and 1112.)

Textual variation among the manuscripts, whether of *Heimskringla* or of the *Separate Saga*, is on the whole not dramatic. It consists most often of orthographic and phonological variants, synonyms, or differences in grammatical expression such as presence vs. absence of definite articles, use of pronouns vs. nouns, or present vs. past tense verbs. On the other hand, there are occasionally more substantial differences in content. For instance, the AM 325 V 4to manuscript of the *Separate Saga* lacks ch. 3 of the saga, and among the *Heimskringla* manuscripts, F lacks a part of *ÓlTrygg* 80 but instead has an interpolation from another text. More substantial interpolations are considered below. There are also differences in the wording of the text or its factual or descriptive detail, particularly in the verse quotations, and chapter divisions may vary, especially among the *Heimskringla* manuscripts (see pp. 60–62 below).

Manuscripts from the later thirteenth, fourteenth and early fifteenth centuries which contain Snorri's sagas of kings show two kinds of expansion: interpolation into Snorri's text and inclusion within the same book of other sagas, all biographical and mostly concerning Norwegian kings. Several of the manuscripts of the *Separate Saga* are lavishly interpolated with passages drawn from the work of Styrmir Kárason and others. The chief of these are AM 61 fol., Flateyjarbók (GKS 1005 fol.), Bergsbók, Tómasskinna (GKS 1008 fol.) and AM 73a fol., an eighteenth-century paper copy of the vellum Bæjarbók á Rauðasandi, which otherwise survives only as a five-leaf fragment. The details of interpolation are sufficiently different in the various manuscripts to suggest that several scribes interpolated independently, even if they knew that others had had the same idea (so Nordal 1914, 96). Several other manuscripts, basically 'pure', have been interpolated with *Rauðúlfs þáttr*.

Similarly, manuscripts of *Heimskringla* such as F and members of the J group are interpolated with material from *Morkinskinna*, much of it of the highly fabulous kind which Snorri in general avoided or rationalised. (Chapters present in J but not K are printed as an appendix in *Heims-*

kringla ed. Finnur Jónsson 1893–1901, III 493–517; see also the list in Bjarni Aðalbjarnarson's *Heimskringla* 1941–51, III, xciv n. 1.) The *Hulda-Hrokkinskinna* compilation, named from the two manuscripts which preserve it (AM 66 fol. and GKS 1010 fol. respectively) and put together some time after 1280, is a more wholehearted hybrid. Like the third part of *Heimskringla* and like *Morkinskinna* in its original state, it embraces the reigns of kings from Magnús góði to Magnús Erlingsson, *c.* 1035–1177. It incorporates much of *Heimskringla* III, especially in its coverage of the years from 1130 onwards, but fuses this with material from *Morkinskinna*.

Snorri's sagas are juxtaposed with other, complementary, saga-texts, especially in fourteenth-century codices containing *Ólhelg(Sep)*. 61 and Bb contain *Óláfs saga Tryggvasonar in mesta* (and Bb also preserves the twelfth-century poems about the two Olafs, *Rekstefja* and *Geisli*). Tómasskinna is named from the saga of St Thomas of Canterbury which it also contains, and the lost Bæjarbók included a saga of St Magnús of Orkney. Among the *Heimskringla* manuscripts, J, E and G also take Norwegian history beyond 1177 in sagas of King Sverrir and King Hákon Hákonarson inn gamli. F has the saga of Hákon but not that of Sverrir.

The grand compilation to end all others, however, is Flateyjarbók, written *c.* 1387–94 by Jón Þórðarson and Magnús Þórhallsson. As well as minor interpolations and appendages, whole sagas—*Orkneyinga saga, Færeyinga saga* and *Fóstbrœðra saga*—are inserted in instalments into the main continuum of Norwegian history as told by Snorri, as well as *þættir—Styrbjarnar þáttr, Hróa þáttr, Eymundar þáttr* and several others. Hence it has been calculated, for instance, that there are forty-eight 'detachable sub-stories' in the Flateyjarbók sagas of the two Olafs, accounting for 350 of the 550 pages of the saga of Óláfr Tryggvason and 300 of the 520 pages of the saga of Óláfr helgi (Clover 1982, 35). The compilers' zeal for completeness can even lead them to include two accounts, only slightly differing, of the same event. The sagas of Sverrir and Hákon are also included in Flateyjarbók.

This section began with brief mention of the way in which Snorri's sagas of kings superseded their predecessors. The highly derivative and compendious character of the writings after Snorri spells out the fact that the art of the *konungasögur* was virtually dead. Snorri's nephew Sturla Þórðarson wrote a life of his contemporary Hákon Hákonarson and one of Hákon's son Magnús lagabœtir, of which only a fragment survives. But as for lives of past kings, there seems to have been a sense that

Snorri's work could be supplemented (sometimes in extreme ways) but not bettered. The distance from the events was so great that presumably little would remain in the way of untapped oral tradition, and new tastes for the fabulous and exotic were being served by *fornaldarsögur*, *riddarasögur* and some *Íslendingasögur*. It is therefore not unnatural that the only literary descendant of *Heimskringla* with any claim to independence concerns not Norwegian but Danish history—*Knýtlinga saga*, which tells of Danish kings c. 940–1187 and which is credibly attributed to Snorri's nephew Óláfr Þórðarson, who could have written it some time between 1240 and 1259. Thus Snorri's contribution to Icelandic historiography, as well as being a summit and a meeting of ways, was virtually a dead end.

Editions

After the fourteenth century it seems that Snorri's kings' sagas fell into relative neglect until the mid-sixteenth century brought a new wave of humanistic scholarly activity to the Nordic countries, in which vernacular manuscripts were not only collected and transcribed but also edited and translated. The first printed text of *Heimskringla* was Johan Peringskiöld's, based mainly on the paper manuscript 18, with Swedish and Latin translation, which was published in Stockholm in 1697. It was also this edition which promoted the title *Heimskringla* for the work (see p. 57 below). Almost a century later Gerhard Schöning and Skúli Thorlacius produced an edition with Danish and Latin translation (1777–83), and still later C. R. Unger published the first Norwegian edition (1864–68).

It was not until this century that the work was published complete in Iceland, edited by Steingrímur Pálsson (Reykjavík 1944), but it is Icelanders who are to be thanked for the two current standard editions of *Heimskringla*: the indefatigable Finnur Jónsson and the painstaking Bjarni Aðalbjarnarson. Finnur's critical edition, in three volumes with a fourth devoted to interpretation of verses, appeared in 1893–1901, and its text was reproduced, without critical apparatus, in one volume in 1911. Bjarni's was published in the *Íslenzk fornrit* series in 1941–51, also in three volumes, the second of which includes chapters peculiar to the *Separate Saga of Óláfr helgi*. The texts of both editions are normalised, and, apart from slight differences in orthographic practice, they appear at first sight very similar. Bjarni for the most part preserves the chapter divisions adopted by Finnur and bases his text on the same manuscripts. There are, however, inevitably points where the two editors have made opposite decisions when choosing between variant readings or interpreting manuscript spellings. An example where a real difference of meaning between the printed texts results is in the passage about Óláfr Haraldsson's death-wound in *Ólhelg* 228. According to Finnur's text it was disputed where (*hvar*) Kálfr [Árnason] wounded Óláfr, whereas according to Bjarni's (and the Finnur Jónsson text of 1911), the dispute was as to which (*hvárr*) Kálfr [Árnason or Arnfinnsson] dealt the wound. More generally, there are important differences in editorial policy which make Bjarni's edition, albeit designed for a more general readership, the more satisfactory of the two (see e.g. Louis-Jensen 1977, 34–35). Bjarni regards the K transcripts as somewhat less sacrosanct than Finnur does, and so tends to be more willing to adopt a reading from other manuscripts, notably from F and 39, especially when supported by readings from the J group. In *Óláfs saga helga* he is more ready to go to the manuscripts of the *Separate Saga*, but on the other hand avoids Finnur Jónsson's error of treating the J text as a *Heimskringla* text for this saga. For *Heimskringla* III he sets more store than Finnur did by E and G and the *Hulda-Hrokkinskinna* text.

The two editions differ more obviously in respect of the 'extras' offered than in their basic texts. Finnur's edition satisfies scholarly needs inasmuch as it offers a full, though not exhaustive, critical apparatus, which covers orthographic and phonological variants as well as more substantive ones. Other helps to the reader, though, are rather sparse. The introduction in vol. I is concerned almost exclusively with manuscripts, and there is nothing like the detailed introductions to the sources, chronology and historicity of individual sagas which appear in Bjarni's three volumes. These also offer information on the authorship and title of *Heimskringla* (in vol. I) and on the manuscripts and later history of the text (vol. III). Again, although Finnur devotes the whole of his fourth volume to explication of the verse texts, there is virtually no explanatory comment on the prose, whereas Bjarni, writing for a wider Icelandic audience as well as for Icelandic and foreign scholars, offers many points of explanation and information. Thoughts on the ideal attributes of a future critical edition to replace Finnur Jónsson's are offered by Jonna Louis-Jensen (1977, 36–37), and plans for a new edition are outlined by Vésteinn Ólason (1988).

The *Separate Saga of Óláfr helgi* was first published in the *Fornmanna sögur* series, vols IV–V, in Copenhagen, 1829–30. It was printed from AM 61, with normalised orthography. The first edition faithful to the manuscript spellings was that of Stockholm 2 by P. A. Munch and C. R. Unger in 1853, now superseded by that of O. A. Johnsen and Jón Helgason (*Den Store Saga om Olav den Hellige*, 1941). This, as well as being the definitive text, offers a full critical apparatus—which almost invariably occupies more space than the text itself—and discussion of manuscripts. The many interpolations in texts of the saga are also printed in full.

Translations

Heimskringla was actually translated before it was edited, for Laurents Hanssøn made a Dano-Norwegian version up to *ÓlTrygg* 50 in 1550–51. This remained unpublished until edited by Storm in 1898. A summary text in Danish was produced by Mattis Størssøn and published by Jens Mortensen in Copenhagen 1594 (edited M. Sørlie 1962), and a more complete Danish translation, of the first and third parts of *Heimskringla* and the *Separate Saga of Óláfr helgi*, was made by the Norwegian Peder Claussøn Friis c. 1599 and published by Ole Worm in Copenhagen 1633 (edited G. Storm 1881). In 1670 Jón Rúgmann made the first Swedish translation (of the *Separate Saga* and *Heimskringla* III), and since then there have been many translations, of *Heimskringla* complete or its component sagas, into Scandinavian languages, German (as early as 1835–7) and into remoter languages such as Finnish, French, Czech and Russian.

There are four complete English translations of *Heimskringla*, and a brief characterisation of each one is given here, illustrated from their various renderings of the prelude to the battle of Stamford Bridge in *HSig* 87–91. The three older translations should be approached with some caution since, especially in the sagas of *Heimskringla* III, they contain passages from interpolated manuscripts which are not Snorri's work; many of them are ultimately from *Morkinskinna*.

Samuel Laing's three-volume *The Heimskringla, or, Chronicle of the Kings of Norway* (1844) was based on Schöning's edition. In general it reads quite well, although it naturally carries the stylistic stamp of its own period, and occasionally gives the impression of sticking rather nervously close to the phrasing or word-order of the original, as in 'the most able and best beloved by the king of all the lendermen' for *ágætastr ok kærstr konungi allra lendra manna, HSig* 87. Further, many of the details of the translation are slightly off-target, e.g. 'laid aside their armour' for *lǫgðu eptir brynjur sínar* (*HSig* 87), or 'without doubt is . . .'

for the suppositional *mun vera* (ch. 88). Indeed, Laing freely acknowledged that he lacked any 'considerable knowledge or great familiarity with the Icelandic' and had often had recourse to modern Scandinavian translations (the imprint of which is especially clear in the proper names of Laing's version). The translations of verses, moreover, are often far distant from their originals in both sense and metre.

Laing's translation is still readily available and, at the time of writing, still in print in the Everyman Library: *Part One, The Olaf Sagas* (in two volumes) with an introduction by Jacqueline Simpson (1964), and *Part Two, Sagas of the Norse Kings* with an introduction by Peter Foote (London 1951, further revised 1961). The revising editors were obliged to reprint Laing's text with little change except for the correction of major errors (and revision of verses in the case of the Olaf sagas), and their main contribution is their new notes and indices and their excellent introductions.

In 1893–1905 William Morris and Eiríkr Magnússon added the four-volume *The Stories of the Kings of Norway called the Round World* (*Heimskringla*) to their Saga Library, the translation being based on Unger's edition. It is in general quite accurate, but Morris was so bent on capturing what he saw as the romantic, antique aura of the original that he favoured English words which were archaic and often closely cognate with the Old Icelandic, e.g. *hight* 'called', *louted* 'bent' or *rede* 'counsel'. The same can apply to idioms, e.g. 'he let blow to land-wending' for *lét hann blása til landgǫngu* (*HSig* 87), and to word-order, e.g. (a few lines later) 'but behind, for the guarding of ships, were Olaf . . .', rendering *en eptir váru til skipagæzlu Óláfr* . . . This idiosyncratic style has a charm of its own but can be a barrier rather than an aid to understanding, especially for readers not able to translate the translation through knowledge of Old Icelandic vocabulary. The use of ornate and archaic diction comes more into its own in the verse translations, which are often both effective in their own right and reasonably true to the originals. The fourth volume of the set contains a life of Snorri and very comprehensive indices which still provide full and fascinating guides to subjects from battles to houses and from pilgrimages to drinking.

Erling Monsen's illustrated single-volume *Heimskringla or the Lives of the Norse Kings* (1932), translated with the assistance of A. H. Smith, takes a sensible middle course. Usually quite accurate, it neither follows the original too slavishly nor too loosely, and its style is neither too archaic nor over-racy. *HSig* 87 contains, for instance, 'the men left behind to watch the ships were Olav . . .' (compare Morris's rendering of the same clause, *en eptir* . . . , above) or 'the most renowned of all the landed men and dearest to the king' (compare Laing's rendering of *ágætastr* . . .). The verses are treated with the same moderation. Their vocabulary lacks the exuberance of the skalds' originals, but has the merit of not sounding forced or causing the reader undue difficulty.

The most recent translation is Lee M. Hollander's (1964), which again comprises a single, illustrated, volume. Based on Bjarni Aðalbjarnarson's *Íslenzk fornrit* text, it was saluted by one reviewer as 'a masterpiece of translation' (Janzén 1966, 155), and although not all were quite so euphoric, its generally high level of accuracy and happy choice of English idiom makes it a translation to be valued. Hollander's long interest in skaldic poetry equipped him well for the verse translations, which are a tour de force, although some may feel that by mimicking much of the style of the original Hollander has made things too difficult for the modern reader.

One translation of a single saga deserves mention since it both exemplifies a slightly different stylistic approach and makes very accessible to English readers one of the best and most enjoyable of the *Heimskringla* sagas. This is Magnus Magnusson and Hermann Pálsson's *King Harald's Saga* (Penguin Classics 1966). The readability and accuracy of this volume reflect the journalistic and scholarly skills of its authors, as well as their Icelandic origins. The vocabulary is contemporary—it will have 'you' where many translations have 'thou', 'armour' for 'byrnies' and so on—and the constructions are always idiomatic. There is a clear will to explain and interpret where necessary. Where most translations have 'thing-men's troops' or an equivalent for *þingamannalið* in *HSig* 91, this has 'the English king's company of House-carls'. In *HSig* 87, where Morris rendered *sá þeir jóreykinn* as 'saw they the horse-reek' and Hollander 'they saw the cloud of dust raised by horses', Magnus Magnusson and Hermann Pálsson explain, 'they could see the cloud of dust raised by the horses' hooves'. Sometimes this will to interpret makes the translation more flowery than necessary. In *HSig* 87 *fagra skjǫldu* and *vápnin glóuðu* are rendered 'the gleam of handsome shields' and 'their glittering weapons sparkled'. Hollander here has the more modest 'fine shields' and 'weapons shone'. Sometimes, too, the translation is rather free. The English king Harold, watching the splendid figure of his Norwegian namesake as his horse stumbles, comments that it seems more likely than not that his luck is out (*ok er vænna, at farinn sé at hamingju, HSig* 90). The Penguin translation's 'let us hope his good luck has now run out' obscures the laconic subtlety of the original. The verse translations are in tune with the prose and hence perhaps err on the prosaic side. The introduction is readable and useful.

SOME MAJOR ISSUES IN THE TEXT

At every word the reader of a printed edition, if suspicious and tireless enough, might pause to wonder whether what he is reading comes from the pen of the original author or from that of a later scribe or modern editor. The remainder of the present chapter explores some important general aspects of the text, especially with a view to estimating how closely the form of the printed editions approximates to Snorri's original conception of his kings' sagas. It is not primarily concerned with particular readings. Short of collating the manuscripts afresh, the only way to investigate these is to use the available critical editions: Finnur Jónsson's 1893–1901 edition of *Heimskringla* and the 1941 edition of the *Separate Saga*.

The Separate and Heimskringla *sagas of Óláfr helgi*

Snorri's *Separate Saga of Óláfr helgi* has a dual nature. On the one hand it is truly a separate work, independent of any cycle of sagas and distinct from the *Heimskringla* saga of Óláfr. On the other, by far the greater part of its text is so closely comparable to that of the *Heimskringla* saga that the two can be seen as redactions of the same work.

Following the Prologue, the *Separate Saga* opens with seventeen chapters, headed *Upphaf ríkis Norðmanna* (v.l. *Frá Haraldi konungi* 68), which cover in synopsis the reigns of Haraldr hárfagri and his sons and grandsons, with some reference also to the dynasties of the kings of the Upplǫnd districts and the jarls of Hlaðir, and occasionally to the kings of Denmark and Sweden. There is nothing in the *Separate Saga* which corresponds to *Heimskringla*'s account, in *Ynglinga saga*, of the legendary predecessors of Haraldr hárfagri, or to *Hálfdanar saga svarta*.

Ch. 18 is headed *Upphaf Óláfs sǫgu*, and it covers, summarily, events of the end of the tenth century: the birth of Óláfr Haraldsson to Ásta Guðbrandsdóttir; her re-marriage to Sigurðr sýr; the death of Hákon jarl Sigurðarson; and the reign of Óláfr Tryggvason and his Christianising efforts, which included standing godfather to the infant Óláfr Haraldsson. The end of the chapter is almost identical with *Ólhelg* 1 and 2 in *Heimskringla*. Ch. 19 treats of Óláfr Tryggvason's death, the succession of the jarls Eiríkr and Sveinn Hákonarsynir, and the moves of

King Sveinn of Denmark and his son Knútr to secure themselves a North Sea empire.

From ch. 20 down to about ch. 40 the text of the *Separate Saga* is recognisably akin to *Heimskringla*, but there are some significant differences. *Ólhelg(Sep)* 22, for instance, lacks the detail found in *Ólhelg(Hkr)* 10 about the battle which Óláfr and Þorkell inn hávi fought against vikings in Suðrvík (Søndervig), while on the other hand *Ólhelg(Sep)* 26 contains information about Gǫngu-Hrólfr which appears in *Heimskringla* in *Hhárf* 24, but is lacking from the corresponding point in *Ólhelg(Hkr)* (ch. 20). Occasionally there is a slight difference of detail, as when Aðalráðr of England flees to Flæmingjaland in *Ólhelg(Sep)* 23 but to Valland in *Ólhelg(Hkr)* 12; and there is some difference in ordering of material, as when *Ólhelg(Sep)* 27–31 correspond to *Ólhelg(Hkr)* 21, 24–29, 22–23.

Variations of this sort continue from ch. 40 right through the main part of the saga up to and beyond the death of Óláfr, but they become even less frequent and are usually on a trivial scale. The overwhelming impression is that the average level of textual variation is scarcely more than is usual between two manuscripts of the same work.

From the close of *Ólhelg(Sep)* 245 (which corresponds to *Ólhelg (Hkr)* 245) to *Ólhelg(Sep)* 251 (which corresponds to the last two chapters of *Ólhelg(Hkr)*, 250–51), the two works again show more divergence, although the basic coverage is still very similar.

The final section of *Ólhelg(Sep)* (chs 252–78) has two principal threads: the reigns of Óláfr helgi's descendants down to the sons of Haraldr gilli, and the posthumous miracles of Óláfr. Chs 251–65 cover the reign of his son Magnús and have much material in common with the *Heimskringla* saga of Magnús. Some of this is given relatively fully, for instance the tense scene between Magnús and Kálfr Árnason at Stiklarstaðir (*Ólhelg(Sep)* 259, cf. *Mgóð* 14) or the miraculous victory at Hlýrskógsheiðr (*Ólhelg(Sep)* 265, cf. *Mgóð* 26–28). Some events, though, are more rapidly summarised, including the ten-year-old Magnús's journey from Garðar (N.W. Russia) back to Norway (*Ólhelg(Sep)* 252, cf. *Mgóð* 1–4). The reigns following Magnús góði's are given ever more scant treatment, becoming in effect little more than a regnal list which, given in episodes, forms a chronological framework for the often quite elaborate accounts of the Olaf miracles. The end of the *Separate Saga* hence has very much the character of a series of *acta* appended to a saint's life. In *Heimskringla* these miracles are retold in virtually the same manner and same chronological sequence, but because the accounts of later reigns are so much more substantial, the miracles punctuate rather than dominate them.

The differences between the *Separate Saga* and *Heimskringla* have given rise to much scholarly rumination over the question, which came first? The prevailing opinion in the later nineteenth century, expressed for example by Munch and Unger in their 1853 edition of the *Separate Saga* (xxxi–xxxiv) and by Gustav Storm (1873, 6–7), was that the *Separate Saga* was Snorri's reworking of the *Heimskringla* saga. Finnur Jónsson in his *Heimskringla* edition (1893–1901, I xxxii–xl) also thought *Heimskringla* primary, but believed the *Separate Saga* was the work of another—not always skilful—reviser, probably after Snorri's death. Meanwhile, other scholars inclined to the view that the *Separate Saga* was the earlier version of Snorri's *Óláfs saga helga*, among them Konrad Maurer and Eiríkr Magnússon. It was Sigurður Nordal's *Om Olaf den helliges saga* (1914, 166–98), however, which presented the fullest discussion of the whole question and established it as a near-canonical truth that the *Heimskringla Óláfs saga helga* was Snorri's revision of the *Separate Saga*, and that the *Separate Saga* was conceived before any of Snorri's other kings' sagas. Some of Nordal's points could in fact be turned round and taken as proofs of the opposite, that the *Separate Saga* is derived from *Heimskringla*, but cumulatively they form a convincing case. The most persuasive appear to be the following:

1. At numerous points (fourteen are listed by Nordal, 1914, 175–83) a difference of detail between the *Separate Saga* and *Heimskringla* suggests that *Heimskringla* was revised in the light of new or fuller information. Thus, where *Ólhelg(Sep)* 11 reports vaguely that certain of the sons of Eiríkr blóðøx were said to have been present at the burning of Sigurðr Hlaðajarl, *Hgráf* 5 in *Heimskringla* offers a definite statement that Haraldr and Erlingr were there.

2. Some people or things appear, often without ceremony, in the sagas of *Heimskringla* I, only to appear again, now properly introduced and explained but without cross-reference to the earlier time, in *Ólhelg(Hkr)*. Cases in point include Þórarinn Nefjólfsson (*ÓlTrygg* 81 and *Ólhelg* 85; Nordal does not insist on the significance of this, pp. 193–94) and the settlement of Orkney (*Hhárf* 22 and 27 and *Ólhelg* 96; see Eiríkr Magnússon (*Heimskringla* 1893-1905, IV, lxxxii–lxxiv) for further examples). These are most plausibly interpreted as resulting from the fact that Snorri's *Óláfs saga helga* was first conceived as a separate work, before even *Heimskringla* I, and that the *Separate Saga* then

formed the basis for *Óláfs saga helga* in *Heimskringla*, without being perfectly revised for its new setting.

3. *Óláfs saga helga* in both its versions is set apart from the *Heimskringla* sagas of other kings by its richness of dramatic episode and narrative detail, which Sigurður Nordal epitomised in his *Snorri Sturluson* (1920) in the word *frásagnargleði* 'delight in narrative'. Snorri's approach to historical writing appears to have grown more restrained with time.

4. A final consideration is motivation. If *Heimskringla* were already in existence when the *Separate Saga* was written, it is perhaps unlikely that Snorri (or anyone else) would think it necessary to furnish the *Separate Saga* with a summary of the reigns before and after Óláfr helgi's.

The Prologue(s)

There exist three Prologues, or rather three versions of one Prologue, to Snorri's kings' sagas: one to *Heimskringla*, and alternative long and short ones to the *Separate Saga of Óláfr helgi*. They are not preserved in all manuscripts. For the *Heimskringla* Prologue, F and J2 are the main sources. If the vellum K originally contained a Prologue, it was lost before the paper copies were made, for those which contain a Prologue have it in a version apparently copied directly or indirectly from J2 (see Finnur Jónsson, *Heimskringla* 1893-1901, I 3n). Of the *Separate Saga* manuscripts which cover the beginning of the saga, three from the 'A' class (2, 73 fol. and Codex Resenianus) contain the longer Prologue, and partial texts are also found in 325 VI and the fragment AM 921 4to. Two 'C' class manuscripts (325 V 4to and Bb) have the shorter version. The 'B' class manuscripts apparently never had a Prologue (Johnsen and Helgason 1941, 1127). The medieval title, where available, is *Prologus*.

The content of the *Heimskringla* Prologue is, in summary, as follows:

1(a) The work concerns Scandinavian rulers.

(b) It rests on the narratives of well-informed (*fróðir*) men, genealogies and poems.

(c) Þjóðólfr's *Ynglingatal* and Eyvindr skáldaspillir's *Háleygjatal*.

2 In the legendary past, an age of cremation (*brunaǫld*) was followed by one of inhumation in mounds (*haugsǫld*).

3(a) The skalds of Haraldr hárfagri.

(b) Skaldic verse is an especially reliable source.

4 The historical writings of Ari Þorgilsson; his life; his informants.

5 (brief sentence only) Skaldic verse is most reliable when uncorrupted in transmission and correctly interpreted.

The longer of the two Prologues to the *Separate Saga* is substantially similar, although the ordering and weighting of the various subjects differs, as follows:

4 On Ari: virtually identical.

1(a) and (b) (On subject and sources): closely similar.

(c) On *Ynglingatal* and *Háleygjatal*: briefer, and some difference of detail, e.g. Yngvi-Freyr is called Ingunar-Freyr and the name *Ynglingar* is consequently not derived from him; *Ynglingatal* is not named.

2 On the ages of cremation and inhumation: much briefer and slightly more straightforward, e.g. memorial stones or *bautasteinar* belong only to the *haugsǫld*, not to both ages as, confusingly, in *Heimskringla*.

3(a) On Haraldr hárfagri's skalds: similar, though more emphasis on the transmission and preservation of (prose?) narratives about Haraldr between Norway and Iceland.

(b) On skaldic verse: more detailed treatment of its advantages over oral tradition in prose.

A similar statement to *Heimskringla*'s point 5 (above) is included here.

6 (not paralleled in *Heimskringla* Prologue)

(a) *Óláfs saga helga* introduced.

(b) The quantity of material about Icelanders is defended on the grounds that they brought many first-hand accounts about Óláfr to Iceland.

(c) The work is mostly based on the verses of skalds who were with Óláfr helgi.

The shorter version of the Prologue to the *Separate Saga* again contains all the remarks on Ari but thereafter is extremely brief. It mentions only that the work is based on verses by Sigvatr and Óttarr, who were with Óláfr, and on Ari and other learned men, and concludes with the same comment on skaldic verse as *Heimskringla* (point 5 above).

Various questions arise from the texts of the Prologue, particularly, is it by Snorri himself, and was the *Separate Saga* version original to the work or is it a later re-writing, by Snorri or others, of the *Heimskringla* one? There have, as usual, been disparate opinions on these matters (see Sverrir Tómasson 1988, 379–83), but they have now been resolved into a fair measure of agreement. Concerning the *Heimskringla* Prologue, most would accept Wessén's view (1928–9, 58) that it is in keeping with Snorri's spirit and style; and if the progression of ideas is jerky in places it is not much more so than in the Prologue to *Gylfaginning*. The intelligent appreciation of skaldic verse, so clear in the *Heimskringla*

Prologue, is characteristic of no one more than Snorri, and, finally, Laurents Hanssøn twice in his Dano-Norwegian translation refers to the Prologue as Snorri's (see p. 14 above).

It seems probable that the *Separate Saga*'s Prologue is not original to the work. The references to the *brunaǫld* and *haugsǫld* are relevant to *Ynglinga saga* but not to anything in the *Separate Saga*, and for the rest the *Separate Saga* Prologue reads like a revised version of the *Heimskringla* one, abbreviated where necessary and at some points improved in coherence. Whether it was Snorri himself who made the revision is difficult to establish. Wessén (1928–9, esp. 62) thought it was; Sigurður Nordal (1914, 172) and Sverrir Tómasson (1988, 383) assume that both the *Separate Saga* Prologues are the work of later redactors. The shorter version in particular seems almost certain to be the work of a later scribe.

Saga-divisions, chapter-divisions, and their titles

In modern editions of *Heimskringla* the text is printed as a Prologue and sixteen discrete sagas with titles declaring the reigns covered by them. The sagas are further divided into chapters, which in some editions have titles but in others only numbers. Some of these sagas and chapters may strike us as arbitrarily thrown together, while others may seem carefully shaped, with uniformity and continuity of subject matter and perhaps a dramatic curve of prelude, climax and resolution. What is the likelihood that the structural divisions and the headings assigned to them are part of Snorri's design?

Heimskringla as a whole. Grand though *Heimskringla*'s present-day title may be, there is no denying that it is a relatively modern invention. Ole Worm remarked in his preface to Peder Claussøn's translation (printed 1633) that people call the chronicle *Kringla Heimsens*, 'from the first two words in the book'. The fuller context is: *Kringla heimsins, sú er mannfólkit byggvir, er mjǫk vágskorin*, 'the circle of the world which is inhabited by man is much indented with bays.' It is not clear whether Worm was here thinking of the title in relation to the work itself or to the manuscript, but certainly in 1697 Peringskiöld gave the title *Heims Kringla Eller Snorre Sturlusons Nordländske Konunga Sagor* to the first printed edition, and the single-word title *Heimskringla* moved closer to established usage when used for Schöning's edition a century later.

Whether Snorri gave the work an 'official' title, and if so what it was, cannot now be known. The manuscripts give only sparse hints. Before the Prologue in Stockholm 18 and in the manuscripts representing Jöfraskinna we find the heading *Konunga sǫgur eru hér ritaðar*. Before *Yng* 1, F has the rubric *Hér hefr upp konunga bók eptir sǫgn Ara prests fróða. Ok hefr fyrst um þriðjunga skipti heimsins, en síðan frá ǫllum Nóregs konungum*, 'Here begins the book of kings according to the narrative of the priest Ari the learned. It begins with the threefold division of the world, and then [tells of] all the kings of Norway.' In other medieval Icelandic works reference is made variously to *Ævi / Ævisaga / Ævisǫgur / Sǫgur / Bók Nóregskonunga* (p. 13 above), and it is usually assumed that *Heimskringla* is meant. As Bjarni Aðalbjarnarson points out, the diversity of designations suggests that the author had not given the work a definitive title (*Heimskringla* 1941–51, I, vi), and since Snorri uses such a diversity of names to refer to the sources he used (*bók, saga, ævi* etc.), we cannot know what his preference would have been.

Finally, although the sixteenth-century translators Laurents Hanssøn and Peder Claussøn Friis recognised Snorri's authorship of *Heimskringla*, they had no fixed way of referring to the work, and some of their references contain the words *Chronica / Chrønicke* and (as a Latin genitive) *Historiographi*. However, Hanssøn more than once refers to the 'book of kings', including one context where, speaking of Fríssbók, he describes it as 'a chronicle written in the Old Norwegian (*Norske*) language which was called in olden times *Konnga Bogh*' (quoted *Heimskringla*, ed. Bjarni Aðalbjarnarson, 1941–51, I, vi n. 1).

Sagas. The division of *Heimskringla* into individual sagas as shown in the standard editions has become canonical, and probably rightly so, since on the whole it has common sense and the evidence of the best manuscripts on its side. Most of the sections now recognised as sagas are announced in the manuscripts by headings which contain the word *saga*, e.g. *Haralds saga ins hárfagra / Hér hefr upp sǫgu Óláfs konungs Tryggvasonar / Saga Óláfs konungs kyrra*, or the word *upphaf* 'beginning', e.g. *Upphaf Haralds konungs harðráða / Upphaf Magnússona*, this being the favoured style in *Heimskringla* III. The two may both occur together, as in *Upphaf sǫgu Hákonar góða*. These verbal indicators of a new and important section are often accompanied by signals in the format of the manuscripts. At the opening of *Haralds saga Sigurðarsonar*, for instance, K has a blank half-page, while 39 and F have large initials occupying 7 or 8 lines. The J2 scribe or rubricator, however, characteristically makes no special effort to alert the reader's attention, simply proceeding with the heading 'Haraldr Sigurðarson healed' (*Græddr Haraldr Sigurðarson*).

Nevertheless, the saga-divisions are not without complications. History itself was far from neat. Co-rulers and pretenders disturb the succession of reigns so that there cannot be a whole, independent saga for every ruler of Norway during the period covered. (Overlaps between reigns and sagas are further discussed in Chapter Five: Formal units.) Further, headings containing the words *Saga* and *Upphaf* also occur in the middle of what we normally regard as sagas. *Upphaf* frequently announces the entry of an important character, e.g. *Upphaf Sigurðar slembidjákns* (*MblokHg* 13) or *Upphaf Eysteins konungs Eysteinssonar* (*MErl* 36), or else the start of an important event, especially a battle. In *ÓlTrygg* 105, for instance, *Upphaf orrustu* introduces the sequence of nine chapters about the battle of Svǫlð which closes the saga. Major sections like this within the saga of a particular reign are especially noticeable in *Óláfs saga helga*. Common to both versions of *Óláfs saga helga* are *Upphaf friðgerðar sǫgu* (*Ólhelg(Sep)* 51 = *Ólhelg(Hkr)* 68) and *Upphaf Orkneyinga sagna / Jarlasaga* (*Ólhelg(Sep)* 81 = *Ólhelg(Hkr)* 96), and there are others. Both of these chapters are heralded in the main manuscript of the *Separate Saga* by ornamented green and red initials, and occasionally elsewhere headings containing *saga* or *upphaf* are highlighted in the manuscripts, as when *MErl* 9 is preceded in K by a blank half-side and the heading *Upphaf Sigurðar konungs*.

These complicating factors do not invalidate the concept of an individual saga within *Heimskringla*, but they may caution us to pause before praising or blaming the structure of any particular saga. Possibly Snorri did not intend the breaks between sagas to be as clear cut as they now appear, or possibly he would have put some of the breaks in different places.

There is nothing sacrosanct about the wording of particular saga headings, for the manuscripts do not always agree, or even always have a heading. The very short saga of Óláfr kyrri is preceded by *Saga Óláfs konungs kyrra* in the K transcripts, by *Upphaf Óláfs kyrra* in 39 and by a very large gap but no title in F. (J2 eccentrically has a chapter heading *Óláfr til konungs tekinn* five lines earlier, and no signal except a rather large capital 'O' where the other manuscripts start the new saga.) Further, the nickname *harðráði* used in the K title for the previous saga would suggest that these titles are scribal rather than authorial since Haraldr Sigurðarson is never called *harðráði* in Snorri's account of his life.

It is therefore not surprising that printed editions do not always agree about saga titles. Finnur Jónsson normally follows the wording of the Kringla transcripts (K and 18), but for the saga of Haraldr gráfeldr he adopts the (already in his day conventional) title *Sagan af Haraldi konungi gráfeld*, although the manuscripts have *Upphaf Eiríkssona* (K), *Upphaf sona Eiríks ok Gunnhildar* (F), or *Einvald Eiríks sona* (J1). Bjarni Aðalbjarnarson adopts the style *Hákonar saga góða* or *Haralds saga Sigurðarsonar* for all the saga titles in his edition, and like Finnur departs from the guidance of the manuscripts for *Haralds saga gráfeldar*. He also takes the slight liberty of replacing the manuscripts' *Upphaf Magnúss blinda* (and minor variants) with *Magnúss saga blinda ok Haralds gilla* and *Upphaf Inga konungs* (and variants) with *Haraldssona saga*. Bjarni's titles are used throughout this book simply because his edition is the most widely available.

Chapters. Divisions between chapters tend to be signalled in the manuscripts by titles and/or by small gaps and large coloured initials. In the Stockholm 2 manuscript of the *Separate Saga*, for example, there is a neat alternation of green and red initials, with only occasional departures. There is on the whole a high degree of accord among manuscripts as to where chapter divisions fall. Thus, among the *Heimskringla* manuscripts, the divisions in the main manuscript, K, are usually confirmed by the remaining manuscripts, although F and 39 tend to break up long chapters into shorter units. (This is especially noticeable in the earlier part of *Heimskringla* III.) J1 and J2 often lack divisions or are out of step with the consensus of manuscripts about where they lie.

Among the manuscripts of the *Separate Saga* there is again reasonable agreement, though some variation (see Johnsen and Helgason 1941, 853–70). The evidence of Stockholm 2 is usually confirmed elsewhere, but 325V and 325VII, 68, 4, 75a and 75c may lack a division present in it (although these also have some extra breaks within what are single chapters in 2). In some cases, especially in 321, it is difficult to tell where the chapter boundaries are.

A comparison of the sagas of Óláfr helgi in the *Separate* and *Heimskringla* redactions where the text corresponds closely (approximately *Ólhelg(Sep)* 40–245 = *Ólhelg(Hkr)* 48–245) also reveals a large measure of agreement in chapter divisions. Near the beginning of this section, however, the *Separate Saga* chapters are sometimes longer, embracing two to three equivalent chapters in *Heimskringla*, whereas later the reverse is frequently the case, with one chapter of *Heimskringla* corresponding to two in the *Separate Saga*.

In view of this evidence, then, the chapter divisions shown in printed editions do seem to rest on a solid tradition, which may go back to Snorri. In order to judge whether this holds good for particular chapters, though, it would be necessary to check either in manuscripts or in the apparatus of critical editions.

The wording of chapter headings in both *Heimskringla* and the *Separate Saga* tends to follow certain stereotyped formulas, which are rather reminiscent of newspaper headlines. The two commonest in *Heimskringla* are the following (examples from *Óláfs saga Tryggvasonar* and based on Finnur Jónsson's edition, which in turn draws its headings mainly from Stockholm 18):

(a) Common noun + name/noun referring to a person in the genitive, e.g. *ferð Ástríðar* 'Ástríðr's journey' (ch. 3), *seiðmanna brenna* 'the burning of the sorcerers' (ch. 62). This accounts for over two-fifths of the total in *Heimskringla*.

(b) *Frá* + name/noun referring to a person in the dative, e.g. *frá Gunnhildarsonum* (ch. 2). Or, much less frequently, *frá* + some other noun phrase, e.g. *Frá íþróttum Óláfs konungs* (ch. 85). Very occasionally, *af/um* is used instead of *frá*. This accounts for about one third of the *Heimskringla* chapters.

The treatment of chapter titles in manuscripts is often erratic. F, for example, frequently lacks titles altogether, and of those present many are of unlikely lengths, suggesting that, in line with common medieval practice, they were concocted by a scribe or rubricator in order to fill a space left for them in the manuscripts. There is also often marked disagreement between scribes about the main import of particular chapters. To give a single example, the following headings are given to *Hákgóð* 18: *Blótveizla á Mærinni* (18, written *mori*), *Hákon kastaði kristni* (J1), *Frá blótum Innþrænda* (F), *Neyddr Hákon konungr til blóta* (39); there is no title in K.

The same formulas for chapter headings are represented in manuscripts of the *Separate Saga* as in *Heimskringla* manuscripts, though (judged by Stockholm 2) preferences differ, pattern (b) being clearly the most popular. There is considerable variation over chapter headings among the *Separate Saga* manuscripts (see Johnsen and Helgason's 1941 edition, 853–70), and between those and the *Heimskringla* manuscripts. In fact the total amount of variation is such that one can certainly agree with Bjarni Aðalbjarnarson that not all the chapter headings can descend from the same root (*Heimskringla* 1941–51, III, xcii).

Nevertheless, there is reason to think that some of the titles may be very ancient, perhaps even stemming from Snorri himself. For the titles to the chapters of *Heimskringla* the most consistent source is 18, a transcript of K, and it is from there that almost all of Finnur Jónsson's chapter titles, their spelling normalised by the editor, are taken. Ásgeir Jónsson's transcripts of K contain next to no chapter titles, but it is still likely that the titles preserved in 18 were original to K, since when Árni Magnússon used K to correct Ásgeir's transcription of *Ynglínga saga* in AM 35, he added chapter titles, and these usually confirm those of 18. (Although Bjarni Aðalbjarnarson does not print chapter titles in his edition, he thinks the titles in 18 are assuredly derived from K (*Heimskringla* 1941–51, III, xcii).)

CHAPTER FOUR
SOURCES AND INFLUENCES

INTRODUCTION

UNTIL recently, the great majority of *Heimskringla* scholarship took a literary-historical approach, aiming to discover Snorri's sources, acknowledged or unacknowledged, extant or lost, and to characterise his particular use of them.

There are various difficulties in the way of doing this accurately. First, some presumed sources have not survived, and those which do (e.g. *Morkinskinna* or *Orkneyinga saga*) are now extant in rather different redactions from the ones known to Snorri, so that it may not be possible to pinpoint exactly what Snorri's own changes are. Second, even when a complete episode in *Heimskringla* lacks a known source, it is difficult to gauge exactly how far Snorri is recasting traditions, and how far inventing out of nothing. A case in point is the famous *landvættir* episode (*ÓlTrygg* 33), in which a sorcerer sent by Haraldr Gormsson of Denmark to avenge the poetic insults (*níð*) of the Icelanders approaches their shores in the shape of a whale but is driven away by the monstrous protectors of the land. All are agreed that, except for the germ of the story—the Icelanders' *níð*—which is found in *Jómsvíkinga saga*, the episode is found nowhere in earlier works; but there have been many guesses as to where Snorri got the constituent ideas from. A bewildering range of parallels has been cited, from the symbols of the four Evangelists to the shapeshifters and fetches of sagas and Eddaic poems (see, e.g., Almqvist 1965, 135-54, and Einar Ól. Sveinsson 1976). Third, there is the whole slippery question of oral tradition, which is discussed later in this chapter.

Despite these and other difficulties, and despite the fact that many readers nowadays may find the scholarly arguments about lost sources frankly dull, source-study has much to offer. Above all, it is a means of identifying what belongs to the common stock, and what is distinctive, in any given work. In the case of *Heimskringla*, it helps to define many special qualities. First and foremost, it demonstrates that *Heimskringla* uniquely combines the broad chronological sweep of the synoptic histories, in *Ynglinga saga* reaching farther back in time than any of them, with the depth of individual *konungasögur*. It integrates the sagas of individual reigns by chains of causation and recurrent themes and character traits. Most readers have also agreed that *Heimskringla* often surpasses its antecedents in presenting the personality of kings and the problems of their reigns, both by paring down tales of Icelanders and other extraneous matter (see Storm 1873, 98–99) and by artful use of description and direct speech. Further, several of the most vivid moments appear to be unique to *Heimskringla*, such as the anecdote of Þórarinn Nefjólfsson's ugly feet (*Ólhelg* 85; Almqvist 1975) or the speech of Einarr Þveræingr (*Ólhelg* 125).

On the other hand, the survival of parallel episodes in other sources can remind us that Snorri's work represents a high point in a continuously developing tradition and that Snorri does not have a monopoly of narrative flair. There is a beautifully controlled picture in *ÓlTrygg* 101 of Óláfr's allied enemies sitting in the sun on a small island, watching Óláfr's ships sailing into view, and speculating which one is the renowned Ormr inn langi. The episode is better told in *Heimskringla* than elsewhere, but in outline it is derived from Oddr Snorrason (pp. 198–205), who may in turn have modelled it on a totally unrelated episode in a chronicle of Charlemagne by a monk of St Gall (see *Heimskringla* 1941–51, I, cxxix–cxxx). In the same way, some of the most vivid moments in other great battles in *Heimskringla*—Stiklarstaðir, Niz and Stamford Bridge among them—are traceable to earlier accounts.

Snorri's reliance on sources varies throughout *Heimskringla*. A great deal of material in *Óláfs saga Tryggvasonar* can be matched in earlier written sources including *Ágrip*, Oddr Snorrason's saga of Óláfr, *Jómsvíkinga saga* and *Fagrskinna*, while the sagas in *Heimskringla* III, especially those after Sigurðr Jórsalafari, are closely dependent on *Morkinskinna*. For *Ynglinga saga*, on the other hand, it is thought that Snorri had only scanty sources and had to deduce and reconstruct much of what he wrote.

Snorri's treatment of the passages he chose to use also varies. At one extreme, a passage may be incorporated more or less verbatim. The two parts of *Kristni þáttr* (the tale of Dala-Guðbrandr in *Ólhelg* 112–13 and Óláfr helgi's miraculous journey through Skerfsurð or Sefsurð in *Ólhelg* 178–79) are transcribed with little change from a source very like the *Legendary saga of Óláfr helgi* (chs 31–36 and 67 respectively; further instances are given in Chapter Five: Variety). More usually, though, source-material is altered in some major way—streamlined, re-ordered or totally recast.

Snorri himself makes no secret of his debt to tradition, and it is worth looking at his own words on the subject—tantalising though they sometimes are—before proceeding to a fuller and rather more orderly review of sources. In the opening sentence of the Prologue to *Heimskringla*, Snorri proclaims his book to be a record of ancient traditions gathered from learned men (*svá sem ek hefi heyrt fróða menn segja*). He refers particularly to genealogy and poetry among his sources and, speaking of *Ynglinga saga*, notes again that he has had to supplement the evidence of the poet Þjóðólfr with 'the accounts of learned men' (*sǫgn fróðra manna*). Of these kinds of evidence it is only skaldic verse that receives detailed comment. This is the only instance in extant Icelandic saga-writing of an author directly referring to verse in a prologue, although the Norwegian Theodoricus and the Dane Saxo, both writing in Latin, had done so (Sverrir Tómasson 1988, 211–12).

About half of the Prologue is taken up with a tribute to Ari Þorgilsson, whom Snorri refers to as the first Icelander to write down 'native lore, both ancient and new' (*frœði, bæði forna ok nýja*) in the Norse language. He found much to admire in Ari: intelligence and acuteness of memory applied in the careful use of first- or second-hand accounts of important events. His praise, however, seems greatly out of proportion. Ari's work was probably too short to have supplied much of the material for *Heimskringla*, and his restrained, scholarly approach is not wholeheartedly followed by Snorri. (The two are compared by Sverrir Tómasson 1988, 279–90.) On the other hand, more recent works such as *Ágrip* and *Morkinskinna* which Snorri used intensively are never mentioned by him. The possible explanations for this are several. Snorri may have intended (whether duplicitously or not see Sverrir Tómasson 1975, 285) to establish his work within a respectable scholarly tradition, rather in the manner of medieval Latin historiographers naming classical or medieval *auctoritates*. He may alternatively be identifying ideal forms of evidence without pretending that they were always available to him; or it may be that he does not spell out his dependence on *Ágrip* and *Morkinskinna* because he knows that his audience will recognise it. In any event, it would be an exceptional medieval author who gave an exhaustive account of his sources.

Eiríkr Oddsson's *Hryggjarstykki* is also valued by Snorri for its nearness to events, witnessed by the author himself or acquaintances of his. Other written sources named by Snorri are *Skjǫldunga saga*, *Jarla saga* / *sǫgur* (i.e. *Orkneyinga saga*), sagas, now lost, of Sigurðr hjǫrtr of Hringaríki (mentioned in *Hálfdsv* 5) and of Knútr inn gamli (i.e. inn ríki, mentioned in *Mgóð* 22), and a work written by, or for, King Sverrir. There are also less specific references, including one to a miracle story written by an unnamed witness (*Msona* 31), one to the many written accounts about Óláfr Tryggvason's strength and agility (*ÓlTrygg* 85), and one to the records of Óláfr helgi's miracles (*Ólhelg* 245).

INDIVIDUAL LIVES OF KINGS

Snorri's *Heimskringla* is both a series of individual kings' lives and a unitary history of Norway. As such it represents the confluence of two streams of tradition, individual biography and synoptic history, both of which were powerfully in evidence in the decades around 1200. Snorri's main written sources are discussed below within the framework of this twofold distinction, although it would be equally admissible to treat the contemporary accounts of Norwegian kings in works like *Hryggjarstykki* and *Sverris saga* as a third, separate category (cf. Jónas Kristjánsson 1988, 160).

Of all Norwegian kings, two were the most esteemed in Iceland: Óláfr Tryggvason (reigned 995–1000) as the missionary king who initiated the conversion of Iceland, and Óláfr Haraldsson (1015–30) as the saint-king ('helgi') whose shrine at Niðaróss (Trondheim) formed the hub of Norwegian and Icelandic Christendom, especially after Niðaróss was promoted to an archdiocese in 1152–3. Talk of miracles sprang up around the name of Óláfr Haraldsson shortly after he fell fighting a rebellious and reputedly heathen army at Stiklarstaðir. These wonders were commemorated in (oral) poetry by his contemporaries Sigvatr Þórðarson and Þórarinn loftunga, much of which survives. There were quite probably also written legends by the monks of Niðaróss before the end of the eleventh century. Two twelfth-century legends in Latin are still extant, the *Acta Sancti Olavi regis et martyris* (published by G. Storm in *Monumenta Historica Norvegiæ* 1880) and the *Passio et Miracula beati Olaui* which is the work of Augustinus (Eysteinn Erlendsson), archbishop of Niðaróss 1161–88 (published by F. Metcalfe, 1881). Many of the same stories are rendered into Norse in the *Norwegian Homily Book* (*Gamal norsk Homiliebok*). There appears also to have been a work about the translation of Óláfr's body and the ensuing miracles, now lost but used by Theodoricus (see below). Writings such as these doubtless fed, at least indirectly, the earliest vernacular histories.

The so-called *Oldest Saga of Óláfr helgi* exists now only in six fragments in NRA (Norsk Riksarkivet) 52, a manuscript of *c.* 1225. (A further two fragments published by Gustav Storm as belonging to the saga have been dismissed by Jonna Louis-Jensen (1970) and Jónas Kristjánsson (e.g. 1976, 284)). These fragments concern central political issues of Óláfr's reign—relations with Norwegian magnates such as Þórir hundr and Erlingr Skjálgsson, and his dealings with Knútr of Denmark and England and Ǫnundr of Sweden; but there is also a manifest taste for more peripheral tales about the fortunes of Icelandic skalds at the courts of Óláfr and Knútr. The author of the *Oldest Saga* is thought to have known *Ágrip* (below), and to have been working around or very shortly after 1200 (Jónas Kristjánsson 1988, 160). His work was quite quickly taken up and a version of it became the basis for other lives of Óláfr—the so-called *Legendary Saga* and Styrmir Kárason's saga.

The *Legendary Saga of Óláfr helgi* is thought variously to be the work of a Norwegian or of an Icelander, but with interpolations from Norwegian works (Jónas Kristjánsson 1976, 293, Ólafur Halldórsson 1979, 134). The author, it seems, shortens the narrative of the *Oldest Saga* overall, but adds new material from other sources, especially the so-called *Kristni þáttr* and posthumous miracles of Óláfr helgi. Being the only other saga of the saint-king from Snorri's time which survives in complete form, it is an important text for comparison with Snorri's *Óláfs saga helga*. The two works have so much material in common that it is clear that Snorri had a work very like the *Legendary Saga* before him, although not the *Legendary Saga* itself (Bjarni Aðalbjarnarson, *Heimskringla* 1941–51, II, ix; Jónas Kristjánsson 1976, 288). The treatment of material is, however, often sharply different in the two works, and the ramshackle structure, fantastic episodes and distinctly clerical tone of the *Legendary Saga* set off the relative restraint and elegance of *Heimskringla*.

Styrmir Kárason, also the author of a version of *Landnámabók*, compiled a *Lífssaga Óláfs helga*. Some excerpts from it, which seem to evince a zeal for the legendary stories, are given as an appendix in *Flateyjarbók* (III 237–48), and others are inserted into the text of Snorri's *Separate Saga* in the same codex and in four other manuscripts (see Johnsen and Helgason's 1941 edition, 683–95), but it is otherwise lost. Sigurður Nordal's reconstruction (1914, 69–133) is widely accepted, but may be over-confident (Heinrichs 1976, esp. 18, and her 1982 edition of the *Legendary Saga*, 12–13); and the often-repeated view that Styrmir's *Lífssaga* was a, even the, main source for Snorri's *Óláfs saga helga* probably owes as much to the circumstance that Styrmir was a trusted friend of Snorri's as to textual evidence.

Snorri certainly wrote his *Óláfs saga helga* first of all his sagas of kings (see the discussion of the *Separate* and *Heimskringla* sagas on pp. 54–5 above), and probably only afterwards conceived the idea of a cycle of lives. In this way, he provided his own inspiration for his lives of other kings. But there were also external models. Oddr Snorrason wrote a life of Óláfr Tryggvason (c. 1190) which was originally in Latin but soon translated into Icelandic. Oddr manages to make his hero a near-saint and his work a near-hagiography, with the emphasis very much on Óláfr's missionary efforts and his struggle against heathen chieftains and sorcerers. According to Icelandic belief (followed also by Snorri, *ÓlTrygg* 60), Óláfr Tryggvason was Óláfr Haraldsson's godfather, and Oddr in his Prologue casts him as the John the Baptist to his namesake's Christ. Snorri knew and used this work, in a text which was evidently not identical with either of the two versions now extant.

Gunnlaugr Leifsson, a fellow monk of Oddr at Þingeyrar and a most learned man, produced a saga about Óláfr Tryggvason, probably before 1200. It was partially based on Oddr's, and filled out with marvels, with detail about the missionary ventures and with rhetorical embroidery. Again originally in Latin, this is now lost and known to us chiefly through the excerpts included in *Jómsvíkinga saga* (AM 291 4to version), in *Kristni saga* and in *Óláfs saga Tryggvasonar in mesta* (*The Great Saga of Óláfr Tryggvason*). Snorri may also have made some use of Gunnlaugr's work but it was, in the words of Gabriel Turville-Petre, 'too far removed from reality to be of great use to Snorri' (1953, 196).

Other separate sagas of kings and jarls may well have influenced Snorri, although they are either lost or their existence only conjectured. Fragments of a saga about Haraldr Sigurðarson's contemporary and rival Hákon jarl Ívarsson survive. It has been suggested that there may also have been early sagas about Hálfdan svarti, Haraldr hárfagri (possibly a joint saga of these two), Eiríkr blóðøx, Hákon góði, Magnús góði, Haraldr Sigurðarson, Magnús berfœttr, the sons of Magnús, and possibly one filling the gap in the mid-twelfth century between *Hryggjarstykki* and *Sverris saga* (Bjarni Aðalbjanarson, *Heimskringla* 1941–51, I, xvi and lviii).

Not all the early lives of kings known to Snorri were written at a great distance in time from the events. Indeed, the earliest datable kings' sagas are contemporary accounts. *Sverris saga*, the life of King Sverrir of Norway (1177–1202), was written by the Icelander Karl Jónsson partly at the dictation of the king himself, and Snorri's reference, *svá hefir Sverrir konungr rita látit* (*Hsona* 32), seems to be to this work. The fact that the account was a contemporary one made for a richness of detail which may have influenced Snorri in his writing. Certainly the literary speeches in *Sverris saga* did so. The existence of *Sverris saga* may also have been one of the reasons why *Heimskringla* stops (like *Fagrskinna*) at 1177.

HISTORICAL SURVEYS

The precedents for a series of royal lives covering a long sweep of time were just as abundant as those for separate lives. The earliest of these were summary in their treatment of individual reigns and in English go under the heading of synoptic histories. After that there is a discernible movement towards greater breadth of treatment, culminating in *Heimskringla*. It is virtually certain that Sæmundr inn fróði 'the Learned' (1056–1133), grandfather of Snorri's foster-father Jón Loptsson, wrote a Latin history of Norwegian kings which is now lost but which opened the way for his successors. First of these was Ari Þorgilsson inn fróði (1067/8–1148). Ari in the Prologue to his *Íslendingabók* refers to an earlier, now lost, version of his work, which contained *konunga ævi* as well as Icelandic history, and these accounts of reigns must have been used by Snorri. He refers to Ari's authority for points of chronology in *ÓlTrygg* 14 and *Ólhelg* 246, and there is a similar use of Ari in ch. 11 of the *Separate Saga*. In a fuller passage in *Ólhelg* 179 Ari is praised in terms reminiscent of the Prologue. Despite much speculation, however, the exact scope and literary character of Ari's *konunga ævi*, and hence of Snorri's debt to them, cannot now be known.

Another work which must have been known to Snorri was the versified tally of Norwegian kings, *Nóregs konungatal*, composed in the *kviðuháttr* metre for Jón Loptsson (d. 1197) as a celebration of his royal forbears (*Skjaldedigtning* A I 579–89, B I 575–90). The poet, pausing at v. 40, acknowledges his debt to Sæmundr's accounts of Norwegian reigns (*intak svá | ævi þeira | sem Sæmundr | sagði enn fróði*). Although the poem survives, it contains very little detailed information, and its main importance to Snorri must have been in encouraging his enthusiasm for Norwegian royal history.

It appears that, in its early stages, interest in dynastic history flourished more in Norway than in Iceland. Shortly before 1180 the monk Theodoricus wrote a *Historia de antiquitate regum Norvagiensium*. The author presents himself as the first writer of history in Norway, and mentions Icelandic poems as especially valuable vehicles of tradition. He is thought to have been working from oral sources and to a lesser extent from foreign written sources. His work spans the period from the late ninth century (reign of Haraldr hárfagri) to 1130. Another Norwegian product, the *Historia Norvegiæ*, used to be thought to have been written shortly after 1211 (Bjarni Aðalbjarnarson 1937, 20–29; Holtsmark 1938, 161), but it could be contemporary with Theodoricus (Jónas Kristjánsson 1988, 155). In its now defective state it covers the reigns of Norwegian kings down to Óláfr Haraldsson's arrival in Norway, with a summary prelude about the Yngling kings in Sweden. Although it cannot be demonstrated that these two Norwegian works were used by Snorri, they—or in the case of *Historia Norvegiæ* another redaction of the same work—were known to him indirectly through one of his most important sources.

This was *Ágrip af Nóregs konunga sǫgum* 'Summary of the histories of the kings of Norway', a (probably) Norwegian work from the end of the twelfth century preserved in AM 325 II 4to, an Icelandic manuscript of *c*. 1225. It now covers the reigns of kings from Haraldr hárfagri to Ingi (d. 1161). Despite its slightly defective text, the work has great importance as the earliest surviving vernacular history of Norway. While the writer shows something of the ecclesiastical viewpoint of Theodoricus and *Historia Norvegiæ* (both of which he used as source-books), he also follows the secular tradition of praising kings and demonstrating their glorious ancestry and the rights attendant on it. The style is generally concise and plain, often pointed by witty exchanges of speech, and hence not unlike that of the *Íslendingasögur* and *Heimskringla*, but there are also more ornate passages containing rhetorical antitheses, alliterating synonym pairs and other devices. *Ágrip* was quite well known in Iceland and gave much to *Heimskringla*—not merely an overall scheme but perhaps also (along with other works) the running themes of the conflict of religions and the conflict of dynasties which united the succession of reigns. Moreover, within *Ágrip*'s rather patchy coverage of history some episodes are polished enough for Snorri to have incorporated them more or less verbatim in *Heimskringla* (see Chapter Five: Variety).

Though silent about the existence of *Ágrip*, Snorri fulsomely acknowledges his debt to *Hryggjarstykki* 'Backbone-Piece' by Eiríkr Oddsson. In each of his four references (*Hsona* 7, 10, 11 and 12), Snorri names Eiríkr's (highly reliable) informants, and in *Hsona* 11 the citation leads into an extended appreciation of the work. *Hryggjarstykki* is now lost, but is known to have been a source for *Heimskringla*, *Morkinskinna* and *Fagrskinna* and can up to a point be reconstructed from them. It dealt, as Snorri says, with the reigns of Haraldr gilli and his sons, and with Magnús blindi and Sigurðr slembir or slembidjákn, d. 1139. It thus began at 1130, but whether it ended at 1139 or 1161 is uncertain, and hence whether it was a single biography or a synoptic work. In a recent study, Bjarni Guðnason considers it to date from *c.* 1150—hence to be the first Icelandic saga—and thinks that it was essentially a saga of Sigurðr slembir (1978, 174 and 168). Bjarni points out that Snorri (in *MblokHg* 13–*Hsona* 12) alters the *Hryggjarstykki* narrative relatively little, for it is written in a quite developed 'saga-style' (1978, 150).

In the thirteenth century brief synoptic works gave place to compilations such as *Fagrskinna* and *Morkinskinna* which showed a delight in detailed narrative and, in the case of *Morkinskinna*, incorporated a great many *þættir* 'strands' or 'short stories' of a kind which had already found their way into the oldest sagas of Óláfr helgi. Whether this was because the increasing distance from the events deseribed made it more crucial to make a detailed record, because the proliferation of written texts gave authors more materials to work from, or simply because tastes changed, bringing historical writing quite close in narrative texture to the newly flourishing *Íslendingasögur*, cannot be known—doubtless all three contributed.

Morkinskinna was originally written *c.* 1220 or a little earlier. The end (from *c.* 1157) is now lost, but the work is thought to have spanned the period 1035–1177. Several pages are also missing from the *Morkinskinna* sagas of Magnús góði and Haraldr Sigurðarson, but the text here can be supplied from the copy in *Flateyjarbók*. *Morkinskinna* provided Snorri with much of the material for the third part of *Heimskringla*. The extant *Morkinskinna* contains many *þættir*, especially about Icelanders at the Norwegian court, and much fabulous material; most of this is lacking from *Heimskringla*. Since the extant *Morkinskinna* is an expanded version of the original work it is difficult to gauge the extent to which Snorri deliberately omitted material which did not suit his purpose or taste, and to what extent he simply did not know it. (On the narrative art of *Morkinskinna*, see Kalinke 1984.)

Fagrskinna, also known as *Nóregs Konunga Tal*, with the consequent danger of confusion with the poem of the same name, is believed to have been written *c.* 1220–30, by an Icelander or Norwegian, probably working to a commission from King Hákon Hákonarson and in

Trondheim (Bjarni Einarsson, *Ágrip* 1984, cxxvii–cxxxi). It follows a chronological scheme which goes back to Sæmundr fróði, and spans the reign of Hálfdan svarti in the ninth century to the battle of Ré in 1177; there are now two lacunae towards the end. The emphasis on battles (or rather, certain battles, since some, including Stiklarstaðir, are underplayed) at the expense of other matter, such as anecdotes illustrating the character of kings, leads Bjarni Aðalbjarnarson to see it as a 'battle-saga' (*Heimskringla* 1941–51, I, xviii).

The textual relations between *Fagrskinna* and *Heimskringla* are elusive. It is generally accepted that the authors of *Fagrskinna* and *Heimskringla* used common sources which are now lost, in addition to the known ones such as *Hryggjarstykki* and *Morkinskinna*. It is also likely, though less easy to prove, that Snorri used a version of *Fagrskinna* for *Heimskringla* I and III, but not for his *Óláfs saga helga* (see Bjarni Einarsson, *Ágrip* 1984, cxxv–cxxvii). Of all the synoptic histories *Fagrskinna* is perhaps the closest in literary character to *Heimskringla*, in its abundant use of skaldic verse (a feature shared with *Morkinskinna*), its streamlined style, graphic detail and bold repartee, and its avoidance of irrelevant and fabulous episodes. It provides a valuable reminder that some of the most striking touches in *Heimskringla* are inherited rather than invented by Snorri. Compared with *Heimskringla*, however, *Fagrskinna* shows fewer signs of authorial planning and control. Coverage of events can be patchy, and individual episodes less fully drawn, and where the two works follow a common source, *Heimskringla* tends to modify the original more radically than *Fagrskinna* (see *Heimskringla* 1941–51, I, xvii).

Other compendious works which played their part in the genesis of *Heimskringla* are not directly devoted to Norwegian rulers. *Orkneyinga saga*, to which Snorri refers under its older title of *Jarlasǫgur / saga* (*Ólhelg* 103 = *Ólhelg(Sep)* 89), and *Færeyinga saga* concern the island territories colonised by Norsemen and taxed by Norwegian kings. Both sagas were in existence by c. 1210 (*Orkneyinga saga* probably no later than 1200) and both were used by Snorri, especially in *Óláfs saga helga*, although the particular redactions he knew are now—as usual—lost. The textual relations between *Heimskringla*, *Morkinskinna* and *Orkneyinga saga* are—again as usual—complex, but it seems likely that the main *Orkneyinga saga* passage which Snorri used (chs 13–19, cf. *Ólhelg(Hkr)* 96–103 and *Ólhelg(Sep)* 81–89) came to be replaced by Snorri's rewriting of it, so that the original no longer survives for comparison (see *Orkneyinga saga* 1965, xxvii–xxx). Further, Finnbogi Guðmundsson has suggested that the saga was revised under Snorri's supervision (*Orkneyinga saga* 1965, xlii–xliii) and that the three-chapter prelude devoted to legendary Nordic ancestors was written by Snorri himself and modelled among other things on *Ynglinga saga* (*Orkneyinga saga* 1965, xiv–xvi). *Færeyinga saga* was certainly known to Snorri in some form, and his mention of *stórar frásagnir* about events in the Faeroes (*Ólhelg* 143) doubtless refers to a version of the saga. The saga only survives now in fragments (though large ones) in *Óláfs saga Tryggvasonar in mesta* and in *Óláfs saga helga* in *Flateyjarbók*, but it seems that where Snorri has followed *Færeyinga saga* (notably *Ólhelg* 127, 135 and 142–43) he has retained the cryptic and dramatic character of the narrative (see Bjarni Aðalbjarnarson, *Heimskringla* 1941–51, II, xliii–xlvii).

Skjǫldunga saga is believed to have been written c. 1180–1200 (Bjarni Guðnason 1963, 142–45), but it is now known chiefly through a Latin digest made by Arngrímur Jónsson (1568–1648). It concerned the legendary past of the Danish royal house, going back to Skjǫldr, son of Óðinn. The exact scope of the original is now unclear, although some clues suggest that it was quite extensive (*Heimskringla* 1941–51, I, xlix–l). The saga is cited by Snorri as a source for the battle on the ice-covered Vænir (Lake Vänern) and for the career of Hrólfr kraki (*Yng* 29), and its influence is thought to be especially strong in the middle chapters of *Ynglinga saga* (17–29, the reigns of Dyggvi to Aðils; see Magerøy 1976, 360). It may also have been the main spur to Snorri to begin his *Heimskringla* with a treatment of the prehistorical Swedish and Norwegian rulers in *Ynglinga saga*, although some scholars believe in an earlier saga of the Ynglings.

Other synoptic works—a saga about the Norwegian jarls of Hlaðir and an early *Jómsvíkinga saga*—are thought to have existed in Snorri's day and to have influenced his writing, especially in *Óláfs saga Tryggvasonar*, but their exact form is difficult to reconstruct.

A final source of influence on Snorri's kings' sagas, as on the *Íslendingasögur*, is genealogical material, which we may perhaps regard as the ultimate in synoptic biography—mere naming of individuals of whose lives the consumers of genealogy may have known much more—as well as the ultimate expression of the potency of kinship ties and of family characteristics. It is clear, among other things from the reference to *áttvísi* 'genealogy / family lore' in the so-called *First Grammatical Treatise* (mid-twelfth century), that this was among the first matter to be preserved in writing in Iceland. Snorri must have known the genealogical lists (*langfeðgatal*) appended to Ari Þorgilsson's *Íslendingabók*—which may or may not have been contemporary with the work itself—as well as others such as genealogies of the Oddaverjar.

To summarise, the three most important prose works for comparison with *Heimskringla* are the compilations *Ágrip*, *Fagrskinna* and *Morkinskinna*. They are important because they survive (in something like the versions known to Snorri), and because of their scope. *Ágrip* and *Fagrskinna* span almost as much time as *Heimskringla* if *Ynglinga saga* is set aside, and *Morkinskinna* covers most of the reigns in the third part of *Heimskringla*. We have a much less clear picture of sagas of individual kings as antecedents of *Heimskringla*, except that Oddr Snorrason's saga and the *Legendary Saga* give some idea of the lives of the two Olafs which Snorri must have known. What is striking about Snorri's known sources is that they are all vernacular. Unlike most medieval writers of history, Snorri cannot be shown to have made direct use of any Latin source, and indeed the extent of his knowledge of Latin has still not been satisfactorily gauged, although investigations such as those by Amory (1978), Clunies Ross (1987) and Sverrir Tómasson (1988) represent important moves in this direction.

OTHER PROSE WORKS KNOWN TO SNORRI

As well as producing lives of Óláfr helgi and Óláfr Tryggvason which lie on the boundary of hagiography and royal biography, Icelanders had miracle-working saints of their own in the persons of the bishops Jón Qgmundarson (d. 1121) and Þorlákr Þórhallsson (d. 1193). Writings about them attended the recognition of their sanctity (in 1200 and 1198 respectively) and Snorri must have been aware of this kind of literature and was possibly in some degree influenced by it.

Synoptic histories of ecclesiastical leaders are less common than their secular counterparts, but one, *Hungrvaka* 'Hunger-rouser, Appetiser', may well have been known to Snorri since it is believed to have been written at Skálaholt at some time in the first two decades of the thirteenth century. It is an account of the bishops of Skálaholt (1056–1193) and, glancingly, of Hólar (1106–93). Another survey, *Kristni saga*, is now only extant in a version probably made by Sturla Þórðarson and preserved in *Hauksbók*, but there may have been an earlier version which furnished Snorri with material about the conversion of Iceland for his saga of Óláfr Tryggvason.

Íslendingasögur, Sagas of Icelanders or (commonly, but inexactly) Icelandic Family Sagas, have a narrative style in some ways very like

Heimskringla. Dating them is difficult, but it is certain that four of the five great 'classical' sagas (*Njáls saga, Laxdœla* saga, *Grettis saga* and *Eyrbyggja saga*) cannot have existed in anything like their present form when *Heimskringla* was written (although Madelung, 1972, argues for Snorri's authorship of *Laxdœla*). The *Íslendingasögur* considered to be the oldest include *Heiðarvíga saga, Kormáks saga, Bjarnar saga Hítdœlakappa* and possibly *Reykdœla saga* (Clover 1985, 247–49), but definite proofs of the influence of any of these on *Heimskringla* are elusive. There is, however, a chance that *Hallfreðar saga* was known and used by Snorri in the account of Hallfreðr's conversion at the court of Óláfr Tryggvason (*ÓlTrygg* 83; see *Vatnsdœla saga* 1939, lxiii and n. 2). Between *Heimskringla* and the other saga of the 'great five', *Egils saga*, there is an especially close relationship which suggests that Snorri both used sources in common with *Egils saga* and knew the saga itself (Bjarni Einarsson 1975, 29–43). Many further believe that Snorri was himself the author of *Egils saga* (Clover 1985, 245 and 249–50 for references). The shorter *þættir*, so close to the *Íslendingasögur* in subject-matter and style, doubtless also influenced Snorri's writing.

SKALDIC VERSE

On many counts it is natural that Snorri's kings' sagas should include an abundance of skaldic verse. In the preliterate society of pagan Scandinavia, poetry had been a fitting means of commemorating great deeds for posterity, and this rôle of poets is made explicit in Óláfr helgi's command to his skalds to take their place in the wall of shields at Stiklarstaðir (AD 1030) and afterwards to compose about what they saw (*Ólhelg* 206). Whether or not Óláfr's words are a literary fiction, it remains true that very many skalds composed eye-witness accounts of battles, and that three skalds died with Óláfr at Stiklarstaðir. The metrically tight and complex *dróttkvætt* form lent itself to easy memorisation and accurate transmission so that panegyrics in the metre were highly valued as historical sources. Indeed, they have survived principally because they were quoted in historical or quasi-historical prose narratives.

Verse quotations figure sporadically in Ari's *Íslendingabók*, the *Oldest saga of Óláfr helgi* and *Ágrip*, but it is in the encyclopaedic histories, *Fagrskinna, Morkinskinna* and *Heimskringla* itself, that their use reaches its peak and their function is fully established. In the earliest works the quotations are mainly of *lausavísur*, occasional verses which form an integral and dramatic part of the narrative. Uttered, supposedly, by the protagonists at high points in the action, they are introduced by tags such as *þá kvað Sigvatr*. The later quotations are more commonly extracts from long encomia which serve an authenticating function, confirming and embellishing the facts of the narrative. These are typically introduced *svá segir Sigvatr*, or *þess getr Óttarr*.

Snorri's interest in skaldic verse is amply attested. His *Prose Edda* is a textbook for skalds, a valiant attempt to preserve skaldic metres and diction in the face of changing tastes. Its final part, *Háttatal* with its 102 verses illustrating almost as many variations of form, attests great knowledge and exuberance, even if it impresses more as craftsmanship than art. *Háttatal* praises King Hákon and Skúli jarl, and Snorri is also credited with further verses about Skúli jarl, as well as poems about King Sverrir and his two nephews Ingi and Hákon galinn, Hákon's wife Kristín, and Guðmundr, bishop of Hólar, although next to nothing survives of these poems. Skaldic verse seems to have been a family strength, for Snorri's nephews Óláfr Þórðarson hvítaskáld and Sturla Þórðarson were among the last known Icelandic poets to visit Scandinavian courts.

The breadth of Snorri's memory for skaldic verse and his agility of recall is shown by the sheer number of verses or parts of verses cited in *Heimskringla*. There are some six hundred, from over sixty skalds, usually cited in ones or twos but occasionally as longer stretches, as when twenty-one verses from Eyvindr skáldaspillir's *Hákonarmál* are quoted at the end of *Hákonar saga góða* (ch. 32) and nine verses each from Þórarinn loftunga's *Glælognskviða* in *Ólhelg* 245 and Sigvatr Þórðarson's *Bersǫglisvísur* in *Mgóð* 16. It is also shown by the particular verses cited. When writing of Óláfr helgi's ravaging of Upplǫnd (*Ólhelg* 121) Snorri cites a verse of Arnórr jarlaskáld which mainly concerns Haraldr Sigurðarson but alludes to Óláfr. (A further example is given by Nordal 1920, 141.) Nor is Snorri content to take over his predecessors' choice of authenticating verses when he can muster better ones. A verse from Arnórr's praise of Þorfinnr, jarl of Orkney, somewhat irrelevantly quoted in *Morkinskinna*, *Fagrskinna* and *Hulda-Hrokkinskinna* to illustrate the formalities of Óláfr kyrri's feasts, is replaced by a more suitable verse by Stúfr blindi (*Ólkyrr* 3). Elsewhere, Snorri may choose to paraphrase rather than quote, as when *ÓlTrygg* 17 has an echo of Einarr skálaglamm's *Vellekla* (Nordal 1920, 141–42).

The verse quotations in *Heimskringla*, and Snorri's comments on verse in the Prologue, always suggest that his priorities in choosing and using the verse are historical rather than aesthetic, and for that reason

Sources and Influences 77

discussion of some further aspects of skaldic sources is postponed to Chapter Six.

ORAL TRADITION

The delight and despair of scholars, 'oral tradition' offers almost unlimited scope for speculation, but is notoriously difficult to quantify or characterise, and can at worst become a dumping-ground to which anything not directly traceable to a written source may be assigned. The wording of Snorri's text is not always helpful on the matter of oral sources. It is quite liberally peppered with tags like *svá er sagt* and *þat er sǫgn manna*, but these are ambiguous. Words such as *saga / sǫgur, sǫgn / sagnir, frásǫgn* or *fyrirsǫgn* are based on the same root as *segja* 'to say, tell', and can in general Old Norse usage mean written texts (and then either fully-fledged sagas or parts of compendious works), or else more or less fluid oral reports. In some cases the meaning of these words is made clear by the context. In *Hákherð* 20, for instance, *sagði hann [Eindriði ungi] þessa sǫgu í Nóreg* seems to mean an oral report, and twice in *Hsona* 11 Snorri seems to distinguish spoken report (*segja fyrir / fyrirsǫgn*) from written (*segja frá / frásǫgn*): Hallr . . . *sagði Eiríki Oddsyni fyrir, en hann reit þessa frásǫgn* and *suma frásǫgn reit hann eftir fyrirsǫgn Hákonar maga*. But elsewhere things are less clear-cut. Snorri refers to one and the same authority, Ari Þorgilsson, with the verbs *segir* (*ÓlTrygg* 14, twice) and *ritaði* (Prologue), and the nouns *sǫgn* (Prologue), *bók* (Prologue), pl. *bœkr* (*Ólhelg* 179), and *ævi Nóregs konunga* (Prologue). *Sǫgn* definitely means a written work here, but in *Ólhelg* 179, in the phrase *alþýðu sǫgn*, it seems to mean a looser kind of common opinion or report. It is therefore extremely difficult to know what Snorri means when he refers to a *lǫng saga* about Sigurðr hjǫrtr (*Hálfdsv* 5) or to *miklar frásagnir* about the sons of Þorfinnr hausakljúfr (*Ólhelg* 96, corresponding to *miklar sǫgur* in *Ólhelg(Sep)* 81).

Recognising passages as primarily oral or written in origin on the basis of style or vocabulary can also be hazardous, because many of the features commonly associated with oral narrative, such as lavish and unspecific use of third person pronouns or rapid alternation between past and historic present tenses, became a customary part of written Icelandic prose style, and it is always easier to demonstrate written origins·than it is to prove or discount oral origins. For example, Bjarni Aðalbjarnarson (*Heimskringla* 1941–51, I, lviii, following Nordal) suggests that when the verb *venda* 'turn, go', not favoured elsewhere in *Heimskringla*, occurs three times in the opening of *Haralds saga hárfagra*, this points to the likelihood that Snorri is closely following an earlier *þáttr* about Haraldr which is preserved in *Flateyjarbók*, and which has *venda* at the relevant point.

The distinction between oral and written sources can, further, be blurred by what has been called 'secondary oral tradition' (Holtsmark 1938, 161), in which material already written down then gains wider (and cheaper) circulation by being passed on orally from the reader to others. Such a process would account for the fact that a sentence or sentences from one work, fully or partly remembered, can turn up in a quite different context, often to the bafflement of source-hunting scholars.

What traces of oral tradition, then, can be found in *Heimskringla*? We would not perhaps expect to find a great deal. Snorri, writing a century after Ari and almost as long after Eiríkr Oddsson, must have recognised that what were to them original, fresh oral reports of events were now only available to him in processed—presumably written—form. Nevertheless, he does in some measure follow their example in naming the ultimate sources for some of his narrative—men and women such as Þórir hundr, who attested to the unnatural beauty and healing power of Óláfr helgi's corpse (*Ólhelg* 230), or Þorgils Snorrason and Guðríðr, Steigar-Þórir's granddaughter, who knew the later history of Haraldr Sigurðarson's gifts to Steigar-Þórir (*HSig* 24). There are also some references to groups rather than individuals as sources of information, for instance the Væringjar (*HSig* 13), Haraldr Sigurðarson's warriors at a later stage in his life (*HSig* 99), or the men of Vík (*Hsona* 32).

Further, there is information given in *Heimskringla* which is not found in earlier written sources, and may be Snorri's own contribution to what was set down in writing and known in Iceland. The most convincing arguments for this identify fairly coherent bodies of such information and suggest routes by which it could have come to Snorri's notice. Thus Didrik Arup Seip (1954) investigated material in *Heimskringla* which is connected with Túnsberg (Tønsberg) and seems based on local tradition. Comparing the treatment of incidents before the life of Óláfr helgi in the *Separate Saga of Óláfr helgi* and in *Heimskringla* I, Seip noted considerable refinement in the latter and surmised that Snorri had already written this material for the *Separate Saga* before he reached Norway, and revised it on learning local traditions during his stay in Tønsberg (1954, esp. 156). Another interesting suggestion is that, since *Heimskringla* III has little in the way of Tønsberg tradition until the description of the siege of the town (so graphic that it must rest on an eyewitness account), Snorri may have conceived the idea of covering the reigns after Óláfr Haraldsson at a later stage (1954, 159–60). There is, however, another explanation of the relative sparseness of Norwegian local traditions in *Heimskringla* III, which is simply that *Morkinskinna* was such a rich source that it left Snorri with little scope for addition (Berntsen 1923, 225).

Swedish traditions are naturally less in evidence in *Heimskringla* than Norwegian ones, but scholars have detected the fruits of Snorri's journey to Västergötland in 1219. They include his knowledge of Swedish legal arrangements, and his story in *Yng* 42–43 of how Óláfr trételgja fled from Uppsala to Vermaland (Värmland) and was burned to death there, which is lacking from older Icelandic sources (discussed by Wessén in his edition of *Ynglinga saga*, 1952, xvi–xvii).

It was probably not only Snorri's visit to mainland Scandinavia which gave him access to fresh information, but also his life in Iceland. There was a steady trickle of news from Norway, as seen in the report in *Hungrvaka* that Magnús Einarsson, bishop of Skálaholt 1134–48, on his return from Norway declaimed the news from the forecourt of the church at Þingvǫllr (*Biskupa sögur* I 77). Possibly new talk about past events was also brought back by travellers. More certainly, Snorri had a good informant in Jón Loptsson, who was not only a grandchild of King Magnús berfœttr but had been brought up until the age of eleven in Konungahella (Kungälv, now in Sweden). It may have been Jón above all that Snorri was thinking of when he undertook in the Prologue to write down traditions *svá sem ek hefi heyrt fróða menn segja*. Undoubtedly, Snorri's detailed accounts of twelfth-century events in Konungahella are partly thanks to Jón, and quite probably much of the material about Magnús berfœttr is too. It is also possible that there were traditions current in the Sturlung family about Haraldr Sigurðarson, stemming from his one-time henchman Halldórr Snorrason, son of Snorri's distinguished ancestor Snorri goði (cf. *HSig* 9).

Finally, Toralf Berntsen fashioned a theory of mixed oral and written tradition behind some of the apparently fresh material in *Heimskringla*. He examined the treatment there of events and characters from Hálogaland (e.g. the chieftains Hárekr ór Þjóttu and Þórir hundr), and from the Trøndelag and Gudbrandsdal, and suggested that the density of place-names and other details must derive not from Icelandic written sources but from a rich body of local Norwegian tradition (1923, esp. 122–23 and 141). He noted also that Snorri's summer in Scandinavia

(1219) was spent in Sweden, not Norway, which must have reduced his time for first-hand research in Norway (1923, 96–97). For these and other reasons, Berntsen surmised that Snorri had access not just to scattered oral reports but to written works quite like the *Íslendingasögur*. In the absence of further evidence for written Norwegian vernacular material, it might be rash to go so far as to postulate Norwegian family sagas, but it certainly seems that there must have been Norwegian local sources, oral or written, for some of the material in *Heimskringla*.

OTHER INFLUENCES

Another way of looking at the influences on *Heimskringla* is not just to consider direct literary links between particular texts but to go back a stage further and examine the ways in which the materials inherited by Snorri had already been shaped by tellers of tales, both popular and learned.

Folktale

Several episodes in *Heimskringla* are closely paralleled by independent folktales from within or outside Scandinavia, and their roots in folktale are often still evident on the surface of Snorri's narrative. Many of them concern the early careers of kings—Haraldr hárfagri, Óláfr Tryggvason and Haraldr Sigurðarson among them—before their deeds took on sufficient political importance to be commemorated in skaldic verse or story. The tales about Haraldr hárfagri's youth are probably the best example of this. Haraldr's vow not to cut his hair until he is supreme over Norway finds parallels in tales in many languages (*Hhárf* 4 and 23; Koht 1931, 135), as do the stories of his encounter with the Finn after the theft of King Hálfdan's Yule provisions (*Hálfdsv* 8) and of his infatuation with the Lappish beauty Snæfríðr (*Hhárf* 25). The two last-mentioned episodes are based on *Ágrip*.

Folktale motifs are not confined to the early careers of kings in *Heimskringla*. Several Irish analogues have been found by Bo Almqvist (1975) to the tale of Þórarinn Nefjólfsson's ugly feet (*Ólhelg* 85), which has no known antecedents in Norse. Similarly, Alexander Bugge made a case for Irish influence on such anecdotes as Óláfr Tryggvason's presentation of the huge angelica plant to his queen (*ÓlTrygg* 92) or the *mannjafnaðr* of Kings Sigurðr and Eysteinn (*Msona* 21; Bugge 1909, 111–12). Although Bugge's argument may have been overstated, it did demonstrate the presence of international folktale patterns in *Heimskringla* as in other kings' sagas.

Clerical writings

The influence of the Latinate style which characterised some Icelandic clerical writings is rarely noticeable in *Heimskringla* and is mostly confined to a few strikingly anomalous passages (see Chapter Five: Variety). A more significant contribution is of story patterns (some of them folktales in origin) which, with characteristic mobility, can be seen to have flowed through learned religious channels, surfacing especially in the parts of *Heimskringla* relating to Christian missions. The account of Óláfr Tryggvason's baptism in *ÓlTrygg* 31 credits a pious and prescient hermit on the Scilly Isles with the king's conversion, explaining that the king first tested the hermit by sending his henchman to him, disguised in the king's clothing. Snorri's narrative, once more, depends heavily on *Ágrip*, but the story pattern ultimately goes back to the conversion of the Gothic king Totila by St Benedict of Nursia as told in the *Dialogues* of Gregory the Great (*Heimskringla* 1941–51, I, civ; it is also attached to Óláfr helgi in the *Legendary Saga* ch. 18). Similarly, the fabulous happenings which attend Óláfr helgi's Christianisation of Guðbrandsdalr have been traced via the *Legendary Saga* to a Norse version of Ælfric's *De Falsis Diis* (now preserved in *Hauksbók*; Frankis 1976).

There may also be occasional traces of influence from the Bible itself on the narrative of *Heimskringla*. It has been suggested that the twelve chief priests (*hofgoðar*, v.l. *hǫfðingjar*) in Ásgarðr (*Yng* 2) and the twelve advisers to the Swedish king at Uppsala (*Ólhelg* 94) are influenced by the New Testament (Faulkes 1978–9, 121).

Poetic paradigms

The influence of poetry on *Heimskringla* is difficult to assess, but it certainly goes beyond the large and obvious contribution made by skaldic verse to the factual content of the work. The Niebelung legend, vividly preserved in the poems of the *Elder Edda*, has been suspected as the ultimate source for the portrayal of the powerful lady, Sigríðr stórráða, in *Óláfs saga Tryggvasonar* (see Chapter Six: Factual accuracy). Sigurður Nordal (1920, 175–76) suggested that when Óláfr Tryggvason plucks the feathers from his sister's hawk and sends it to her there may be an echo of Randvér's similar action of plucking his own hawk and sending it to his father Jǫrmunrekkr, who has ordered his execution, as a sign of the desolation Jǫrmunrekkr is causing to his own life and realm. The story is preserved in *Snorra Edda* (*Skáldskaparmál* ch. 51, 1931, 132–33), but may well be based on earlier poems.

It is possible, too, that some of the ideas and ideals in *Heimskringla* are tinged by early Norse poetry. It is doubtless over-simple to see the Icelandic saga-writers as akin to the Germanic poets of the migration period—as warriors of noble birth and in royal service with a duty to heroicise (so Fleischhauer 1938, 90), but certainly there are heroic sentiments in common between the kings' sagas (and *Heimskringla* in particular) on the one hand and Eddaic and skaldic poetry on the other. There are the compelling duties of loyalty to one's lord or to one's word (sometimes, as for Finnr Árnason or Tósti Guðinason, in tragic conflict with loyalty to one's kin), of courage in the face of death, and of choosing glory rather than shame whatever the cost. Occasionally the influence from poetry is obvious, when Snorri includes a heroic motif in his narrative which he clearly derives from verse he quotes. An example is Magnús góði's vow, in ch. 18 of his saga, to possess Denmark or die, which matehes the accompanying verse by Arnórr jarlaskáld.

CHAPTER FIVE
STYLE AND STRUCTURE

HEIMSKRINGLA AND SAGA-STYLE

SNORRI has often been acclaimed as one who helped Icelandic saga style to reach maturity. This may be rash, for our picture of the nature and development of saga-style is still rough and incomplete, but certainly *Heimskringla* comes closer than any of the *konungasögur* to the style of the 'classical' *Íslendingasögur*, although it predates most of the latter.

'Saga-style' is really an abstraction, a shorthand term used to refer to a range of features which, with some variation between individual works, characterise much medieval Icelandic saga-writing, but especially the *Íslendingasögur* of the thirteenth century. The term tends to be applied both narrowly, to details of lexical and syntactic usage within the smaller linguistic units of phrase and sentence, and to broader features of the narrative such as the presentation of character, motive and action. For convenience of description the discussion in this chapter moves from the narrower to the broader features, but the two groups of features are largely interdependent, and taken together they embrace many aspects of the presentation (as distinct from content) side of the work.

In its narrower features saga-style is concise, essentially unpretentious in vocabulary and syntax, and sparing with descriptive and evaluative epithets and rhetorical devices. It has the effect of everyday language shaped and polished by the influence of oral narrative (as suggested by such characteristics as the use of historic present verbs and swift transitions between indirect and direct speech) and of clerical writings in Latin and the vernacular (suggested, perhaps, by such rhetorical devices as the use of parallel and antithetical clauses). It brings together 'much of the simplicity of colloquial speech with the richness of the language of books' (Hallberg 1962a, 68, quoting Nordal). In the broader features of classical saga-style there is again a kind of equilibrium—between scholarship and art, information and entertainment, fact and fiction. The characters and events are mainly kept within the bounds of possibility. They are shown externally, often dramatically through vividly realised scenes, and the narrative voice is in general so detached as to be inaudible.

The above description fits the style of *Heimskringla* well. A century has elapsed since Ari Þorgilsson produced his *Íslendingabók*, and the accumulated Icelandic experience of translating saints' lives and writing the lives of Norwegian kings and Icelandic bishops, poets, farmers and warriors matures in *Heimskringla* into a confident, even-paced narrative, while history, freed from the constraints of Ari's scholarly but mainly summary treatment, takes life.

That style is rather an intractable topic is manifest from the nervously scant treatment it often receives, whether in scholarly books or student examination scripts. As already noted, the evolution of style in Icelandic saga-literature still needs much fuller examination, and there are few comprehensive stylistic studies of particular works. For *Heimskringla*, there exist several studies, either of small portions of the text compared with cognate sources, or of particular stylistic features, and some of these have identified what we might take as 'Snorri hallmarks'. There is only sparing use of the historic present tense; there is frequent use of the conjunction *en* or *en er* in preference to *ok*, of passives but not impersonal constructions, of relative clauses, of verb-initial sentences, of unannounced transitions from indirect to direct speech, and so on. But it is difficult at present to draw these disparate findings together in any very illuminating way, and the scale of *Heimskringla* and the complexity of its sources render it very difficult to make meaningful generalisations about aspects of its style. The observations which follow do not pretend to achieve statistical precision or to break wholly new ground, but it is hoped that they provide a fair starting-point for the appreciation of *Heimskringla*'s style.

DETAILS OF STYLE

Economy

A leading feature of Snorri's writing is its economy of expression. Few passages in *Heimskringla* could be rewritten more briefly without some loss of content or emphasis. This can be illustrated at the level of individual words from the account of the battle of Hjǫrungavágr. *Jómsvíkinga saga* ch. 33 and *Flateyjarbók* I 193 portray the Jomsviking Búi striking a Norwegian opponent in the words *Búi hǫggr (þá) í mót til Þorkels*, but *Heimskringla* lacks *í mót* 'against': *Búi hjó til Þorsteins* [sic]. The other two sources, but not *Heimskringla*, go on to specify that the ship was slippery with blood, and Þorkell fell while trying to get away, so that Búi's blow hit him in the waist and scythed him in two against the gunwale. The only detail in *Heimskringla* is that Búi struck

Style and Structure

útan á síðuna svá at sundr tók manninn í miðju, 'into his side, so that he sliced the man through the waist' (ÓlTrygg 41). This tendency of Snorri's not to make explicit every component link in a chain of action is manifest elsewhere in his account of Hjǫrungavágr. About the storm which brought about a reversal in the battle he writes: Þá gerði illviðri ok él svá mikit, at haglkornit eitt vá eyri. 'Then foul weather and a sharp storm blew up, so great that a single grain of hail weighed an ounce' (ÓlTrygg 41). The Flateyjarbók account of this moment, by contrast, occupies eight lines of print, ending: En menn hafa farit af klæðum um daginn ok var mǫnnum heitt. En nú var veðrit ǫðruvís ok tekr nú at kólna veðrit, 'But the men had taken clothes off during the day since they (literally, the men) were hot, but now the weather had changed and it (literally, the weather) was starting to grow cool' (I 192). This adds little of substance to the idea of a storm getting up. It is only rarely that the Heimskringla narrative edges forward in steps as small as these.

One detail in the Flateyjarbók passage (also in Jómsvíkinga saga ch. 33 and Fagrskinna ch. 22) specifies that the Jomsvikings had to fight in the face of the storm. This is lacking from the Heimskringla account, and its absence is paid for with a certain loss in clarity. Often, though, the relative terseness of the Heimskringla narrative implies no such loss, and indeed its vigour and starkness have been much admired. In the account of the battle of Svǫlð which concludes Óláfs saga Tryggvasonar, the doomed king, seeing Eiríkr jarl and his forces among his enemies, utters a speech of mingled respect and bitterness, ending with the words Þeir eru Norðmenn, sem vér erum (ch. 104). Some might feel that there is a tragic starkness here which surpasses that of Oddr Snorrason's saga, where further remarks follow (p. 218).

A further aspect of the economy of Snorri's writing is the comparative scarcity of narrative formulas such as svá er sagt 'it is said', or nú er eigi sagt fleira frá hjali þeira 'now nothing more is told about their talk'. This trait is revealed in a comparison of the tale of Dala-Guðbrandr (Guðbrandsþáttr) in the Legendary saga and Snorri's Separate Saga of Óláfr helgi made by Anne Heinrichs (1976, 15–16). Narratorial comments in Heimskringla are further examined in the section on the Narrator, pp. 92–3 below.

This verbal economy is by no means personal to Snorri (it is matched, for instance, in Fagrskinna or in the 'O' text of Hallfreðar saga), but it does seem to be the product of a definite, if not necessarily conscious, sense of style.

Unobtrusiveness

The lexical resources of Old Icelandic were possibly better known to Snorri, as the author of the *Prose Edda*, than to any of his contemporaries. But in *Heimskringla*, as elsewhere in 'classical' Icelandic sagas, the impression is of a rather modest use of vocabulary. The words selected often denote exactly what is necessary, and no more. A sentence such as that which opens *ÓlTrygg* 38 would be typical of much of *Heimskringla*: *Jómsvíkingar heldu liði sínu til Limafjarðar ok sigldu þaðan út á hafit ok hǫfðu sex tigu skipa ok koma at Ǫgðum* . . . 'The Jomsvikings brought their fleet into the Limfjord and from there sailed out to sea. They had sixty ships, and they came to Agder . . .' As frequently in early prose literature (Old English, for example), repetition is not a cause for embarrassment. *Ólhelg* 38 reads: *En er hann kom norðr til fjalls, þá byrjar hann ferð sína, kømr norðr um fjallit ok fór til þess, er hann kom norðr af fjallinu*, 'and when he came north to the mountains (literally, mountain), he begins his journey, goes north over the mountains and kept on until he got north of the mountains.' Yet such repetition of nouns where pronouns might have been substituted is used sparingly compared with the *Legendary saga*, and this forms part of Anne Heinrichs' case for seeing *Heimskringla* as farther from the interface between oral and literary cultures than the *Legendary Saga* (1976, 15–16). At the other extreme from the case of *Ólhelg* 38, a celebrated speech of Kálfr Árnason contains five different words for 'army', four for 'unafraid' and three for 'leader' (*Ólhelg* 220, discussed by Lie, 1937, 115). The vocabulary of direct speech, indeed, tends throughout the work to be both more varied and more markedly 'literary' than that of the third-person narrative, although the contrast is not always as sharp as between the two examples above. We are more likely to find poeticisms in direct speech, as for instance in Einarr þambarskelfir's anguished *of veykr, of veykr allvalds bogi* 'too weak, too weak the sovereign's bow' as his master's bow snaps at the critical moment in the battle of Svǫlð (*ÓlTrygg* 108), or in the words of Haraldr Sigurðarson over Úlfr stallari's grave: *Þar liggr sá nú, er dyggvastr var ok dróttinhollastr*, 'There lies the one who was most valiant and most loyal to his liege' (*HSig* 79).

Epithets are sparingly used, characteristically broad rather than precise in their reference, and functional rather than decorative in effect, indicating size, colour or materials (of objects) or age, wealth, nationality, stature, strength or religious status (of persons). *Mikill, góðr, stórr, ríkr, fagr, gǫfugr* and *ágætr* are among those most frequently used.

Where attributes are mentioned they may well be significant in the unfolding of the action. At the opening of *ÓlTrygg* 78 Rauðr inn rammi is described as *maðr stórauðigr . . . ríkr maðr . . . blótmaðr mikill ok mjǫk fjǫlkunnigr* 'a man of great wealth, a powerful man . . . a great man for sacrifices and very skilled in magic'. We are not being given a portrait so much as the reasons why Óláfr must convert or crush him. Even this degree of attention to traits of appearance or personality is rare outside formal (usually introductory) portraits of the *dramatis personae*. This is not to say that the narrative is totally bare of decorative detail. Rauðr's ship with its gilded dragon-stems is described briefly later in the chapter and more elaborately two chapters farther on when confiscated and renamed Ormr by the king (and see section on Events, pp. 96–9 below). But description for its own sake is rare.

At the syntactic level too the general impression is of relative simplicity. An analysis of *Ynglinga saga* and *Óláfs saga Tryggvasonar* in the *Íslenzk fornrit* text yields the following provisional information. Some 64% of the sentences in *Ynglinga saga* contain no subordinate clauses. Nearly 43% consist of a single main clause. No more than 9% of all the sentences have more than one subordinate clause. In *Óláfs saga Tryggvasonar* some 53% of sentences contain no subordinate clause, and nearly 34% consist of a single main clause. At most 17% of sentences contain more than one subordinate clause. Insofar as subordination is a gauge of syntactic complexity, therefore, straightforwardness is the norm. The extreme of this can be illustrated by *Yng* 22. The first sentence of the chapter contains two subordinate clauses, but the remaining nineteen sentences have none at all. The middle of the chapter has a succession of seven sentences consisting of a single main clause each, including the staccato: *Þeir hittusk á Fýrisvǫllum. Varð þar mikil orrosta. Fell brátt lið Hugleiks*, 'They met on Fýrisvellir. There was a great battle there. Hugleikr's forces quickly fell.'

It is probably true to say that Snorri's style is normally terse and syntactically uncomplicated, but a great deal more work on the various manuscripts of *Heimskringla* and on comparative materials is needed before an accurate description emerges. Certainly, like most such statements, this one can very readily be overturned by counter-examples, for complexity too can be found, for instance:

> En fyrir þá sǫk, at atlaga þessi hafði ekki þannug tekizk sem Knútr konungr hafði til skipat, hǫfðu skipin ekki þannug fram lagt sem til var skipat, þá varð ekki af atróðrinum, ok kǫnnuðu þeir Knútr konungr lið sitt ok tóku þá at skipa liðinu ok bjoggusk um.

(But because this assault had not turned out as King Knútr had commanded, the ships had not advanced as had been commanded; then nothing came of their attack, and King Knútr and his men surveyed their force and then started to put it (lit. the force) in order, and made ready.) (*Ólhelg* 150.)

However, allowance should be made for the difficulties of imposing modern conventions of punctuation (and even of syntactic analysis) on a text which was composed without reference to them. In this instance the construction would be made simpler by the insertion of a full stop after the second *skipat* 'planned', so that *þá varð* begins a new sentence. Further, it should be borne in mind that the text was in all probability written down from dictation and designed for reading aloud. As a further example of complexity, we might take Finnr Skoptason's remonstration to Magnús berfœttr (*Mberf* 18). It contains thirteen finite verbs, which are linked by four coordinating conjunctions (*ok* and *en* 'than' twice each) and eight subordinating (*þá er* and *at* once each and *er*, *ef* and *sem* twice each).

Rhetoric

Figurative language is only sparingly used in *Heimskringla*. At least in the third-person narrative prose, it is irony, chiefly in the form of cool understatement, which is most in evidence. Emundr lǫgmaðr is 'known as a devious man and only moderately trustworthy' (*kallaðr undirhyggjumaðr ok meðallagi trúr*, *Ólhelg* 94). Þórarinn Nefjólfsson's hideously ugly foot is 'in no way lovelier' (*engum mun fegri*, *Ólhelg* 85) than his other, ugly, foot which has already been revealed. Again, two rulers who part 'angry' (*reiðir*) in *Morkinskinna* p. 263 are 'not wholly in agreement' (*ekki mjǫk sáttir*) in *Heimskringla*, *HSig* 78). Simile is rare, metaphor even more so. These figures are usually drawn from the world of nature—animals, weather or the elements—and when used in third-person narrative they are normally associated with striking sights or violent actions. The sail on Hárekr's ship is 'white as fresh snow' (*Ólhelg* 158), the gilded ornament on another approaching ship is 'like fires blazing' (*HSig* 35), while men in battle may rage or howl like dogs or wolves (*Yng* 6, *MblokHg* 11) or be felled like cattle and piled up like waves or jetsam (*unnvǫrp*, *Mgóð* 28). They are rare enough to give great emphasis to such statements as that the crippled King Ingi, learning of the death of Grégóríús Dagsson, 'wept like a child' (*Hákherð* 15).

Patterning of the language, especially by the use of repeated words or word-stems or of parallel syntactic structures, is a device used more in

Heimskringla than in other *konungasögur*, and it is more common in direct speech than elsewhere. It may be used within a single speech, sounding a keynote, as when Sigurðr sýr repeatedly refers to his stepson Óláfr Haraldsson's *kapp* '(rash) bravery' in *Ólhelg* 35, but it is most often to be noticed in dramatic exchanges between two speakers at moments of climax and crisis. (Lie gave the term *responsjon* to such repetition—'repartee' is perhaps the nearest in English.) Óláfr Tryggvason's queen Þyri throws his words back at him when, egged by her to recover her estates in Wendland, he arrives in her chamber offering nothing more than affection and an armful of angelica (*ÓlTrygg* 92). Oddr Snorrason's telling of the anecdote (pp. 185–86) lacks the verbal tension and neat staging of Snorri's version. In ch. 42 of the same saga Hávarðr hǫggvandi, learning that he has shot not Hákon jarl but only one of his *lendir menn* says: *Þá varð minna happit en ek vilda*, 'Then it wasn't such good luck as I hoped.' *Œrit var óhappit*, 'It was bad luck enough', say his enemies, *en eigi skaltu vinna fleiri*, 'and you won't cause any more,' and kill him. Peter Hallberg's comment on the direct speech in Snorri's work certainly seems justified, that here 'we find combined his outstanding qualities as historian, judge of characters, and artist' (1978, 137).

Variety

Stylistic variety in *Heimskringla* is mainly provided by the alternation of a norm of third-person narrative, lucid and unpretentious, with direct speech which is typically rather more 'literary', and with skaldic verse quotations most of which are ambitiously elaborate in lexis and syntax. However, these simple distinctions by no means capture the range of style, for although the character of the third-person narrative is fairly homogeneous, there is also much variation. This is attributable to, among other things, the range of sources used. Certain passages seem to leap out of the page as we read them, their style seems so uncharacteristic. In these cases we suspect an underlying source which has been transcribed closely, and we can often prove the suspicion. *HSig* 56 begins like this:

> Greifi einn var í Danmǫrku, illr ok ǫfundfullr . . . En sá greifi, er áðan gat ek, tortryggði allt þat, er honum var sagt frá þess helga manns jartegnum, kvað ekki vera nema kvitt ok pata einn, gerði sér at gabbi ok at gamni lof ok dýrð þá, er landsfólk allt veitti þeim góða konnngi.
> (There was a count in Denmark, evil and envious . . . And this count, whom I mentioned just now, disbelieved everything that was told him about the holy

man's [St Olaf's] miracles, saying that it was nothing but gossip and rumour, making a mock and a joke of the praise and glory which all the people of the country gave to that worthy king.)

Attention is arrested here by many untypical features, notably the epithets, word-pairs and first-person pronoun and verb, and more generally by the uncompromising moral weighting that these devices produce. It therefore comes as no surprise to find that the passage is an only slightly diluted version of a legend of St Olaf preserved in the *Norwegian Homily Book* (*Gamal Norsk Homiliebok*, p. 115). Similarly, the often highly-wrought periods of the Snæfríðr episode are from the pen of the *Ágrip* author, not from Snorri's. The last sentence of the episode, in which Haraldr recovers from his excessive grief at Snæfríðr's death, is the clearest and probably most famous example of borrowing:

Seig hon svá í ǫsku, en konungrinn steig til vizku ok hugði af heimsku, stýrði síðan ríki sínu ok styrkðisk, gladdisk hann af þegnum sínum ok þegnar af honum, en ríkit af hváru tveggja.
(Thus she sank to ash, but the king rose to wisdom and turned his thoughts from folly, then steered his kingdom and gained strength, took joy in his retainers and they in him, and the kingdom in both.) (*Hhárf* 25, cf. *Ágrip* ch. 4.)

It appears from these and other passages that, although Snorri's normal procedure was to impart his own style to the material, he must on occasions have instructed his amanuensis to import part of a previous narrative more or less verbatim.

Stylistic variation is produced by the use of diverse sources, but it is also to some extent a reflection of the different kinds of action portrayed. A plethora of verbs in paratactic structures can, for example, mimic swift and decisive action. The visit of a troll-wife is described thus: *Síðan greip hon mann þann, er næst henni var, reif ok sleit allan, kastaði á eldinn,* 'Then she seized the man who was nearest her, tore and rent him whole, threw [him] on the fire' (*Ólhelg* 141). The description of the battle of Forminterra in *Msona* 6 provides further examples. As seen here, swiftness of tempo is effected by placing the verb first in the clause and hence linking it with the preceding one, with which it shares a subject. This is especially noticeable in battle scenes but also, for instance, when the attempted murder of Haraldr Sigurðarson by night is described in *HSig* 22.

Elsewhere, the use of parallel structures and of paired synonyms or antonyms may give a formalised, 'official' ring to the narrative, as when Óláfr Haraldsson's punishment of the recalcitrant pagans of Upplǫnd is described :

Suma rak hann brot ór landi, suma lét hann hamla at hǫndum eða fótum eða stinga augu út, suma lét hann hengja eða hǫggva, en engi lét hann óhegndan, þann er eigi vildi guði þjóna ... Jafnt hegndi hann ríka ok óríka.
(Some he drove from the land, some he had maimed in hand or foot or their eyes pierced out, some he had hanged or beheaded, but he let none go unpunished who would not serve God ... He punished great and small alike.) (*Ólhelg* 73.)

In more subtle ways, too, the character of the *Heimskringla* narrative may be a product both of the nature of the events described and of the sources available to Snorri. The greater syntactic simplicity of *Ynglinga saga* as compared with *Óláfs saga Tryggvasonar* which was observed above may perhaps reflect the nature of the two sagas, one summarily depicting a large tract of the remote and largely unknown past, the other presenting in detail a reign about which Snorri had a great deal of information.

The cumulative effect of the details of style surveyed here is a narrative which is swift, lucid and restrained. Snorri describes Haraldr Sigurðarson fighting for England and his life at Stamford Bridge thus:

Hann hljóp fram allt ór fylkingunni ok hjó báðum hǫndum. Helt þá hvártki við honum hjálmr né brynja. Þá stukku frá allir þeir, er næstir váru. Var þá við sjálft, at enskir menn mundi flýja. Svá segir Arnórr jarlaskáld ...
(He ran right forward, out of the battle-line, and struck blows with both hands. Neither helmet nor mail-coat could hold against him. Then all the men nearest at hand scattered. It nearly reached the point where the English fled. So says Arnórr jarlaskáld ...) (*HSig* 92.)

The corresponding passage in the near-contemporary *Morkinskinna* makes fuller use of, among other things, descriptive and evaluative epithets and of figurative language.

Þá spennir hann báðum hǫndum meðalkafla sverðsins, ok hǫggr á tvær hendr, bíðr ekki merkjanna, ryðr svá stiginn fyrir sér, ok veitir mǫrgum manni bana. Þat segja allir menn eina lund, at eigi hefði sét drengiligri framgǫngu, ok háða með jafnmikilli hugprýði. Hafði hann báðar hendr blóðgar, ok gekk svá milli óvina sinna náliga sem hann œði vind. Ok sýndisk at hann hræddisk hvártki eld né járn. Sem Stúfr segir ...
(Then he grasps the hilt of his sword with both hands and strikes blows on both sides, not waiting for the standards, and so clears a path before him, and deals death to many a man. All men say the same, that they had never seen a more valiant attack, carried out with such great boldness of spirit. He had both hands bloody, and in this way went through his enemies almost as if striding through wind, and it was made clear that he feared neither fire nor iron. As Stúfr says ...) (*Morkinskinna* 1932, p. 277.)

Heimskringla

BROADER FEATURES OF STYLE

The narrator

The events described in *Heimskringla* are overwhelmingly left to speak for themselves without overt comment—moral or partisan—on the part of the narrator. Nevertheless, there are ways in which we are made aware of the process of narration, and these are explored in the following paragraphs.

Explicit reminders of a guiding hand are mostly of a routine and impersonal kind, expressed in formulas such as the introductory *en þat er at segja frá* or the cross-referencing *svá sem fyrr er / var ritit / ritat*. A handful of more extended comments in the first person concern the selection of material. Two important ones appear to be original to Snorri: the statement in *ÓlTrygg* 80 that the author is more concerned with Óláfr's Christianization of Norway and other lands than with his encounters with trolls and other evil creatures; and the affirmation of the value of recounting the miracles of St Óláfr in *Ólhelg* 246. Frequently, however, they are inherited more or less verbatim from a source, e.g. *Hsona* 22: *Nú gerðisk mart þess í með þeim brœðrum, er til sundrþykkis var, en ek mun þó hins eins geta, er mér þykkir mestum tíðendum sætt hafa*, 'Now much passed between the brothers of a kind to cause disagreement, but I shall only mention what seems to me to have been the most important.' *Morkinskinna* p. 453 has virtually identical wording, and the *ek* may well be Eiríkr Oddsson.

The narrator sometimes draws attention to himself and his antiquarian interest in customs of the past by commenting on details of government, court life, religion, sea battles or drinking, introducing them by phrases such as 'it was the custom' (*þat var siðvenja / siðr / siðvandi*) or *í þann tíma* or simply *þá*. Predictably enough such comments are most common in *Heimskringla* I, examples being found in *Yng* 34, *Yng* 37, *Hhárf* 11 and *ÓlTrygg* 21, but they occur sporadically later, e.g. *Msona* 24. Another category of statement also draws attention to the temporal distance between narrator and events, and hence to the act of narration itself, but this time by stressing the continuity of past and present. A handful concern the survival of traces of the past (graves, burial mounds and memorial stones) down to Snorri's own day. Statements that monuments are still visible or located at named sites are framed around present-tense verbs (*sér, liggr, standa*, sometimes accompanied by *enn* or *nú*), and these suggest the presence of the narrator in the text, as well as the possibility that Snorri had visited these sites himself (*Hhárf* 42,

Hákgóð 27, *ÓlTrygg* 88, *Ólhelg* 111). Still another, rare, linkage of past and present is exemplified in *Hhárf* 24 where, mentioning Gǫngu-Hrólfr, Snorri draws attention to his descendant Vilhjálmr bastarðr, king of England, and adds *ok frá honum eru síðan komnir Englakonungar allir*, 'and all the subsequent kings of England are descended from him.'

Generalisations about human behaviour, cast again in the present tense, also give periodic reminders of a narrator's presence. When Haraldr Sigurðarson washes himself in the Jordan it is 'as the custom is with other pilgrims' (*sem háttr er til annarra pálmara, HSig* 12, cf. *MblokHg* 13). The discomfiture of Álfhildr, who cannot endure the rivalry for prestige at her son Magnús's court, is 'as can happen to many who gain power' (*sem mǫrgum kann verða, þeim er fá ríkdóminn, Mgóð* 7). A more moralistic, even gnomic tone can be heard, but it is rare and is probably always an echo of a source. When a young Dane in *Msona* 31 is captured a third time without ransom we hear: *Vel hefir sá maðr, er eigi bíðr slíkt illt þessa heims, sem hann þóttisk þá beðit hafa*, 'It is well for the man who never endures such trial in this world as he felt he endured then.' The words are inherited from a miracle tale. Outright statements of opinion about particular people or events are also extremely sparse, and tend to be used only to correct a false interpretation voiced by one of the characters. Thus in *Ólhelg* 181 Snorri defends Óláfr against the reported charge of being niggardly; rather he was very generous—more so than the two-faced briber Knútr. When Halldórr Snorrason in the heat of battle jibingly accuses Haraldr Sigurðarson of cowardice, Snorri, as well as inserting the adverb *óvitrliga* 'foolishly', adds that Halldórr was talking in anger not truth, 'for Haraldr was the most daring with weapons' (*því at Haraldr var inn vápndjarfasti maðr, HSig* 9). However, it should again be stressed that this, like the other categories of statement mentioned in this section, is quite a rarity, and that the norm in *Heimskringla* is for events to proceed without overt steering or judgement from the narrator.

Character

The approach to character portrayal in *Heimskringla* is closely akin to that of the *Íslendingasögur*. The formal descriptions which appear as introductions, obituaries or at other salient points list features of character and appearance in a summary and often stereotypical way. Sigurðr slembidjákn is:

allra manna vaskligastr ok sterkr, mikill maðr, ok á alla atgørvi var hann um fram alla jafnaldra sína ok náliga hvern annan í Nóregi. Sigurðr var snimma ofsamaðr mikill ok óeirarmaðr. Hann var kallaðr slembidjákn. Manna var hann fríðastr, heldr þunnhárr ok þó vel hærðr.
(the boldest of men, and strong, a big man, and one who surpassed all of his age and nearly everyone else in Norway in all accomplishments. Sigurðr was from an early age a thoroughly overbearing and ruthless man; he was known as *slembidjákn* (sham-deacon?). He was the most handsome of men, rather thin-haired but with good hair all the same.) (*MblokHg* 13.)

The third-person narrative is seldom used to analyse the motives and feelings of characters, and generally the audience is left, as in real life, to size up characters on the basis of externals. The heart-searchings of Óláfr Haraldsson, in exile in Garðar, are exposed (*Ólhelg* 87–88), but this is exceptional. Normally when the ruminations of characters are glimpsed they are practical rather than existential (e.g. Þyri in *ÓlTrygg* 92; Sigurðr slembidjákn in *MblokHg* 14).

It is through the actions and words of the protagonists and the comments of others on them that character, motive and mood are most subtly and vividly revealed. The speech of the young Óláfr Haraldsson in ch. 35 of his saga ranges through heroic gesture, political generalisation and Christian regret for a Viking career, and the responses of his parents add further dimensions. His step-father Sigurðr provides a royal reception but also, in his speech, a pragmatic counterpoint to Óláfr's words, while his mother Ásta offers affectionate welcome and support for his grand ambitions. No less than a quarter of *Óláfs saga helga* is taken up by direct speech—a proportion only exceeded in *Heimskringla* by the brief *Hákonar saga herðibreiðs* (Hallberg 1968, 214, Table 9), although it is matched by the *Legendary Saga of Óláfr helgi* (Hallberg 1978, 117). Although direct speech has many functions, including the distillation of ideas and information and the pointing of climaxes, the revelation of character is among the most vital. The high proportion of direct speech in *Óláfs saga helga* is due not to the number of individual utterances but to their length. By comparison with *Fagrskinna* and the *Legendary Saga* there are twice as many words in each 'speech situation', and often the extended utterances have no counterpart in the other two works (Hallberg 1978, 117–18).

Individual utterances, even brief ones, add zest to the narrative. Often they do double service, simultaneously casting light on the speaker and the person on whom he or she is passing comment. Thus in the conversation about Magnús Óláfsson's hasty baptism without his father's presence or consent, Óláfr Haraldsson, melted by Sigvatr the skald's argument says, *Gæfumaðr ertu mikill, Sigvatr. Er þat eigi undarligt, at gæfa fylgi vizku,* 'You are a man of great good luck, Sigvatr. It is not surprising that good luck should go with wisdom' (*Ólhelg* 122). The generalisation leads us to reflect on Óláfr's own nature and career as well as Sigvatr's. Another example is Finnr Árnason's bitter outburst to Haraldr Sigurðarson in *HSig* 45.

There is no doubt that Snorri's writing, free from hagiographic zeal or overt political partisanship, offers portraits very much more complex and true to life than are to be found in most of the other kings' sagas. The presentation of two enemies of Óláfr Haraldsson, the deposed and blinded King Hrœrekr and the embittered Þórir hundr is, for instance, masterful and penetrating compared with that of other sources. Finnr Árnason is portrayed with strength and compassion in a number of emotionally taut scenes, and Bergljót, wife of Einarr þambarskelfir and only a name in *Morkinskinna* and *Fagrskinna*, makes a dramatic appearance at the scene of her husband's and son's murder in *HSig* 44. Nevertheless, few of the personages are drawn in sufficient detail to emerge as credible human beings (though imaginative effort on the reader's part may make them so) and it has often been remarked that the characters in *Heimskringla* do not necessarily speak with an individual voice. Thus Þorviðr stammi 'the Stammerer' is true to his name, but Haraldr gilli, mocked for his halting Norse, actually expresses himself perfectly fluently (Lie 1937, 123–24).

It is certainly worth considering other ways of seeing the character portraits of *Heimskringla* than as attempts at psychological authenticity, and most readers have recognised the presence of some kind of stereotyping or idealisation in them. Hallvard Lie thought that recurring ideal types could be found in *Heimskringla*, including the farmer-magnate (Ásbjǫrn af Meðalhúsum, Þorgnýr lǫgmaðr) and the representative of wisdom and sense (Rǫgnvaldr jarl, Sigurðr sýr; 1936, 91). More recently, Ingebjørg Sogge, in a detailed study of Þórir hundr, finds symbolic value as well as individual psychology in his portrait. As she points out, his rôle is that of an intransigent enemy to Óláfr helgi, associated solely with the downward curve in his fortunes. At Stiklarstaðir he uses black magic against Óláfr, but is the first to benefit from a miracle of healing by him. Although his portrayal is considerably more subtle in *Heimskringla* than in earlier works, he appears, spiritually, as the opposite pole to Óláfr Haraldsson (1976, esp. 107–109). Further and more broadly, while the *Heimskringla* narrative has much to offer in the illumination of human character and behaviour, its interest often lies in the representation of ideas and situations. Among those who oppose Óláfr Haraldsson, Hrœrekr and Þórir hundr are interesting as people, but Einarr Þveræingr and Bishop Sigurðr are scarcely people at all, rather mouthpieces for alternative opinions on the saint-king's career. It is not Bergljót's personality (of which we learn nothing except its strength) but her situation which moves us in *HSig* 44. That it is often the total situation which is especially well captured in *Heimskringla* is also confirmed by a comparison of the oratory of *Heimskringla* with that in *Sverris saga* (Knirk 1981, 82, citing Sveinn Álfífuson's speech in *Mgóð* 4 as an example).

Events

The handling of particular events in *Heimskringla* ranges from the swift and spare to the rich and leisurely. (Cf. Allen's discussion of degrees of reportage in *Njáls saga*, 1971, 30–34.) *Mberf* 11 in about a dozen lines covers Magnús taking possession of the Hebrides, marrying off his son and returning to Norway. It also records the deaths of the earls of Orkney in Norway and introduces Skopti Ǫgmundarson and his family, who are to play a leading part in later chapters. However, it is the episodes which are cast as developed scenes (especially those containing direct speech) which imprint themselves most strongly on readers' memories. Few could fail to relish the picture of the Norwegian army as, cheered by recent victories, they leave their armour at the ships and march in warm sunshine towards the city of York, only to sight and speculate on the dust and glint of approaching cavalry (*HSig* 87), or the beautifully staged parley between the English Haraldr (whose identity is unknown to his Norwegian namesake) and his brother Tósti (ch. 91).

The reasons why some episodes are highlighted by full narrative treatment and others not would repay more detailed examination than is possible here. Certainly centrality to Scandinavian history is an important criterion. A battle fought on the margins of the world of *Heimskringla* (Úlfreksfjǫrðr in Ireland, *Ólhelg* 86, Helsingjaport / Hastings in England, *HSig* 96) may be dismissed in a handful of lines, which report only in the vaguest terms on a 'great battle', 'far larger force', 'victory' or 'fall'. In other cases the richness of tradition—the sheer appeal of the story—seems critical. This must account for the amount of space dedicated to Haraldr Sigurðarson's conquests of four Sicilian towns (*HSig* 6–10).

Some of the most compelling narrative moments are characterised by a manipulation of viewpoint so that events are experienced through the perceptions of the protagonists. This technique of the 'restricted viewpoint' (discussed, with related phenomena, in Lie 1937, 36–52) is particularly suited to the narration of events involving suspense such as attacks and conspiracies. Sigvatr skald feels something wet (blood?) on the steps at night (*Ólhelg* 83), Þóroddr Snorrason lies in the firelight in an isolated cottage, watching and listening as a man of strange and distinguished appearance talks with his peasant hosts (*Ólhelg* 141), and we share their ignorance of what is to come. This withholding of privileged or hindsight information can effect the surprise of sudden action, but also produce intense impressions of atmosphere or mood. Thus we can experience the growing dismay of the princess Ingigerðr as her father Óláfr Svíakonungr maintains his morose silence on the subject of her betrothal to Óláfr Haraldsson (*Ólhelg* 88), or the apprehension of Kálfr Árnason as Magnús Óláfsson prepares the show-down with him at the site of his father's slaying (*Mgóð* 14).

Particular examples of the technique of limited viewpoint can often be traced to a source, and the example of *Færeyinga saga* may have encouraged Snorri in his use of it (Bjarni Aðalbjarnarson, *Heimskringla* 1941–51, II, xlv n.; Foote 1965, 16), but it is certainly something he excelled in, as comparison with other tellings of the same incident frequently shows. In *HSig* 10 the Varangians, besieging a Sicilian city, are allowed in with a funeral cortège for their dead leader Haraldr, and although the saga-audience (who probably knew the story already) could not have been taken in by this Trojan horse as readily as the citizens were, they could relish the chaos as Haraldr and his men spring into action and sack the town. The *Morkinskinna* author (p. 73) spoils the story by having Haraldr explain his plan of feigned sickness and death to his troops at the outset. Similarly, in *HSig* 64 there is a detailed and highly entertaining account of the escape of 'Vandráðr', also called 'the man in the hood', *hattarmaðr*, after the battle of Niz. It is not until ch. 67 that it is made explicit that this was Sveinn Úlfsson of Denmark, but once more, the game is given away in *Morkinskinna* (p. 214), as it is in *Fagrskinna* (ch. 57), with the unequivocal *Sveinn konungr flýði nú á land upp.*

On the other hand, there are occasions where the outcome is anticipated. We know that the English Haraldr is marching north before the Norwegians do (*HSig* 86), and the assassination of Haraldr gilli in his sleep is given away in *MblokHg* 15. A vassal of Haraldr asks the king, supposedly to settle a bet, whether he will be spending the night with his wife or his mistress. The king tells him *hlæjandi ok var mjǫk óvitandi at* þessi spurning væri með svá mikilli vél, 'laughing and quite unaware that this question contained such great deceit'. Here both the uncharacteristic use of the participial construction and the lack of suspense suggest that the narrative is imported direct from a source, and comparison with *Morkinskinna* (p. 412) confirms this.

Another feature of the *Heimskringla* narrative which is frequently acclaimed is its striking visual effects: Magnús berfœttr in military splendour on Ulster terrain of bog and brushwood (*Mberf* 24), Sigurðr Jórsalafari and his men riding haughtily through the splendid streets of Constantinople (*Msona* 12), the ice-bound ship beside which Hallr Koðránsbani meets his death (*HSig* 72), and many others. Often it can be shown that the addition of scene-setting details, especially those referring to weather or time of day, is part of Snorri's own contribution to particular episodes. The descriptions in *Mberf* 24 are only slightly more elaborate than the corresponding passage in *Morkinskinna* (pp. 334–35), but they are enlivened by Snorri's indication that Magnús and his company came ashore as the sun came up and that the day was sunny and windless. Again, in the highly-charged scene before the battle of Stiklarstaðir, *Heimskringla* has *þá rann dagr upp* (*Ólhelg* 208), pre-echoing *Dagr es upp kominn*, the opening line of *Bjarkamál* which Þormóðr Kolbrúnarskáld is about to recite. The *Legendary Saga* has merely *þá* (quoted by Lie 1937, 13, within a more extended discussion of this feature).

On the whole, though, the events stand out starkly, with next to no scenery or props to distract attention from the action and dialogue. What scene-setting details there are, whether inherited or introduced by Snorri, are typically brief and highly functional, contributing directly to the action of the saga. The ice-covered river in *Hákherð* 14 provides the opportunity for Grégóríús Dagsson's death and the hot sunny day in *Msona* 28 enables Sigurðr Jórsalafari to have his vicious swimming contest with an Icelander. In *Mberf* 24, referred to above, it is the landscape which enables the Irish to stage their fatally successful ambush. The lavish description of Magnús may conceivably have symbolic or at least dramatic force, suggesting pride before a fall, or it may be included merely because it was part of the inherited tradition.

Themes and opinions

The author's concern in *Heimskringla* is above all with kingly power—the winning and keeping of it. This grand theme is in turn woven from smaller themes or running threads—such issues as internecine rivalry, the relations between the royal successors of Haraldr hárfagri and the earls of Hlaðir, kingly versus chieftainly power, native versus foreign rule, Norway's relations with neighbouring lands, or the fate of Christianity in Norway and its colonies. To the extent that *Heimskringla* reflects actual events of the past, these issues are real rather than artistic fabrications. Yet they are also a product of the writing process, partly pre-formed in Snorri's sources but also presented by him with greater depth and cogency than by his predecessors. Sometimes a vital thread will be highlighted directly in the narrative, as when eternal fratricide among the Ynglingar is predicted by the seeress Hulð in *Yng* 14. Elsewhere more indirect means are used, as Snorri, either in third-person narrative or through the voices of the *dramatis personae*, draws implicit or explicit parallels and contrasts between events, and highlights essential threads by eliminating trivia. The text itself thus forms a rich thematic texture, but also Snorri's preoccupations are thrown into sharper relief by comparison with parallel accounts. The Christianisation of Norway by the two King Olafs, for instance, a major preoccupation of *Heimskringla*, is given very scant coverage in *Fagrskinna*.

A vigorous debate took place in the early decades of this century as to whether *Heimskringla* embodies any unitary view or theory of Norwegian history. Halvdan Koht (especially 1914) maintained that the objectivity of the narrative in the sagas of kings was more apparent than real and that they frequently have partisan standpoints. In *Morkinskinna*, for example, he found a distinctly ecclesiastical bias. Snorri, he maintained, had a very definite, and actually erroneous, theory, namely that the driving force in early Norwegian history was the conflict between monarchy and aristocracy. He believed Snorri's view to be influenced by Norwegian politics since the reign of Sverrir. Koht's thesis was extremely influential, and important variations on it have been produced. Gudmund Sandvik also demonstrated the importance of the conflict between king and aristocracy in reigns such as that of Óláfr helgi in *Heimskringla*. He too felt that, compared with historical actuality, the conflict was exaggerated, ascribing this especially to Snorri's standpoint as an Icelandic aristocrat (1955, esp. 98–99). Siegfried Beyschlag (1956 and 1966) similarly emphasised the relations of king and magnates and believed that *Heimskringla* showed the movement from conflict to collaboration between them as the feudal state emerged and matured. A different response came from Fredrik Paasche (especially 1922a and 1922b), who shared Koht's scepticism about the importance of king-chieftain conflicts in Norwegian history, but challenged his theory of strongly partisan viewpoints in *Heimskringla* and others of the kings' sagas. As he points out, Snorri may show eminent landed men taking sides with Knútr of Denmark against Óláfr Haraldsson, but this does not necessarily imply opposition by the landed men as a class, nor does it necessarily extend to other sagas in *Heimskringla* (1922b, 13). Overall, he maintained that Snorri had views of history, but not a single view (1922b, 17), and that on the whole he 'let the past remain peacefully alone' (1922a, 331; cf. also Gurevich 1971, 42).

The question whether particular political opinions are promoted in *Heimskringla*, and, if so, what they are, is a peculiarly challenging one. *Heimskringla* is celebrated among kings' sagas for its evenhandedness. The scope given to King Hrœrekr, Þórir hundr and Bishop Sigurðr to speak out against (the mainly admirable) Óláfr Haraldsson, or Ásbjǫrn af Meðalhúsum's eloquent opposition to Hákon góði's Christian mission are classic examples. The appraisal of Hákon jarl Sigurðarson (especially *ÓlTrygg* 45 and 50) breathes wisdom and balance, and the issue of Icelandic independence, potentially a focus of passionate debate in Snorri's day, is dealt with rather moderately (see Chapter Six: Author's standpoint). Therefore although certain sympathies may be detectable, it would be difficult to avoid the general conclusion that what *Heimskringla* offers is something very much more interesting and complex than forthright opinions. Certainly, as Bjarni Einarsson has pointed out, *Heimskringla*'s royalist sympathies are less fervent than those of *Fagrskinna*, which might indeed have been composed for Hákon Hákonarson himself (*Ágrip*, 1984, cxxii–cxxiii). It is even possible to argue for a consciously ambivalent, or at least mediatory, message about the values of the feudal monarchy and independent chieftainly power in an episode such as the *Friðgerðarsaga* in *Óláfs saga helga* chs 68–94 (Lönnroth 1976, discussed by Andersson 1985, 224, who remarks on the paucity of published work on the ideology of the kings' sagas).

On issues of a more broadly social or ethical kind Snorri's sympathies may again be guessed at from the narrative, but they are rarely simple and rarely made explicit. Haraldr hárfagri's sexual appetite, and the resulting glut of sons, creates a disastrous scramble for the succession after his death and Snorri may have deplored it, but he does not say this outright. Snorri's attitude in larger matters such as the rivalry of the old and new religions is generally quite complex. No sympathy is wasted on pagan sorcerers, such as Eyvindr kinnrifa in *ÓlTrygg* 76, who, it seems, fully deserve the grisly deaths they receive from Christian monarchs. Yet there is a touch of the noble heathen about Haraldr hárfagri (*Hhárf* chs 4,

42), and Snorri sees, especially in Hákon góði's reign, how Christianity can come into collision with ancient rights and laws. Again, Snorri's comment that Hákon Sigurðarson's career was ill-starred especially because the days of paganism were over seems neutral, without anti-pagan sting (*ÓlTrygg* 50). To take another sphere of ideas, it might be difficult to discover a coherent attitude to women in *Heimskringla*. The few women who appear are mainly either passive nonentities or viragos, but what in this portrayal are the relative contributions of Snorri's thought, literary stereotypes and the actual status of women in Snorri's time or the time of the sagas? It is even difficult, finally, to say what qualities Snorri most admires in a king. The verve and artistry lavished on the major battles and their heroes (Svǫlð, Stiklarstaðir and Stamford Bridge among them) might suggest an admiration for warrior kings, yet Snorri has no zest for the details of slaughter, the last campaign of the dashing Haraldr Sigurðarson is manifestly condemned as foolish, and the military glamour of Sigurðr Jórsalafari is set off by Eysteinn's building programme. Another builder, Óláfr kyrri, gets only a three-page saga, but he is described in his obituary as 'a most popular king, and Norway had grown much in wealth and splendour under his rule'. On the whole, it seems likely that Snorri's ideal king is such a one as Magnús góði, in whom military prowess is tempered by wisdom and moderation and whose battles are in a just cause (see his necrologue in *HSig* 30).

Despite the difficulty, even the futility, of trying to discover coherent points of view in *Heimskringla* which will account for all the evidence, there are many individual episodes where the balance of sympathies is very clearly tipped one way or another. The presentation of Haraldr Sigurðarson's killing of Einarr þambarskelfir and his son Eindriði (*HSig* 40–45) shows Snorri—consciously or not—deploying some of the available tactics to present this as an act of calculated violence arising from political paranoia. Among the devices used are direct character description (Eindriði is admirable and popular); clear depiction of causation (political rivalry is more manifest than in the *Morkinskinna* account, pp. 178–80); narrative detail (Haraldr indicates willingness for reconciliation with Einarr, then has him killed as Einarr enters a shuttered room saying *myrkt er í konungs málstofu* 'it is dark in the king's council-chamber'); individual phrasing (brutality expressed in *lǫgðu sumir en sumir hjoggu* 'some thrust and some hacked'); and public opinion (Haraldr is very unpopular because of this action, and Finnr Árnason makes an outspoken attack on Haraldr; neither detail is in *Morkinskinna*).

A brief treatment of the question of themes and opinions in *Heimskringla* is bound to be inadequate, and much work remains to be done in this area. The challenge of it lies especially in the need to attempt important but elusive distinctions: between those themes or recurrent preoccupations which arise naturally from the material and those which are in some sense put there, or emphasised, by the author; between detached interpretations of events and attempts to use events persuasively to promote a particular (religious or political) party line; and between casual sympathies and coherent patterns of bias.

STRUCTURE

Ordering of material

It might seem self-evident that historical material should be organised in chronological order, and indeed this is the dominant principle in *Heimskringla*. The method serves well as long as there is clearly one main protagonist and one significant set of actions, and at its simplest it can yield a neat, numbered sequence. Fourteen early battles of Óláfr Haraldsson occupy, virtually without interruption, *Ólhelg* 6–19, and there are four conquests of Sicilian cities by Haraldr Sigurðarson in *HSig* 6–10, and eight triumphs of Sigurðr Jórsalafari in Spain and the Balearic islands in *Msona* 4–7. The first and last sequences had been pre-packaged by the skalds Sigvatr Þórðarson in his *Víkingarvísur* and Halldórr skvaldri in his *Útfarardrápa*.

Even when the arrangement is basically chronological, however, the effect is more than merely annalistic, for events are not merely noted and left behind, but seen within larger patterns of development and causal link, as illustrated in the section on Formal units, pp. 104–11 below. Further, chronological order is by no means the only principle of arrangement. Often there is a minor disturbance of the basic time sequence—a swift flashback, a recapitulation or a reference forward. For instance, in *Ólhelg* 137, about the rival claims of the Norwegian and Swedish King Olafs to the loyalty of the Jamtr, it is necessary for Snorri to retrace the previous history of Jamtaland and Helsingjaland, which has also been mentioned in *Hhárf* 19 and *Hákgóð* 12.

In this particular instance the handling of time is not particularly adept, since ch. 137 launches into the time before Haraldr hárfagri's reign without providing the reader with any chronological orientation. In other ways, too, the ordering of information is not always ideally coherent. Sometimes the memory of the reader is overtaxed. In *Mberf* 5 Steigar-Þórir goes raiding north in Bjarkey and we are told that Jón and his son

Víðkunnr flee. Even the most attentive reader might be at a loss to recall that Jón Árnason and his son Víðkunnr of Bjarkey had already been introduced in *Mgóð* 11—nearly two hundred pages earlier in the *Íslenzk fornrit* edition—for they have not been brought into play since. Another type of minor flaw concerns the introduction of characters. In *Ólhelg* 116 a defiant Erlingr Skjálgsson tells King Óláfr that he will submit to him but not to his slave-born steward Sel-Þórir; but Þórir is not properly introduced until the next chapter. Despite minor flaws such as these, however, it should be said that Snorri's control of his vast body of material is generally impressive.

Chronological ordering of material only reflects actuality by simplifying it into a single, linear strand. Often, important events are in reality taking place synchronously, whether at opposite ends of a battlefield or at opposite ends of the known world. Snorri explicitly recognises this on several occasions. In his account of Stiklarstaðir, for instance, Snorri tells of the death of Þorgeirr af Kvistsstǫðum and others and the arrival of Dagr Hringsson in the confusion of the eclipse which darkened the brightness of early afternoon, then remarks that these things happened more or less at the same time (*Ólhelg* 227). On a larger scale, Snorri may reflect the complex political preoccupations of a reign by using the structural principle of interlacing or stranding two separate threads of narrative. For example, Óláfr Haraldsson must send Bjǫrn stallari and Hjalti Skeggjason east on a diplomatic mission to Rǫgnvaldr jarl in Gautland and Óláfr Svíakonungr (*Ólhelg* 69–72, 77–80), while himself attempting to consolidate his power in Norway and beard the troublesome kings of Upplǫnd (chs 73–76, 81–85). The technique is, indeed, especially common in *Óláfs saga helga*, highlighted by explicit pointers such as *nú ferr tvennum sǫgum fram* . . . (ch. 104) or *nú er þar til máls at taka, er áðr var frá horfit* (ch. 87; further examples in *Ólhelg* 144, 193, 216). The effect of these structures is often initially one of dislocation, as new material is introduced, then of resolution as its relevance to the main thread becomes clear. Thus the lives of Ásbjǫrn Selsbani, the Swedish princess Ingigerðr or Eyvindr úrarhorn at first seem distant from Óláfr Haraldsson's, but they soon prove to have a direct and powerful impact on his fate (Paasche 1916, 365–67). The extent to which stranding occurs varies greatly within the corpus of saga-literature. Oddr Snorrason's saga of Óláfr Tryggvason is richly stranded, for example, Fagrskinna very little (Clover 1982, 167–68, 170–71), while *Morkinskinna* is stranded but in a way that strikes one as random rather than purposeful.

Most of the kings in *Heimskringla*, moreover, either shared rule more or less resignedly with a kinsman or had to defend it against rivals, so that next to none of them has a saga to himself. The literary effects of this complexity are diverse, but can be enriching, as when Sigurðr Jórsalafari's glamorous exploits abroad are graphically contrasted with his brother Eysteinn's achievements in civil works (*Magnússona saga*, especially chs 14 and 21). Elsewhere, things may be more complicated. Hákon góði jostles his way through his saga as through life in rivalry with his brother Eiríkr blóðøx and Eiríkr's sons until he eventually dies of wounds sustained in battle against them at Fitjar on Storð, bequeathing the kingdom to them as he expires. Only in chs 13–18 does the narrative achieve full continuity and tension with a consecutive account of Hákon's moral and political dilemma over promoting Christianity in Norway.

Formal units: chapter, saga, and saga-cycle

As seen in Chapter Two, there is reasonable agreement between the *Heimskringla* manuscripts about the formal divisions of chapter and saga which portion out the text. It is convenient to take these as the starting point for examining the arrangement of the material in *Heimskringla*, and in particular for considering to what extent it proclaims the presence of a guiding authorial hand. These units, though the most consistently marked in the manuscripts, are not the only useful ones for analysis, and some reference will be made to scenes and to chapter-sequences. The discussion moves from smaller to larger units, beginning with the chapter.

The chapter varies in length from three or four lines, e.g. *Yng* 45 or *ÓlTrygg* 23, to six or seven pages (*Ólhelg* 94; counting here and in what follows from the 1911 edition of Finnur Jónsson, since it is uncomplicated by footnotes). Quite often there is a longish even-paced stretch where the chapters are usually between ten and thirty lines (for instance, much of *Óláfs saga Tryggvasonar* or *Magnúss saga berfœtts*). The average length is about two-thirds of a page. *Óláfs saga helga* differs somewhat from the remaining sagas in that its chapters are on average almost a page long, and there are many more especially long chapters in it, which are often labelled as 'sagas' in the manuscripts, e.g. *Saga Dala-Guðbrands, Ólhelg* 112.

Throughout *Heimskringla*, there are certain types of material which suggest a new start and which occur especially frequently at the beginnings of chapters. These include references to 'tradition' or to the business of narration (*Svá er sagt / En nú er frá því at segja*), introduction of a new character (*Rauðr hét maðr, er þar byggði í Eystri-Dǫlum, Ólhelg* 164), or specifications of time and place (*Hálfdan konungr fór um haustit út á Vingulmǫrk, Hálfdsv* 4). The chapter may of course begin with an explicit link to preceding material, e.g. *Eptir þetta* . . . / *Eptir um várit* . . . , a reaction to preceding events (*Gull-Haraldr unði þá miklu verr en áðr* 'Gull-Haraldr was now much more dissatisfied than before,' *ÓlTrygg* 10), or a recapitulation (*Síðan er Óláfr konungr hafði ráðit fyrir sér, at hann vildi snúask til heimferðar, þá bar hann þat upp fyrir Jarizleifi konungi* . . . 'After King Olaf had reached the decision that he wanted to set out on the journey home, he announced it to King Jarizleifr,' *Ólhelg* 191).

There are also types of material which provide a suitable final flourish for chapters—a graphic gesture (the funerary ship lannched blazing onto rough seas after Fýrisvellir, *Yng* 23), a profonnd utterance (*byskup segir, at sú sýn var heilaglig ok stórmerkilig*, 'the bishop said that this sight was holy and most remarkable' after Óláfr Haraldsson's vision of the whole world, *Ólhelg* 202), an unresolved crisis (God and Bishop Sigurðr enlisted against the demonic powers of Rauðr inn rammi, *ÓlTrygg* 79), or foreboding direct from the narrator (the warning that there was more to Óláfr Haraldsson's friendly gifts to the Icelanders, as became apparent later, *Ólhelg* 124). Nevertheless, by no means all of Snorri's chapters leave the reader in a state of either satisfaction or suspense, for some endings are distinctly feeble. Thus *Ólhelg* 152 moves us through Knútr inn ríki's actions after the battle of Áin helga, as he spies on Óláfr Haraldsson's fleet near Eyrarsund, breaks off to visit Úlfr jarl at Hróiskelda, and plays chess with him. The chapter ends prosaically with a brief description of Úlfr, a note that his sister was married to Guðini jarl in England, and a list of their children. The impetus is regained in the next chapter with the chess-game ending in anger and the killing of Úlfr, but it is clear that the chapter is not really the nnit of narration here, and one gains the same impression on many other occasions (*ÓlTrygg* 36-7 for instance) that the chapter break has very little significance.

When we look at the arrangement of whole chapters, and not merely at their beginnings and ends, the same diversity emerges. Some are paratactic in character: strings of genealogical information, for instance, or of character description. Others, containing more miscellaneous information, may have a more haphazardly annalistic ring, a case in point being *Mberf* 11 (described on p. 96 above; a further example of a loosely organised chapter is *Ólhelg* 121).

At the other extreme are chapters which can stand alone as vivid and shapely units of narrative. As such they can be regarded as 'scenes', a word used as a technical term by older scholars such as W. P. Ker and Andreas Heusler and enthusiastically adopted by more recent ones. A scene can be described, adapting a much-used definition (Allen 1971, 65), as a compact unit of sustained and significant action, individual or social, which has a beginning, middle and end. Of these three parts the first (preface or scene-setting) and the third (conclusion) typically consist of brief, informative narration and are, broadly speaking, concerned with static situations, while the centrepiece (the dramatic encounter) portrays change through directly represented action and/or dialogue. The opening frequently contains some reference to time, either absolute (season or time of day) or relative (*Litlu síðar* etc.), or to the writer's time (*Nú er at segja frá* . . . etc.). New characters are also often introduced by formulas such as *Maðr hét* . . . The concluding part also frequently contains certain characteristic features, such as the report of a departure, an end of a conversation, public response to a happening or a statement of passing time. The scene is not an inflexible or indispensable unit of saga-narrative, for there are smaller and larger units such as motifs and groups of scenes which can co-exist with it, and some of the writing may impart information (especially genealogical or character-describing) in a non-scenic and even non-narrative way. But it is employed so liberally throughout all kinds of sagas (religious sagas, kings' sagas from the *Oldest saga of Óláfr helgi* onwards, sagas of Icelanders), and is so often formed around a framework of stereotyped verbal tags, that it has been regarded as a 'fundamental point of contact with oral tale-telling' (Clover 1974, 82).

Scenes in Snorri's narrative are well-defined (see Kossuth 1980), and frequently co-terminous with chapters. An example is the conquest of the fourth Sicilian town, narrated with such verve and irony in *HSig* 10. There are also many 'speech-scenes', including Tósti's diplomatic visits to Sveinn of Denmark and Haraldr of Norway in *HSig* 78 and 79. Ch. 78 comprises the following stages. The situation is laid out (Haraldr Guðinason realises his brother Tósti's ambition for the English throne), there is some action (Haraldr deprives Tósti of power, Tósti goes to Denmark); the centre of the scene is a conversation, beginning in indirect speech and moving into direct (Tósti tries unsuccessfully to persuade Sveinn to invade England); there is a concluding sentence (*Síðan skilðusk þeir konungr ok jarl, ok ekki mjǫk sáttir,* 'Then the king and the jarl parted, and not on very good terms').

The skill of a saga-writer lies not only in his handling of individual chapters and scenes, but also in the manner of their joining, and often a sequence of chapters will form a tightly constructed unit of narration. Óláfr Tryggvason's confrontation of a crowd of farmers from Þrándheimr in *ÓlTrygg* 65–69 is a good example of Snorri's control of audience response in a medium-length narrative. Ch. 65 ends in suspense as Óláfr seems to back down, promising to meet the heathen farmers at their sacred place, and the brief ch. 66 seems anti-climactic as the farmers' spokesman declaims against Óláfr and all go home. Ch. 67 swings the balance towards Óláfr when he says he wants to make a sacrifice—of all the best men of the district; ch. 68 like 65 keeps us guessing when Óláfr says he wants to observe a *blót*, and ch. 69 finally sweeps away all doubts as the heathens, their leader Járn-Skeggi killed and their Þórr effigy smashed, accept baptism.

A rather different kind of chapter sequence is illustrated by *Hhárf* 19–23, where, at a milepost in Norwegian political development, Haraldr reaches a pause and climax in his military accumulation of power. The narrative confirms the position of the new all-Norwegian sovereign in outright statements that there was no more opposition to him in Norway (chs 19, 20) and shows him making a diplomatic marriage (ch. 21), leading an expedition to the British Isles (ch. 22), and setting symbolic seal on his achievements by a hair-cut and consequent change of nickname (ch. 23). Of course this kind of structure to some extent reflects reality. Marriage is quite likely to come as an interlude after military activity; compare Hákon jarl Sigurðarson's marriage to Þóra in *ÓlTrygg* 19 after he had pacified the land in the previous chapter.

The material within sagas is often drawn into tighter coherence not merely by the grouping of successive chapters but by links forged over longer stretches. There may, for instance, be a bridge of motivation, as in the portrayal of Þórir hundr in *Óláfs saga helga*. In ch. 123 Sigríðr, the mother of the slain Ásbjǫrn, presents Þórir hundr with the spear which killed him and challenges him to put it through Óláfr digri. The gesture is vivid enough to be still remembered towards the end of the saga when Þórir acts. In ch. 219 he mentions his nephew Ásbjǫrn as one of the four men he has to avenge on Óláfr, and in ch. 228 he puts a spear—we can guess which—through Óláfr after the king has thrown away his sword. (The spear has already been used against Karli, who was involved in Ásbjǫrn's death, ch. 133.) Another long-range link which is made at

Stiklarstaðir is the reintroduction of Arnljótr gellini, who in *Ólhelg* 215 recalls that he had sent a silver dish to Óláfr as a token of friendly intent—a reference to ch. 141.

Much the same variety can be found in the treatment of the saga as a narrative unit as in the treatment of the chapter. One can find plentiful examples which satisfy modern literary tastes reasonably well: *Óláfs saga helga, Magnúss saga góða* and *Haralds saga Sigurðarsonar*, for instance, all have a coherent narrative, focussed upon one well-drawn character, and a handful of clear thematic threads reflecting the preoccupations of his reign. Moreover, although the individual sagas of *Heimskringla* are not worked according to a formula, most of them do end at or near the death of their hero and on the way depict his rise to power (by fending off enemies or sharing power), his attempts to secure his sons' succession, his relations with neighbouring kingdoms and colonies, and the manner of his death. The extent to which diplomacy or adventures abroad, building works, law-making and religious concerns are covered in the saga varies greatly. However, by no means all of the *Heimskringla* sagas form polished units. The ending of *Haralds saga gráfeldar* (ch. 16), for instance, is indisputably messy. It recounts the fall of King Erlingr, son of Eiríkr blóðøx and Gunnhildr, notes the poor seasons during Gunnhildr's reign and in support quotes Eyvindr skáldaspillir's verse about snow at midsummer. The saga then tails off with an anecdote about the poverty-stricken skald buying herrings with the proceeds from selling his arrows.

If it is only to a certain extent that the individual sagas function as neat, self-contained narratives, this is largely because of the overlaps between kings' lives, joint kingships and rivalries which characterise the period. These complications, do, however, have a positive side. They can produce unity in the cycle of sagas as well as striking literary effects at particular points within it. Thus when Óláfr Tryggvason stands godfather to the three-year-old Óláfr Haraldsson (*ÓlTrygg* 60) a link is forged between the colourful careers of the two missionary warriors. Similarly, the picturesque scene between Óláfr Haraldsson and his young stepbrothers (*Ólhelg* 76) gives a memorable glimpse of Haraldr Sigurðarson's ruthless ambition long before he has any military or political rôle to play. In fact nearly all the kings in *Heimskringla* are introduced before their own sagas begin, sometimes two sagas earlier, as when Haraldr gráfeldr is born in *Hhárf* 43 or Haraldr Sigurðarson is first glimpsed in *Ólhelg* 33. The main exception is Óláfr Tryggvason, who is born in ch. 1 of his own saga. A few other kings are already adult when they first appear, especially those who arrive from abroad as claimants to the throne in the later sagas of *Heimskringla* (e.g. Haraldr gilli in *Msona* 26; the sons of Magnús berfœttr in *Mberf* 7, 8 and 16 are also adult at their first appearance). Other important but non-royal characters can also provide a bridge between the sagas of *Heimskringla*, men such as Einarr þambarskelfir or Kálfr Árnason whose fates are bound up with Óláfr helgi and his two successors.

Another category of unifying devices, entirely fitting in the context of *Heimskringla*'s dynastic preoccupations, is the constant cross-referencing between various kings and their deeds. Within the third-person narrative we find, for instance, comments that Magnús berfœttr was temperamentally much more like his grandfather Haraldr Sigurðarson than his father Óláfr kyrri (*Mberf* 7), and that Eysteinn Magnússon *vann . . . Jamtaland með viti, en eigi með áhlaupum sem sumir hans forellrar* 'won Jamtaland by intelligence and not by aggression like some of his forefathers' (*Msona* 15, evidently following *Morkinskinna* p. 353). The protagonists themselves are also made to show awareness of the traditions of their line, whether naively, as when Haraldr Sigurðarson or Eysteinn Magnússon build ships to the exact dimensions of Óláfr Tryggvason's Ormr inn langi (*HSig* 59, *Msona* 23), or more subtly, as in the splendid verbal fencing-match in *HSig* 78. Here, Tósti jarl thrusts Knútr inn ríki as a model of conquering zeal before Knútr's nephew Sveinn Úlfsson, and is parried by Sveinn's response that he will match his actions *meirr eptir mínu lítilræði en eptir framkvæmð Knúts konungs, frænda míns* 'more to my own mediocrity than to the achievement of my kinsman King Knútr'. One popular point of reference is the reign of Haraldr hárfagri (in *Hgráf* 3, *ÓlTrygg* 15, 45, 58; *Ólhelg* 72, 95, 96, 100 etc.). Whether Norwegian kings really were as conscious of his legacy as the saga-writers suggest is doubtful (Krag 1989), but the recurrent references are certainly a useful literary device which promotes unity in the *Heimskringla* cycle of sagas. That Snorri exploited the theme is clear on many occasions, never more than in *Ólhelg* 35 where, in a speech to Sigurðr sýr, Óláfr not only repeatedly conjures with the name of his ancestor in phrases such as *eigur allra várra frænda, er at langfeðgatali erum komnir frá Haraldi inum hárfagra* 'the possessions of all of us kinsmen who are descended from Haraldr Finehair', but batters out his resolve to recover his legacy in key words such as *arfr, ætt, lǫg, óðalborinn, frændleifð* and *frændaskǫmm*. Further, comparisons between kings are made in the voices of ordinary folk as well as in those of the author and the rulers themselves. Thus we are told that when Hákon

Aðalsteinsfóstri (alias 'góði') returned to Norway people said that Haraldr hárfagri had come back, young again (*Hákgóð* 1); later there are murmerings that Hákon has the family failing of meanness with food (*Hákgóð* 15).

This sustained current of comparisons back and forth between reigns and the rulers' own constant reference to historical precedent to support their own actions encourage the reader to see links of broader kinds, comparing for instance the varying ways in which rulers tackle similar problems. When the farmers threaten to give Óláfr Tryggvason the same treatment as Hákon Aðalsteinsfóstri got for attempting to spread Christianity (*ÓlTrygg* 65), we also compare the situation with the later missionary attempts and eventual downfall of Óláfr Haraldsson. Our reflections become still more complex when, in *Mgóð* 15, the *bœndr* grumble that Magnús is undermining the laws of Hákon góði, and threaten that he will get the same treatment as they have given his father or other rulers whom they have despatched when tired of their tyranny and lawlessness (*ofsi þeira ok lǫglausa*).

A more contrivedly literary source of unity in *Heimskringla* (at least to modern eyes) is the introduction of dreams, oaths or prophecies which are later fulfilled. This can happen over a relatively small span of time, as when Vagn Ákason's vows, made in *ÓlTrygg* 35, that he will kill Þorkell leira and sleep with his daughter, are fulfilled in unexpected ways in ch. 41, but such devices can work over a much longer range. Ragnhildr and Hálfdan's dreams about Haraldr hárfagri and his progeny (*Hálfdsv* 6 and 7) are not only explicitly fulfilled in *Hhárf* 42 but underpin the entire dynastic parade of *Heimskringla*, and much later they are supplemented by Sigurðr Jórsalafari's dream of a great tree washing up on the Norwegian coast (*Msona* 25). In a similar way the curse of the seeress Hulð on the Yngling dynasty (*Yng* 14) draws together into a foreseen gloom the fratricides of Eiríkr blóðøx and the rival kingships of the later sagas of *Heimskringla*. Important as some of these linking devices are for the overall unity of *Heimskringla*, they are not superabundant, and do not contribute to our sense of an author's hand constantly and tightly guiding events, as they do for instance in *Laxdœla saga*.

Scholars have also sought grander running themes as a source of unity in the whole of *Heimskringla*. Koht, for instance, saw the struggle of king and aristocracy as the mainstay of Snorri's conception of Norwegian history. These themes were discussed earlier in this chapter.

Finally, however strong the factors making for unity in *Heimskringla*, there is no question that there are divisions of saga and saga-groups cutting across that unity. The most obvious is the division, reflected in modern editions of the work, into three parts, the first containing the sagas of reigns up to and including Óláfr Tryggvason, the second comprising only the long *Óláfs saga helga*, and the third consisting of the remainder, the sagas from *Magnúss saga góða* to *Magnúss saga Erlingssonar*. The sagas within each of the three parts seem, at least to some extent, to be united by running concerns. Part I sees the rise, within the heathen era, of something like a Norwegian state under the dynasty of Haraldr hárfagri, and the establishment of Christianity. Part II marks a sustained climax in the career of Óláfr Haraldsson, the most famously and turbulently Christian ruler of Norway. Part III marks a falling curve as it traces the fates of the successors of Óláfr and their increasingly tenuous hold on political and moral supremacy.

CHAPTER SIX
FROM HISTORY TO LITERATURE?

INTRODUCTION

IN the nineteenth century, Thomas Carlyle counted *Heimskringla* 'among the great history books of the world' (1875, 1), while Samuel Laing put Snorri, 'as a dramatic historian', on the same bench of 'the Valhalla of European literature' as Shakespeare, Carlyle and Scott— albeit at some distance (in his *Heimskringla* translation of 1844, I 3). In this century Halvdan Koht called Snorri 'the greatest artist of medieval historians . . . the magician of history' (1931, 118), and Einar Ólafur Sveinsson acclaimed him a 'king of saga-writers' (1937–38, 73–74). Still more recently, Njörður P. Njarðvík hails him in the title of an article (1979) as 'Snorri Sturluson: creator of documentary fiction'.

All these accolades, as well as praising Snorri, attempt to define his achievement. They point to a dilemma of modern readers in approaching *Heimskringla*: how is it to be categorised and how read? What can be deduced about Snorri's aims in writing *Heimskringla*? What kind of history (if any) is it, and how does this relate to the 'artistic' or 'dramatic' side? More precisely, can we treat it as a more or less reliable historical source, given its air of imaginative recreation; can we criticise it as literature, given its evident concern with imparting historical information? Issues such as these are explored in this chapter without any attempt to provide final answers, the hope being to open the way for further debate rather than to close the case. In the course of the discussion some of the threads exposed in earlier chapters will be drawn together.

To discuss the nature of *Heimskringla* in relation to the concepts of history and literature is only one of several possible approaches, and it has obvious limitations, but it is a potentially fruitful one. Satisfactory definitions of the two concepts are difficult to formulate, but for present purposes I take 'history' to refer to (i) events of the past; (ii) a record or records of events (i.e. historical writing or historiography). This will normally be a systematic account, based on discerning use of the best sources available, of past events which are of public rather than merely private importance. It will often include analysis or interpretation of the events and their causes. In practice, of course, the distinction between (i) and (ii) is not sustainable, for the past now exists only in the historical record. As Frank Kermode puts it, 'Events exist only as texts, already to that extent interpreted' (1979, 108). By literature I mean writing which is valued for other reasons than for the information it contains. It will frequently afford evidence of the exercise of imagination and of heightened or non-obvious use of language. It will therefore not lend itself to translation or paraphrase without some loss of effect.

History and literature are not sealed or mutually exclusive categories (indeed, history was subsumed under literature up to the eighteenth century, and some modern theoreticians come close to restoring it to that position), and *Heimskringla* is not solely one or the other. It is historical narrative, imaginative historiography, 'a series of saga-histories' (to borrow a phrase from the translators of *King Harald's Saga*, 1966, 13). Indeed, as the materials in the preceding chapter demonstrate, the triumph of *Heimskringla* is above all its way of presenting information both more intelligently and more pleasingly than comparable works. As Sigurður Nordal put it:

> In Snorri's writings the harmony between learning and art [*milli vísinda og listar*] reaches a higher level than in any other Icelandic writings . . . *Heimskringla* is neither as reliable as *Íslendingabók* nor as moving as *Njála*. But it is much more learned than *Njála* and more entertaining than *Íslendingabók*. It is the harmony which gives it its unique value (1920, 128; my translation).

Nevertheless, the fact remains that *Heimskringla* has often been read either as history or as literature (as shown below), and it can be illuminating to consider in what ways it resembles the one or the other, how the two sides blend together, and what needs to be taken into account in approaching the work.

The question posed in the title of this chapter refers to the activity of Snorri and his forebears, transforming the events of the past into a prose saga. It also refers to the reception of *Heimskringla* by centuries of readers, who have progressively come to view it less as a work of history and more as a work of literature. There is, it should be said, no implication intended that the process of transforming history into literature represents either enhancement or impoverishment. Before venturing on consideration of how Snorri went about his task and how we may read the result, a survey of readers' perceptions in the past may be useful.

It is difficult to glean from medieval responses to Snorri's writings how they were regarded. As seen in Chapter One, Sturla Þórðarson makes only the barest mention of them, and the terms by which Snorri's contemporaries and immediate successors refer to them are notoriously vague: saga-books—*sǫgur* or *sǫgubœkr*—or lives of the kings of Norway—*ævi / ævisǫgur Nóregs konunga*. We do not know whether the readiness of scribes to copy *Heimskringla* and the *Separate Saga of Óláfr helgi* shows their appreciation of the information in it, or of the artistry with which it is relayed, or both, or neither—was Snorri's work simply more readily available? However, Snorri is cited as an authority on historical points by his medieval successors, and he is called *fróði* 'the Learned', although the epithet did not stick to him as it did to Ari and Sæmundr, perhaps because his fame was still greater in other areas than in his knowledge of native lore.

Up to the nineteenth century there were few who questioned the historical value of *Heimskringla*. (Among those who did were G. L. Baden, mentioned by Dahl, 1959, 6–8, and E. Jessen, mentioned by Moberg, 1987, 78.) As late as the 1850s P. A. Munch founded much of his monumental history of Norway, *Det norske Folks Historie*, on Snorri's narrative, and while he recognised that there was much detail that either smacked of literary fabrication or conflicted with other saga accounts, he saw *Heimskringla* as essentially a sound historical source which went back to venerable oral traditions. Gustav Storm's perceptive investigation of *Heimskringla*'s written sources (1873) sowed further doubts about the work's historicity, while stressing Snorri's artistic achievement. It was after the turn of the century, at a time when *Íslendingasögur* such as *Egils saga* were also coming under severe scrutiny, that the full-scale onslaught began. Lauritz Weibull disputed the historicity of some central points in Snorri's account of the battle of Svǫlð (1911; see further pp. 117–18 below), while Halvdan Koht (1914) argued that Snorri, in still greater degree than earlier writers of kings' sagas, had a view of Norwegian history deeply coloured by the conflict of king and aristocracy in the time from King Sverrir onwards. Moltke Moe (1926) and others pointed out the kinship of *Heimskringla* (and other sagas) to widely known folktales, and the implausibility of some parts of the narrative. The broadsides of these scholars gave a jolt to what remained of historians' faith in Snorri, and encouraged a more rigorous approach to source-criticism in Edvard Bull and other scholars of the next generation. Many Norwegians of recent generations have expressed their frustration at the inadequacies of the early source-material by turning away from the medieval period and studying the nineteenth and twentieth centuries instead.

Heimskringla, then, has gradually come to be seen in a different light. If regarded as a historical document at all, it is taken as a witness to a thirteenth-century Icelandic view of Norwegian history up to the twelfth century, rather than to the facts of Norwegian history. Erik Gunnes, for instance, whose book of 1976 pays more heed to Snorri's narrative than most recent histories, stresses that the value of *Heimskringla* is not primarily *som dokumentasjon, men som visjon* (p. 10). This shift of perception results both from the uncovering of factual errors and from changing notions about the proper means of reconstructing the past, and both these are explored in the following pages.

Meanwhile, appreciation of the aesthetic aspects of the work has come increasingly to the fore in published work of the last hundred years (especially in Nordal 1920, Lie 1937 and Ciklamini 1978), and doubtless it is for its 'literary' qualities, as well as the more general fascination of the culture it represents, that it is chiefly read today. Professor Ciklamini's book, for instance, contains several chapters in which *Heimskringla* is treated more or less as a literary text. There is some reference to sources, and some occasional mention of actual events, but in many places the discussion reads as though Snorri had as free a hand as a modern novelist, or at least as the author of *Njáls saga*, to give a particular literary cast and/or moral slant to his narrative.

However, the impression *Heimskringla* sometimes gives of unrestrained artistry is as illusory as the impression of historical veracity. The balance between the two sides is continually changing, and the nature of *Heimskringla* as a whole lies somewhere between. The following sections offer materials which may help to place the work, and Snorri's intentions, more precisely.

HOW HISTORICALLY RELIABLE?

Factual accuracy

It only takes a glance at a few pages of *Heimskringla* to see that many of the events cannot have taken place in precisely the way described. Some general categories, such as supernatural events, imagined scenes and conversations, are discussed in the section on medieval historiography below, but there are other kinds of unlikelihood in the text. It seems improbable that Haraldr Sigurðarson's strategem of setting a city ablaze using birds with lighted tinder attached to them could have worked (*HSig* 6), and indeed this is actually a well-known folktale, which also appears twice in the pages of Saxo Grammaticus. According to Bjarni Aðalbjarnarson, the ploy was tried in the eighteenth century, without success (*Heimskringla* 1941-51, III, xvii–xviii; also Blöndal 1978, 71-72.)

At other times our suspicions may be aroused by internal contradictions. As Finnur Jónsson pointed out (1923, 706), the genealogy of the earls of Rouen (*Rúðujarlar*) in *Ólhelg* 20 does not quite match that in *Hhárf* 24, nor does the intelligence in *HSig* 20 that Magnús Óláfsson went to Norway after the battle of Helganes agree with *Mgóð* 35, where he is said to have stayed the winter in Denmark. Another, opposite, cause for suspicion is a too close similarity between different parts of *Heimskringla*. Sigurður Nordal noted the resemblance between the story of Álfr and Yngvi in *Yng* 21 and that of Haraldr Guðinason and Vilhjálmr bastarðr in *HSig* 76 (1920, 174). Examples of more outright duplication can also be found. It seems unlikely that there were in reality two men called Dala-Guðbrandr—the one who plays a rather redundant walk-on part in *Hgráf* 9 and the defiant heathen who plays opposite Óláfr Haraldsson in *Ólhelg* 112-13—or two called Þorleifr spaki (*Hálfdsv* 7 and *Hgráf* 8 and intermittently thereafter), or three female inciters called Sigríðr (*ÓlTrygg* 92; *Ólhelg* 123 and 183; see Jochens 1987).

Once the relatively few discrepancies and unlikelihoods in *Heimskringla* are set aside, the narrative makes fairly convincing reading. But how are we to know whether it is reliable as history? What external checks are there, and what do they reveal about the accuracy or inaccuracy of particular episodes?

There are places where the *Heimskringla* narrative is supported by independent early sources. The broad outlines of Haraldr Sigurðarson's Mediterranean adventures in the service of the Byzantine emperor are substantiated in the *Logos nuthetikos* 'Advice for the Emperor', written by the Byzantine general Kekaumenos in the last quarter of the eleventh century (see Blöndal 1978, 57-74). Similarly, the *Anglo-Saxon Chronicle* and its derivatives confirm many of the essential points of the *Heimskringla* account of Haraldr's fatal English campaign, although they also reveal details which are unconfirmed or simply wrong.

However, the use of written sources to test the truth of *Heimskringla* is usually more complex than this. As seen in Chapter Four, much of the historical writing of medieval Scandinavia is interdependent, one writer either taking material from another or using a common source, so that agreement between texts does not necessarily validate what they say. It is also conceivable that Snorri knew foreign chronicles in Latin, such as those written in England in the twelfth century, and through them the *Anglo-Saxon Chronicle* (see Moberg 1987, 56-60). If this is so, the supply of independent sources against which material can be checked is still more limited. Where on the other hand there is disagreement, it can often be difficult to arbitrate between various accounts—to compose, for instance, a true picture of Óláfr Tryggvason out of Icelandic accounts (including Snorri's) of a missionary hero and German and Danish accounts of a heathen sorcerer (Jones 1968); or to establish the true origins of Eiríkr blóðøx's queen Gunnhildr when the sagas would have her a Lapp-trained witch from Hálogaland while the *Historia Norvegiæ* would have her—more plausibly—a daughter of King Gormr the Old of Denmark and sister of the proudly Christian Haraldr blátǫnn (Nordal 1941a, 141–44).

An analysis of the whole of *Heimskringla* would reveal constantly shifting patterns of agreement or disagreement between it and other texts, Norse and non-Norse, and no side has a monopoly of accuracy. The famous last battle of Óláfr Tryggvason well illustrates how complex these patterns can be. The sources unanimously have Óláfr defeated in a sea-battle against King Sveinn tjúguskegg of Denmark. They share certain details, but they disagree dramatically as to where and why the battle took place. One group of authorities, including Snorri, locates the battle at Svǫlð in Vinðland (Wendland on the Baltic), while Adam of Bremen (Book II, ch. 40), supported by the author of *Ágrip* (ch. 20), places it in Øresund, between Zealand and Skåne. Certainly Snorri has the evidence of Halldórr ókristni's *Eiríksflokkr* v. 2 in his favour when he maintains that Óláfr was sailing north when trapped in battle, not south towards Wendland as Adam of Bremen and *Ágrip*'s author think, but he may be wrong about the actual location (Ellehøj 1958). Concerning the reason for the expedition the balance of probability may also be against him. According to Snorri (and *Fagrskinna* ch. 24), Óláfr went to win back his queen Þyri's possessions from Búrizláfr (Boleslav), king of the Wends, to whom she had been married briefly and against her will. The battle in *Heimskringla* is immediately precipitated by the egging of Þyri (a new development in *Heimskringla*) and of Sigríðr stórráða, wife of Sveinn and once the betrothed of Óláfr (she is already an inciter in Oddr Snorrason's saga). The *Ágrip* account, however, emphasises the military and political motives for the expedition more than the personal ones, and is probably right to do so, given Óláfr's long and grandiose preparations for war (see *Heimskringla* 1941–51, I, cxxx). Lauritz Weibull even disputed Sigríðr's existence and, taking up a hint from Alexander Bugge, suggested that she had, in function, supplanted a Slav princess who is mentioned by Adam of Bremen. He saw her as part of the legendary web woven around Óláfr's fall, a fabrication by Oddr Snorrason inspired by the Sigurðr/Siegfried cycle, so that she became the Brynhildr to Óláfr's Sigurðr, Þyri's Guðrún and Sveinn's Gunnarr (1911, 110 and 125–26). Clerical misogyny, which would have been familiar to the monk Oddr, might also have influenced her portrayal (Jochens 1987, 112–16 and references there).

The case of Sigríðr and Þyri illustrates the presence in *Heimskringla* of material which is poorly supported in other sources. Predictably, the opposite can also be observed. The Svǫlð sequence in *Heimskringla* (and *Fagrskinna*) lacks Oddr Snorrason's account of a two-week pause in which Óláfr Tryggvason, voyaging south, vainly waited for the Swedish King Óláfr at the border (Oddr p. 190). *Ágrip* and *Historia Norvegiæ* also record a wait at the border, although it is for Norwegian reinforcements, so that this may well be a case of *Fagrskinna* and *Heimskringla* omitting a probably well-based episode in the interests of a smooth and uncomplicated narrative, that is, not telling the whole historical truth.

Many of the details from the accounts of Svǫlð discussed so far put the *Heimskringla* narrative in a questionable light. Others could have been mentioned, however, where the branch of tradition represented there seems more reliable than a rival one. A case in point is the famous moment at the turning-point in the battle when the sovereign's bow breaks in the hands of Einarr þambarskelfir; this is appropriated by the author of the *Legendary Saga* for Óláfr Haraldsson's battle at Nesjar (Saltnessand 1963). Moreover, it must be remembered that the tangle of history and legend which surrounds Svǫlð is open to many interpretations, and scholars have differed greatly in their estimates of the veracity of the *Heimskringla* version.

Modern scholars wishing to investigate the historicity of *Heimskringla* have certain other resources, notably archaeological, which were unavailable to Snorri. It is, however, only rarely that archaeological evidence is precise enough to confirm details. One such case concerns Snorri's claim (*Ólhelg* 185 etc.) that Knútr inn ríki systematically sent infiltrators to bribe Norwegian magnates over to his side in the 1020s. As well as being spoken of in skaldic verse and the chronicle of Florence of Worcester (d. 1118), it is further supported by the plentiful occurrence of coins of Knútr in Norwegian finds from the reigns of Óláfr Haraldsson and Magnús góði (Andersen 1977, 115 and 130–31). The claim in *HSig* 58 that Haraldr Sigurðarson founded the market town of Oslo, on the other hand, needs modifying in the light of archaeology. The strategic and economic reasons which Snorri gives for Haraldr cultivating Oslo are sound, but archaeology shows that a market-place existed there in the early eleventh century, and so suggests that Haraldr's part was rather to consolidate it with military, ecclesiastical and royal buildings (Andersen 1977, 154 and 231). On the whole, archaeology is more valuable for illuminating the material context for such general developments as the Christianisation of Norway or the consolidation of a centralised monarchy by the establishment of towns than for checking particular details. The clear traces of heathen burial customs persisting in northern Norway and Upplǫnd into the second half of the eleventh century may, for instance, provide some support for the saga accounts of chieftainly opposition to Óláfr Haraldsson's missionary activities in these areas (Andersen 1977, 128). Finally, inscriptions on Scandinavian rune-stones occasionally make reference to major contemporary events. The time-worn Stavanger III cross is interpreted by Aslak Liestøl as 'the priest raised this stone in memory of Erlingr his lord . . . when he fought against Óláfr' (cited in Andersen 1977, 115 and 129), and so is a precious allusion to the fateful sea-battle in the bay of Bókn described in *Ólhelg* 176.

Use of sources

In terms of factual accuracy, a work can be no better than its sources, and Snorri is limited to sources which are by modern standards hopelessly inadequate. Some scraps of raw documentary evidence now survive from the times covered in *Heimskringla*, among them Knútr's letter of 1027 to the English in which he claims the title *Cnuto, rex totius Angliæ, et Denemarchiæ, et Norregiæ, et partis Swavorum* (Andersen 1977, 129); but it seems that next to no relevant treaties, charters, letters or account books were available to Snorri. Similarly, although Snorri makes glancing reference to archaeological monuments and to the origins of personal and place-names, these do not genuinely substantiate the details of his narrative.

The sources used in *Heimskringla* are of three types: oral traditions in prose, which by definition are no longer directly accessible to us (though see the discussion in Chapter Four), skaldic verse and, the largest contributor of material, written prose narratives. The last two are examined here with a view to assessing Snorri's chances of achieving historical accuracy, and to gauging how far it was his intention to do that.

Snorri's praise of Ari Þorgilsson shows that he considers the accounts of reliable eye-witnesses to be the ideal kind of historical source; yet of the prose writings known both to Snorri and to us Eiríkr Oddsson's *Hryggjarstykki* is the only one written very close to the events. In most of them, layers of oral and written tradition have already been processed according to various artistic and ideological sensibilities, and often with less discrimination than Snorri himself would have applied.

The intelligence with which Snorri uses sources is celebrated. He will often play off one source against another, especially by using skaldic verse to correct an earlier written prose source. Where *Ágrip* ch. 30 and *Legendary Saga* ch. 80 say that Óláfr helgi at Stiklarstaðir wore no helmet or mail-shirt, Snorri cites a verse of Sigvatr containing the words *gekk . . . sœkja . . . fram í brynju* 'he advanced in his corselet' and pictures Óláfr in gilded helmet, ringed corselet and white shield with golden cross (*Ólhelg* 213). But where prose sources disagreed and there was no skaldic evidence to tip the judgement, Snorri's choice may be based on mature reflection but it is not based on fresh or superior information. He adopts, for instance, the version of Hákon jarl Ívarsson's story found in the saga about him rather than that of *Morkinskinna*, but some scholars have doubted his judgement here (e.g. Bjarni Aðalbjarnarson in *Heimskringla* 1941–51, III, xxvi–xxvii). Again, when Snorri rationalises, he is not uncovering new 'facts' but interpreting old ones afresh and translating hagiography into secular narrative. A famous example is the way that he has Óláfr Haraldsson's fleet escape from the Swedes at Lǫgrinn (Lake Mälaren) using a channel produced by manual labour rather than miracle (*Ólhelg* 7, discussed in Evans 1981, 96–103). Another way in which Snorri deals with particulars he found suspect or unimportant was to mention them cursorily and perhaps in a postscript to the main account. The rumours that Hákon jarl sacrificed his young son for victory at Hjǫrungavágr or that Óláfr Tryggvason escaped from Svǫlð and found penance and refuge in a monastery in Greece or Syria are given this compromise treatment (*ÓlTrygg* 42 and 112, respectively).

Still others of Snorri's departures from the detail of his sources are, as far as we can tell, more wholeheartedly independent of tradition. The example of the *landvættir* episode was mentioned in the introduction to Chapter Four, and the marriage of Gefjun to Skjǫldr in *Yng* 5 may be Snorri's own surmise or invention (Clunies Ross 1978, 152).

The other main foundation for Snorri's narrative, the skaldic verse, gives more promise of reliability and, since it is so often quoted verbatim, we have direct access to it and can see for ourselves how it substantiates or supplements the prose narrative. Its advantages are manifold. It was usually composed soon after the event and often—as Snorri emphasises from time to time—by participants and eye-witnesses. Most of the verse (though not some of its most venerable monuments such as *Ynglingatal, Eiríksmál* and *Hákonarmál*) is in the *dróttkvætt* form. The syllable-counting lines are intricately structured by alliteration and internal rhyme, and the formal complexity afforded at least some safeguard against alteration in transmission.

The Prologue to *Heimskringla* shows Snorri's clear grasp of the strengths and limitations of skaldic verse. Speaking especially about the genealogical poems *Ynglingatal* and *Háleygjatal* which stretch far back into myth and prehistory, he makes explicit the uncertainty of the ground. Such poems cannot be proved true, he says, but learned men in the past have taken them for true. It is possible that Snorri's stance here is defensive, and that his contemporary audience, and even Snorri himself, would have regarded such poems as sources of entertainment but not of information (so Sverrir Tómasson 1988, 214–17). Later, speaking of the skalds of Haraldr hárfagri but also of court poetry in general, Snorri says that the most valuable evidence comes from poems which were first declaimed before rulers or their sons, that is, which were contemporary. He takes as true all that such poems tell of royal journeys and battles, recognising that court poetry by its very nature contains hyperbolic flattery, but not downright falsehood, for to credit kings with deeds they have not done would be mockery, not praise. Another comment on skaldic verse, oddly placed and controversial, occurs at the end of the Prologue. Here, Snorri says that he considers poems to be least corrupted (*sízt ór stað fœrð*) when they are correctly composed and can be plausibly interpreted—this being the most likely meaning of *ef þau eru rétt kveðin ok skynsamliga upp tekin*.

The theoretical comments on skaldic verse in the Prologue are on the whole matched by discerning use of verse in the body of *Heimskringla*. Priority is given to poetic sources contemporary with the events deseribed. Snorri quotes extensively from Sigvatr's *Nesjavísur* about Óláfr Haraldsson, and is at pains to point out that Sigvatr was present at the events, that he composed the verses the following summer and that he records the events carefully (*Ólhelg* 49; other skalds in battle are mentioned in *ÓlTrygg* 105 and *Ólhelg* 206). He makes ample use of Einarr Skúlason's verse records of contemporary, twelfth-century, events, but from Einarr's *Geisli* 'Sunbeam', composed in praise of Óláfr helgi over a century after his death, he by contrast takes only a single verse which records a miracle witnessed by Einarr himself (v. 37, in *Msona* 30). Again, Snorri omits fourteen verses from Þorbjǫrn hornklofi's *Haraldskvæði* which are included in *Fagrskinna*, although he does quote from the poem when telling of the battle of Hafrsfjǫrðr (*Hhárf* 18; see further Bjarni Einarsson, *Ágrip* 1984, cxxv). Possibly the verses omitted, some of which mention matters as trivial as jesters and jugglers, were felt to fit ill with the political concerns of Snorri's saga.

Against the many virtues of skaldic sources must be set certain drawbacks, both for Snorri in constructing his narrative and for us in attempting to assess his accuracy. The verse was not written down until the twelfth century at the earliest, and then usually in the form of short verse quotations within prose texts. Either during the oral stage or through scribal transmission verse texts could be mangled by those who did not understand them, or attached to the wrong historical event. Thus Snorri in *HSig* 96 uses a verse of Þorkell Skallason to authenticate his remark about Valþjófr burning a hundred Normans immediately after the battle of Hastings, but the verse actually refers to an event three years later in York (Scott 1953–7, 90; Hofmann 1978–9, 68).

Even if a verse can reasonably be counted authentic (and many can), there are still pitfalls in using it as a historical source. It may be linguistically difficult to interpret because of its convoluted syntax and esoteric diction. Medieval connoisseurs may offer differing interpretations and even make mistakes (e.g. Bjarni Aðalbjarnarson mistrusts Snorri's use of *Glymdrápa*, *Heimskringla* 1941–51, I lxii). The verse may also be propagandist or partisan. Snorri comes close to admitting this in the Prologue to *Heimskringla* and to illustrating it in *Hákgóð* 27. There Eyvindr skáldaspillir is said to have composed a verse about Hákon góði's victory over the sons of Eiríkr blóðøx in response to one exulting in Hákon's fall by Glúmr Geirason. Further, the poetry's content is often vague and stereotyped (although not so much so as some scholars have despairingly claimed), with only sparing mention of details such as names of people or places or numbers of ships or men. This all leaves the saga-writer who quotes the verse with plenty of leeway for exaggeration, and a minor viking raid may be expanded into a major battle or even a conquest. There are signs, though, that Snorri was less prone to this than some saga-writers—indeed he reduces Guthormr sindri's grandiose claim that Hákon góði conquered Zealand to a modest ravaging (*Hákgóð* 8; Nordal 1920, 148). Worse than a vague verse inviting exaggeration is the verse which itself contains a historical misconception. Sigvatr claims, for example, that the sun was eclipsed at the time of Óláfr helgi's fall at Stiklarstaðir in 1030, but the two events probably happened on 31 August and 29 July, respectively, 1030 (see Andersen 1977, 132). Specific errors such as these must have been as good as undetectable for Snorri, and this one at least he takes over in his prose account (*Ólhelg* 227). Elsewhere, he does recognise the possibility of error: there is a tinge of scepticism in his treatment of Eyvindr skáldaspillir's *Vellekla* (*ÓlTrygg* 18; Nordal 1920, 148–9). Finally, if we, as modern readers, had no other grounds for approaching skaldic verse with caution, they would be supplied by the attribution of three verses in *HSig* 80–82, all heard in dreams, to two troll-women and the dead Óláfr Haraldsson.

Looking at both sides of the balance-sheet, it is clear that although skaldic quotations never guarantee the absolute truth of specifics in *Heimskringla*, they greatly enhance the historical value of the work. However stylised, the verses take us closer to the events than any prose narrative can, and, if nothing else, their presence often provides some general assurance that the narrative has a historical basis. (Conversely, the absence of skaldic verse in some episodes in *Heimskringla*—often more fanciful ones such as Haraldr Sigurðarson's conquest of four Sicilian cities in *HSig* 6–10—might well arouse suspicion.) Moreover, everything about Snorri's particular use of verses suggests once more his serious intent to remain as faithful as possible to the best record of events.

Author's standpoint

Apart from its sources, the major limitation on the factual accuracy of *Heimskringla* is one common to all historians: that of the writer's own time and place. Snorri's standpoint in thirteenth-century Iceland inevitably colours the view of the past offered in the *Heimskringla* sagas.

Snorri's debt to specifically Icelandic tradition, and the probability that he is writing primarily for an Icelandic audience, occasionally surface in phrases such as *hingat* meaning 'to Iceland', *oss Íslendinga*, or *þarlandsmenn* meaning 'Norwegians' (*Ólhelg(Sep)* ch. 10). They are also manifest in certain whole episodes. The fate of Hrœrekr, the only king to be buried in Iceland, is dismissed in one sentence in *Legendary Saga* ch. 23, but was evidently a source of fascination for Snorri (*Ólhelg* 81–5). The *landvættir* in *ÓlTrygg* 33 offer material and symbolic defence of Icelandic independence, and Einarr Þveræingr's eloquent, though measured, resistance to Óláfr Haraldsson's designs on the Icelandic island of Grímsey has been held to resound with the urgency of allusion to Snorri's own time (*Ólhelg* 125; Madelung 1973, esp. 24–5).

Icelandic chauvinism is not, however, particularly marked in *Heimskringla* as a whole. The poet Sigvatr's close relationship with King Óláfr Haraldsson and his son Magnús may be exaggerated, but probably not greatly so. Anecdotes about Icelandic skalds at the Norwegian court were in any case plentiful and a stock element in the *konungasögur*, going back at least as far as the so-called *Oldest Saga of Óláfr helgi*. Snorri in the Prologue to the *Separate Saga of Óláfr helgi* acknowledges that to a foreign reader there might seem to be a superabundance of Icelandic material in the saga, but he justifies it on grounds of the richness of traditions brought back from Norway by Icelanders. Outside *Óláfs saga helga* Snorri tells little of the affairs of Icelanders. In narrating the battle of Hlýrskógsheiðr in *Mgóð* 28 he notes the presence of two Icelanders among the twelve men chosen by Magnús góði to heal the wounded. But in the account of Hjǫrungavágr in *ÓlTrygg* 41 he only mentions one Icelander, Vígfúss Víga-Glúmsson, without making a point about his nationality, whereas *Jómsvíkinga saga* ch. 32 draws particular attention to four; *Fagrskinna* ch. 22 also makes more of the Icelanders in the battle. Where Icelanders do figure prominently they almost always either carry out royal plans or influence royal fate, directly or indirectly, an example being Steinn Skaptason, who is the agent through whom the Árnasons become so entangled with the fate of Óláfr Haraldsson. (A ready guide to further materials about Iceland and Icelanders is the index to Monsen's translation of *Heimskringla*.)

Occasionally Snorri's experience as an Icelander seems to lead him into an erroneous view of conditions in mainland Scandinavia. As an example, the evidence of Swedish laws shows that lawmen or lawspeakers such as Þorgnýr, who confronts Óláfr Svíakonungr with the views of the Swedes in *Ólhelg* 78–80, did indeed direct the proceedings of Swedish assemblies already in heathen times (Wessén 1964, 91–92). But Snorri's implication that an all-Swedish assembly existed in Óláfr's day, and that the lawspeaker of Tíundaland dominated all the others has been ascribed to his projection of Icelandic conditions onto Sweden. Some scholars have seen Þorgnýr—a gifted orator and a magnate with a huge following—as Snorri's indirect spokesman for Icelandic independence and hence even as 'Snorri himself, the lawspeaker of Iceland' (Weibull 1964, 247; cf. also Hjärne 1952 for a more complicated explanation).

Nevertheless, a fascination with Norwegian history was also an Icelandic attribute, which Snorri had in full measure, and both by his reading and by his visit to mainland Scandinavia in 1218–20 he quite sucessfully compensates for the potential insularity of his Icelandic viewpoint. Further, his eagerness to link Scandinavian history with world history is shown by his following the tradition that the Æsir, mythical progenitors of the Scandinavian royal dynasties, were 'Asia-men' who came from 'Turkland' which, as he explains in his *Edda*, is Troy. (The early historians of Britain and France do much the same.)

Snorri's geographical knowledge of Norway is on the whole quite detailed and accurate, although he can make mistakes. Fræði (modern Frei), for example, is placed too far south, in Sunnmœrr (Sunnmøre) rather than Norðmœrr (Nordmøre, *Hákgóð* ch. 22). Not surprisingly, the picture becomes more inexact when the narrative moves to Denmark and Sweden and beyond.

The proportions in international politics also tend to be distorted. The importance of Norwegians abroad is probably exaggerated (Sigurðr Jórsalafari is the most glamorous example), and the superior power of Denmark during the ninth and tenth centuries is not given its due weight. On the other hand, foreign monarchs are allowed their voice, as when Óláfr Svíakonungr sneers at the small settlements and petty kings of Norway in *Ólhelg* 72, and in other ways Snorri's interest in, and grasp of, international politics often surpasses that of his predecessors. Snorri in *Óláfs saga Tryggvasonar* sees the conversion of Norway in the context of the mission of the Emperor Ótta (Otto II) in Denmark and Haraldr Gormsson's heavy-handed attempt to encourage Christianity in Norway. The background to the battle of Svǫlð is also widened and sharpened by consideration of events in Denmark, Sweden and Wendland (Andersson 1977).

Snorri's view of the past is coloured by his standpoint in the thirteenth century as well as his Icelandic nationality. Some anachronisms are of a trivial order, as when Óláfr Haraldsson fights behind the emblem of the cross in the manner of a crusader (*Ólhelg* 213), or when Magnús berfœttr is decked with the armorial bearings which are actually proper to King Sverrir nearly a century later (*Mberf* 24; Madelung 1972, 62 and 69). There are also, however, misconceptions about political fundamentals. Snorri almost certainly projects a later, and more highly organised, political system backwards in time when he shows Haraldr hárfagri reigning supreme over a united Norway neatly parcelled out into *fylki*, over each of which a *jarl* ruled, and under him four or more *hersar* (*Hhárf* 6; *Heimskringla* 1941–51, I, lxvi–lxviii).

The evidence surveyed so far shows that *Heimskringla* is not factually dependable; it constantly ranges through the spectrum from the true to the untrue via the unverifiable. Snorri could not make reliable history out of unreliable, except where he had access to fresh skaldic or oral traditions, and his accounts, though typically more credible and more fair-minded than their predecessors, are not necessarily more accurate.

The historical interest of *Heimskringla*, as of all writings from and about the past, goes beyond straightforward information about specific events. It affords much insight into the intellectual life of thirteenth-century Iceland as well as into the earlier centuries with which it is concerned. It creates images of a whole North-European world in which the sea provides many of the links, and which has its own distinctive material culture: ships, houses, weapons, food and clothing. More abstractly, *Heimskringla* has much to say about the political organisation and social relationships of medieval Scandinavia, its ancient religious customs and the protocols of assemblies, feasts and game-playing. These things undoubtedly contribute to the interest and appeal of *Heimskringla*, as of the sagas generally. However, the possibility of distinguishing what particular features belong to the time in which the sagas' events are set and what to Snorri's idea of that time (or to both) depends largely on the availability of other evidence, and as much care is required in extracting pictures of thirteenth-century culture and attitudes from the kings' sagas as in reconstructing the tenth or eleventh centuries from them.

It is clear from what has been said above that it would be an eccentric librarian who would assign *Heimskringla* a shelfmark in the History section. Yet, by the light of its times, *Heimskringla*'s margin of error is a reasonable one, its author's use of sources intelligent and discerning, and the distortion caused by his standpoint in time and space only moderate. Snorri places his work in the scholarly tradition of Ari, and from his methods and his results it seems that his intention was to record and make sense of the best traditions he knew about the Scandinavian past. It therefore seems justified to treat it first and foremost as a piece of historical writing and, in the following pages, to explore further what kind of historical writing it is.

WHAT KIND OF HISTORICAL WRITING?

Narrative

Whatever the specific needs and assumptions which mould the writing of a particular historical work, some general considerations apply to all. The most fundamental is that no historiography can be truly accurate. The 'reality' of history is so complex that the human mind cannot begin to apprehend it. No one can know all 'the facts'; only a fraction can be available to the historian, and even then he will bring preconceptions and subjective judgements to bear in scrutinising the data, selecting, interpreting and assigning relative importance to them. Any sense or pattern he extracts from the data is therefore as much constructed as 'found'. Two intuitively rather attractive assumptions therefore prove fallacious: that historical writing can directly reflect 'what actually happened', and that it consists of two separable layers: the neutral facts and the interpretations and value-judgements imposed upon them.

When the historian puts his findings into writing (or oral account) for others to share, he forces multi-dimensional and simultaneous situations into a single linear sequence and creates the illusion, by the use of the grammatical third person, of a single, fixed intelligence through which the events are perceived. Further (setting aside the spare, abrupt form of the annals or the driest chronicles), in order to give the audience a lucid, 'followable' and pleasing account, the history will be cast as fully fledged narrative, which in many ways takes the writing still farther away from the 'reality' of history. Change and movement may be exaggerated at the expense of continuity and stability, and the memorable at the expense of the important. Minute particles of incident will be shaped into a plot, the writer choosing a beginning and ending and an overall form, perhaps following the fall-rise structure of Comedy or the rise-fall of Tragedy. Links of causation will be made, explicitly or implicitly, and events will be placed in hierarchy, some highlighted by more extensive narrative treatment than others. The work as a whole may be further aligned with current literary models by the use of recognisable plot motifs or the presentation of historical personages according to heroic or romantic stereotypes. All this does not necessarily mean that evidence is wilfully subverted or factual accuracy neglected, but it does mean that the view of the 'whole factual field' (Hayden White's phrase, 1975, 60) will be distorted. (This is a specialised application of the idea propounded by Roland Barthes and others that language does not in any direct, unmediated, way represent or reflect reality.)

The distortion which results from the transformation of events into narrative tends to be more obvious in medieval works than modern. Certainly there are many passages in *Heimskringla* whose basic content is plausible enough but whose narrative presentation is simply too good to be true. The repartee may be too slick, the gestures too dramatic, or the contrasts and parallels of character too clear-cut, to dispel the impression that an authorial hand is guiding, rather than merely recording, events. In the following pages *Heimskringla* is discussed in relation to medieval historical writing, then to Icelandic saga-writing, in order to illuminate the particular kind of narrative shaping that the materials in *Heimskringla* have undergone. The division of the material is made for convenience and is by no means the only one possible.

Medieval historiography

The challenge Snorri took up in *Heimskringla*, of compiling a dynastic and national history stretching back into the mythical and legendary past, had already been faced by Geoffrey of Monmouth (*Historia Regum Britanniæ*) and William of Malmesbury (*Gesta Regum Anglorum*), both working in the first half of the twelfth century, and by Saxo Grammaticus (*Gesta Danorum*) c. 1200. Some early European 'histories' were known in medieval Iceland, conceivably as early as Snorri's time, among them Geoffrey of Monmouth's *Historia*, which was translated as *Breta sǫgur*, the works of Lucan and Sallust, which are adapted in *Rómverja saga*, and the *De Excidio Troiae* of 'Dares Phrygius' which is the basis for *Trójumanna saga*, and it is possible that Snorri was influenced by them. Geoffrey's *Historia*, in particular, may, however indirectly, have been a stimulus to the writing of *Heimskringla* (Clunies Ross 1978, 163–64; Sverrir Tómasson 1988, 288–89), and it has been suggested that Snorri knew the chronicles of William of Malmesbury and Henry of Huntingdon (Moberg 1987, 56–60 and 78–9). The influence of foreign histories on the writing of Scandinavian history in the vernacular, and the extent and nature of Snorri's Latin learning are both areas which still await comprehensive investigation, and there are interesting questions to be asked about where exactly *Heimskringla* is most appropriately to be placed—alongside the *Íslendingasögur* and other, stylistically similar, *konungasögur*, alongside the vernacular historiography which flourished in northern Europe and Italy in the thirteenth century, or even the *chansons de geste* with their meeting of history and entertainment (Hay 1977, 61), or alongside Latin histories by clerical authors. Even a modest comparison of *Heimskringla* with other medieval historiography is outside the scope of this book. All that can be done here is to identify, with some risk of over-simplification, features which are common to much or all of the European (Latin or vernacular) historiography of the Middle Ages. Some aspects of *Heimskringla* which make it unacceptable as 'serious' history today will then be put in perspective, and some features of *Heimskringla* (and comparable saga-writing) which are different from, and more modern-looking than, many medieval works will be thrown into relief.

For Snorri, as for most non-clerical writers up to the nineteenth century, history was above all political history, especially dynastic history. Its course largely consisted of the deeds of great men, and the earliest known titles of *Heimskringla*, *Nóregs konunga sögur / ævi* and variants, encapsulate this view. The work can therefore hardly be blamed if it fails to satisfy the modern historian's taste for a much broader-based view of the past which explores, rather than merely hinting at, the economic and social base of power and its administrative, legal and cultural manifestations, and which interests itself not just in kings and their henchmen but in the life of the common man. Furthermore, when read alongside other Norse accounts of the same events, *Heimskringla* often appears broad rather than blinkered in its view, with greater awareness of international politics and appreciation of causation.

Cicero called history 'the witness of the past, the light of truth, the life of memory, the instructor of life' (*testis temporum, lux veritatis, vita memoriae, magistra vitae, De Oratore* II 36), and this epitomises at least some of the possible functions of history. Historians of all eras are, one assumes, engaged in the pursuit of truth, whatever their understanding of truth. Although modern Western historians are typically professionals employed by academic or other institutions, this will ideally not colour too deeply their view of the past as expressed in their published work. The ideological influences on them will be various and subtle, perhaps even undetectable except to those who disagree with them. The truth they honestly pursue (without ever expecting to attain this Holy Grail) is factual accuracy, based on scrupulous investigation of all the evidence, and their interpretation of trends and causes will be as disinterested as possible. Medieval historiographers, on the other hand, may have a different conception of truth. Fleischmann suggests, for instance, that 'for the Middle Ages and even well beyond, historical truth was anything that belonged to a widely accepted tradition' (1983, 305). Medieval authors also have different motives and assumptions in writing history. They are driven by the desire to preserve the memory of great men and their deeds; Saxo writes so that 'the reputation of our people should not lie forgotten under ancient mould, but be blest with a literary memorial' (trans. Fisher, p. 4). They are frequently alert to the didactic potential of history, which 'tempering character by the agreeable commemoration of past events, stimulates its readers by example to the pursuit of good and the avoidance of evil' (William of Malmesbury, *De Gestis Regum Anglorum* I 103). Many historiographers wish to preserve glories which are specifically national ones, while others, whether overtly or not, have still more pragmatic motives: of ingratiating themselves with a prince, of asserting the material and moral claims of a dynasty, a town or a monastic house, or of providing precedents for particular policies.

How relevant any of these potential motives might be to *Heimskringla* is a subject still to be investigated in full. Certainly Snorri's Prologue, unlike most of its European counterparts (Sverrir Tómasson 1988, 382), gives no outright statement of intent, and his narrative is virtually free of the partisan fulminations and accolades which flow from the pens of some medieval authors. Saxo's 'he darkened the brilliance of his glory with the foul smear of pride' (p. 109), for instance, could have no place in *Heimskringla*. There has been much debate as to whether or not *Heimskringla* promotes a particular political 'line' and, if so, what it is (as seen in Chapter Five, Themes and opinions), and this disagreement might in itself favour the view that there is none. The split loyalties of Snorri's career and the stylistic kinship of *Heimskringla* to other secular saga-writing might also suggest that the *Heimskringla* narrative is really as neutral as it seems. One might compare the case of the *Íslendingasögur*, for which ideological interpretations are fashionable, but inconclusive. The multiplicity of contradictory interpretations of *Hrafnkels saga* is a case in point.

Whatever their specific aims in writing history, medieval European historiographers are almost by definition committed to the premiss that God's hand is at work in human history. The extent to which this is made explicit varies greatly, however, and a writer's stance on this point has profound effects on his history. Snorri would doubtless have accepted the importance of divine will and divine favour in the reigns of the Norwegian kings, and occasionally these forces are manifest in *Heimskringla*, for instance in Magnús góði's spectacular victory at Hlýrskógsheiðr (*Mgóð* 27–28). Miracles, dreams and prodigies such as produced that victory were part of the language of the age, and Snorri spoke it. Yet comparison with other sources shows his approach to be essentially secular. Even his lives of the two missionary kings, Óláfr Tryggvason and Óláfr Haraldsson, are very much kings' saga rather than hagiography, and his treatment of miracles illustrates this secular stance well. Snorri realised the importance of the cult of Óláfr helgi in Norwegian history and perhaps also the value of the miracles as a yardstick against which the unhappy events of later reigns could be measured, and accordingly he retains the posthumous miracles recorded in the *Legendary Saga*. He groups them as an appendix at the end of his *Separate Saga* and in the final third of *Heimskringla* disperses them through the relevant sagas of Óláfr's successors (unlike the authors of *Morkinskinna* and *Fagrskinna*, who retain very few of them). The miracles of Óláfr's lifetime, on the other hand, are either omitted or rationalised (as in the Mälaren episode, mentioned above, p. 120), so that Óláfr's sanctity only emerges in the last, tragic, act of his drama. Even then, there is rationalisation. Snorri inherited the tale that Óláfr, deep in thought one Sunday, began idly whittling away at a piece of wood. Realising his sin against the Sabbath, he burned the wood-shavings in the palm of his hand. Snorri in *Ólhelg* 190 omits the claim found in the *Legendary Saga* and *Gamal Norsk Homiliebok* that his hand was unburned (see further Whaley 1987, esp. 334–41).

Outside the miracle accounts, references to God are rare in *Heimskringla*, and virtually confined to speeches (direct or indirect) by the characters (Hallberg 1978, esp. 125–29). Óláfr Haraldsson asks God's help, thanks him or pledges service to him; but there is no narratorial comment such as is found in the *Legendary Saga* to the effect that a given happening was God's will or that Óláfr succeeded because blessed by God. Still less are there dramatic interventions by God such as the scene in the *Legendary Saga* (ch. 82) where God opens the eyes of Þórir hundr to see the soul of the slain king being carried to heaven by angels.

The modest space given to the transcendental in *Heimskringla*—fate, personal luck or the will of God (see Gurevich 1971)—allows for a more complex appreciation of causation than is found in many analogous histories. As a small example, Óláfr Haraldsson's mission in the Vík goes well, not because of any miraculous demonstration of God's power (though there are such demonstrations elsewhere), but because the men of the Vík are accustomed to the new ideas. They have been exposed to the customs of visiting Danish and Saxon traders and are themselves used to trading in Christian lands or wintering there on Viking expeditions (*Ólhelg* ch. 64).

Similarly, since all is not seen in terms of moral black and white there is more chance that both sides of an issue will be shown. In the *Historia* of Theodoricus, opposition to Óláfr is based on *infelix cupiditas* and still in *Ágrip* Óláfr is first and foremost a Christian martyr. Snorri's *Óláfs saga helga*, by contrast, gives remarkably penetrating accounts of men such as Þórir hundr, Ásbjǫrn Selsbani or Kálfr Árnason and their motives for turning against Óláfr (in contrast also with the *Fagrskinna* author, who takes relatively little interest in them, Fleischhauer 1938, 75), and allows glimpses of less saintly aspects of Óláfr.

Finally, the secular standpoint of *Heimskringla* enables the heathen past to be viewed benignly, or at least with an appearance of tolerant detachment—a view clearly akin to that presented in *Snorra Edda*. It is true that the routing of unrepentant pagans is narrated with some relish, not to say exultation, and that Óðinn appears as a dangerous trickster (*ÓlTrygg* 63–64). But the early chapters of *Ynglinga saga* portray the pagan gods not as demonic powers but euhemeristically as human rulers whose power was interpreted by others as divine (see further Ciklamini 1975), and this is done without the overt contempt of Saxo who, relating how Frigg prostituted herself to obtain gold from Odin's statue, comments: 'Need I add anything but to say that such a god deserved such a wife? Men's intelligence was once made ridiculous by gullibility of this kind' (trans. Fisher, p. 26). Nevertheless, the mainly neutral tone of the saga narrative makes it difficult to gauge exactly how Snorri's presentation of the heathen past in *Heimskringla* is to be read. Weber (1987), examining it in the light of typological interpretations of secular history by Christian writers, finds it less sympathetic, while more sophisticated and schematic, than might at first sight seem the case.

The medieval historiographer's relish for the fabulous is evidenced in *Heimskringla*, but only to a modest degree. Ghosts, monsters and shape-shifters occasionally obtrude on the accounts of kings and their wars, treaties and coups d'état; and a few of these are unique to *Heimskringla*, the *landvættir* in *ÓlTrygg* 33 among them. The reason for their inclusion is perhaps that they served as vividly symbolic demonstrations of political situations or of individual character, or simply as entertaining stories which would otherwise have fallen into oblivion. But Snorri's normal tendency was to curtail the fabulous materials found in his sources. At Hjǫrungavágr the defeated Jomsviking Búi, having jumped into the fjord with his treasure chests, does not, as in *Jómsvíkinga drápa*

v. 37 and *Jómsvíkinga saga* ch. 38, turn himself into a serpent (*ÓlTrygg* 41). There is even, unusually, a statement of policy on this matter, for at the close of *ÓlTrygg* 80 Snorri remarks that he is more interested in writing about Óláfr's Christianisation of Norway and other lands than about the trolls and other monsters which harrassed him and his men on their travels. The policy is, on the whole, maintained in practice. Comparison of Snorri's *Óláfs saga Tryggvasonar* overall with Oddr Snorrason's saga shows suppression or near-suppression of twenty-five chapters containing supernatural materials from the sublime (Óláfr's vision of heaven and hell) to the ridiculous (an assembly of lamenting trolls; Andersson 1977, 83–84).

Like most writers of history up to the nineteenth century, the author of *Heimskringla* brings events to life with picturesque detail and imagined dialogue—a technique which might seem a long way from the detached and cautious analysis and speculation of the modern historian. The *Heimskringla* narrative is generously furnished with material which is more or less unknowable: speeches uttered in the din of battle, private conversations or neatly echoic repartee from speakers who are out of earshot from each other (e.g. the remarks of the English- and Norse-speaking King Haralds in *HSig* 90–91). Even allowing for the verbal agility of the protagonists and a strong folk memory, such material must be the product of literary craftsmanship.

Nonetheless, Snorri does show some caution about introducing material which cannot be validated because no eyewitness account could be available. When in *Yng* 20 the brother kings Alrekr and Eiríkr are found dead from head injuries and without weapons Snorri reports that it is thought (*ok þat hyggja menn*) that they had killed each other with their horse-bridles. Snorri's restraint here is striking, not least since Þjóðólfr's verse on the incident is more dogmatic.

Further, the difference between medieval and modern techniques of presentation may be less sharp than it at first appears (especially in the light of the general considerations about narrative outlined earlier in this chapter). The debate in *Ólhelg* 36 about the relative merits of native and foreign kings in Norway is put into the mouths of the deposed kings Hrœrekr and Hringr, but it contains eminently useful and credible observations about a running problem of the Norwegian people. It is analysis, interpretation, without which writing on historical subjects becomes mere annal-making or antiquarianism, but it is dramatised—the unknowable is supplied from the imagination in a way which is unacceptable in the works of modern academic historians but is the stuff of historical novels, biographies and drama-documentaries. In fact there is a general resemblance to the more 'popular' end of the present-day intellectual and cultural spectrum, especially in the notion that history is made out of the actions of individuals. (Other points of contact between medieval writings and the modern media are touched on by Sørensen, 1977, 154.)

It is even more difficult to generalise about the sources, methodology and resulting accuracy of medieval historiography than about the matters already considered. They are so complex and so specific to individual works, so important too, that they are instead discussed in particular relation to *Heimskringla* above. Here the only point to be reiterated, now in more general terms, is that the sources used by any medieval historiographer will be, to modern eyes, thoroughly inadequate. Authors may have had access to letters, charters and other raw primary documents written 'unconsciously' for some purpose other than the recording of history (and William of Malmesbury incorporates several in his work). More often than not, though, the sources were earlier narrative, interpretative histories, which, given the characteristic respect for written authority in the Middle Ages, may be used with little critical discrimination. There is thus a sharp contrast with the ideal data of the modern historian—documentary, archaeological, onomastic—which are verifiable, classifiable and quantifiable by quasi-scientific methods. Even modern historians studying the medieval period are limited by the paucity of adequate data, and treasures such as the *Domesday Book* which come close to meeting these criteria are relatively scarce.

How far *Heimskringla* belongs within the mainstream of medieval European historiography is, as already said, a question too large to be debated in detail here. My own, provisional, view, is that Norse writings are absent from many handbooks on the subject not because of their want of historical seriousness but more because of their vernacular language and their geographical and cultural remoteness from the centres of European scholarship. Certainly, consideration of *Heimskringla* as a piece of medieval historiography illuminates both its more 'medieval' features (such as the biographical conception of history, the use of imaginative reconstruction and inclusion of marvels) and its more 'modern' ones (the relative impartiality and rationalism). *Heimskringla*'s 'modernity' is closely connected to its essentially secular cast, and reflects both the intellectual taste of Snorri, a secular chieftain of great and many-sided experience, and the literary traditions within which he worked. For out of the many possible historiographical approaches

From History to Literature 135

available from medieval European models the ones which ultimately flourished most convincingly in Iceland were not those of the clerical-hagiographical kind (though these found an ideal focus in some of the lives of the two King Olafs), but the more scholarly and rationalistic ones. There were specifically Icelandic conditions which fostered the adoption of these approaches and their continued evolution into a realistic tradition of saga-writing culminating in *Heimskringla* itself. These included the nature of society under the Icelandic Commonwealth, lacking the domination of a court or unchallenged ecclesiastical hierarchy as patron and focus; legal, genealogical and historical interests rooted in the pioneering days of the settlement period and embedded in scholarly writings going back to the days of Ari Þorgilsson; a view of Norwegian history which combines fascination with detachment; and the importance of storytelling in a land where economic and climatic conditions limited other cultural activities.

Saga

As already seen in the previous chapter, *Heimskringla*'s stylistic attributes place it squarely alongside other Icelandic sagas, and the genre of the work is clearly a vital guide to how it should best be read. The imaginative recreation of history which characterises most medieval historiography here conforms specifically to the kinds of character portrayal and tripartite scenic construction found in the classic *Íslendingasögur*, and it is the 'saga' characteristics as well as Snorri's own rigour which make the narrative more plausible than much other medieval historiography. *Heimskringla*'s place within Icelandic saga-literature needs no defence or further illustration, and the present section will be concerned especially with its relations with particular branches of saga-writing.

The challenge of finding suitable approaches, 'historical' or 'literary', to the whole range of Icelandic saga-writing has been a major preoccupation of scholars over the last century. All the sagas are to some degree concerned with people and events that actually existed, although the nature and degree of remoteness of the recreated past varies dramatically, from the Germanic heroic age in the 'sagas of ancient times' (*fornaldarsögur*) to thirteenth-century Iceland in the 'contemporary sagas' of *Sturlunga saga*. All the sagas are to some extent imaginative, even fictional works. Even *Sturlunga saga*, its dense documentation of the activities of some three thousand named persons notwithstanding, makes use of imagined dialogue, dreams and prophecies which, like the feud structures which prevail in the *Íslendingasögur*, represent actual experience honed into literary conventions. Historicity and literary interest are by no means necessarily found in inverse proportions in these works: some modern readers find little of either in the *fornaldarsögur* and *riddarasögur* but much of both in the *Íslendingasögur* and some *konungasögur*. Yet Liestøl (1930, 89) found that the *Íslendingasögur* contain more dialogue the farther from history they are, and, broadly speaking, the more the sagas have been revealed to be historically inaccurate, the more they have been perceived as sophisticated literary artifacts. This is particularly true of the *Íslendingasögur*, *Hrafnkels saga* being a classic example. Just as authors are seen as having been relatively free of the detailed actualities of ninth- to eleventh-century Iceland, readers of these sagas are now more free than formerly to see them as reflections of the authors' own thirteenth-century world, or to find in them literary qualities and ethical, political or other meanings.

There is much common ground between *Heimskringla* (with others of the *konungasögur*) and the *Íslendingasögur* : an interest in the Scandinavian past, shared tales of Icelandic skalds fêted at the Norwegian courts, and a narrative style which can create a seductively real-seeming world. Snorri himself may have composed within both genres (*Heimskringla* and *Egils saga*), and, since the genres and their names are modern constructs, we do not know with what precision saga-audiences distinguished between them and the kinds of truth offered in them (see Lönnroth 1965; Steblin-Kamenskij 1973, ch. 2). Further, *Heimskringla*'s particular manner of narration makes it the most like the great *Íslendingasögur*—say *Njáls saga* or *Laxdœla saga*—of all the kings' sagas. The formal detachment of the narrative, the scenic shaping of many episodes, the laconic repartee, even particular kinds of stereotyped character and action such as the virago Sigríðr stórráða (*ÓlTrygg* 43, 61 and 98) are all reminiscent of *Íslendingasögur*. May we then expect a shift in readers' perceptions of *Heimskringla* in parallel with the changed approaches to the *Íslendingasögur* referred to at the close of the previous paragraph?

Certainly the parallel is justified in the practical sense that, since *Heimskringla* ceased to be treated as a more or less reliable historical document, its main worth has been literary, or more broadly cultural. However, literary qualities, especially in medieval writings, are by no means incompatible with an intended fidelity to the past, and it is this fidelity which limits the relevance of the rest of the parallel. Thus, although there are traces in *Heimskringla* of thirteenth-century conditions imprinted upon the past, and some possibility of ideological threads, there is little suspicion of anything so deliberate as the 'encoding' of thirteenth-century problems, even specific feuds, into stories of the Saga Age, which some scholars have detected in the *Íslendingasögur* (Madelung 1973 is unusual). Moreover, too close a comparison between *Heimskringla* and the *Íslendingasögur* may be misleading since most of them, certainly the greatest of them, were written after *Heimskringla*. It is not the case that, because the *Íslendingasögur* can be treated as literary fictions, *Heimskringla* should be too, but rather that the *Íslendingasögur* authors learnt the art of verisimilitude from, among others, the *konungasögur*.

Whatever its resemblance to the *Íslendingasögur*, *Heimskringla* borrows from, learns from and belongs with the *konungasögur*, a modern and far from homogeneous grouping but one with, on the whole, more claim than the *Íslendingasögur* to be regarded as history. The kings' sagas are more continuously concerned with events of public, not just private, importance, and with the placing of events in a defined chronology. Their narrators, several of whose names are known to us, whereas all the *Íslendingasögur* are anonymous, are more overtly conscious about the process of representing the past, weighing up the plausibility of tradition and naming informants. Thus, many writers from Ari onwards remark explicitly on the high value they place on reports stemming from reliable witnesses, and many voice suspicion of unauthenticated material. Fragment 3 of the *Oldest saga of Óláfr helgi* contains a declaration that not all the available material is included because not all is attended by acceptable evidence (*at eigi eru svá vitni um þau ǫll er tœkilig eru*), and *Morkinskinna* has a similar statement, taken over in *Fagrskinna* and *Heimskringla* (*HSig* 36), concerning some tales of Haraldr Sigurðarson's exploits. Practice does not always—to modern eyes—keep step with theory, however. As already seen, Oddr Snorrason uses a great deal of fabulous material despite his contempt for 'stepmother-tales which shepherd lads tell', and veracity is not always the first consideration. Styrmir Kárason recognised that not all the materials he recorded were equally credible, and was confident that enjoyable stories about Óláfr helgi would not cause the saint offence, even if they proved false (*Flateyjarbók* III 248). Nevertheless, *Heimskringla*'s kinship with the *konungasögur* marks it out as requiring a different kind of reading from the *Íslendingasögur*, and within the *konungasögur*, *Heimskringla* is more true than most to the stated ideal of avoiding fabrications and trivia; it also has less affinity with hagiography than some others of the group.

To summarise so far: *Heimskringla* is, in some very obvious ways, still the 'history book' that Thomas Carlyle took it to be. It is entirely devoted to events of the past, and much of it can in some degree be independently verified. Chronology is well handled, and the chain of events is tightly forged out of human action and external circumstance. Divine intervention is rarely seen and supernatural exotica only haunt the periphery of the world of *Heimskringla*. Furthermore, the writing gains an air of authority through its detached and coherent style of narration and modern-looking avoidance of propaganda or moralising. Some elements, however—the supernatural beings and the imagined scenes among them, as well as the historical misconceptions—bring parts of the work closer to myth, folk-lore or legend than to history in the modern sense, and given the nature of medieval historiography and of the sources available to Snorri, this is not surprising. Snorri and his audience must have been aware that, especially for the remoter periods, intelligent speculation was the most they could hope for. Moreover, despite the excellence of *Heimskringla* and its convenience as a survey of so great a chronological span, it should not be allowed a status so monolithic that its sources, many of which are extant, are disregarded. If *Heimskringla* is still to be read as history (and it is read by anyone with a serious interest in medieval Scandinavia) it must be read with the widest reference to other sources and with the awareness that the truth about particular episodes is often beyond recovery.

LITERATURE?

Heimskringla is the best of its kind, its scope ambitious, its narrative lucid, purposeful and plausible. While ideological or theological forces leave little imprint on the surface, the aesthetic imperatives of shaping a good story and entertaining the audience are strongly in evidence. The literary interest of *Heimskringla*, moreover, remains however 'historical' or 'unhistorical' the narrative may prove to be, for 'when a great work of historiography or philosophy of history has become outdated, it is reborn into art' (White 1975, 67). If every word of *Heimskringla* were outright fabrication we would still be left with a cultural artifact of great worth— one of the finest products of thirteenth-century Iceland and an image of the Scandinavian past as seen from that standpoint. The literary qualities of *Heimskringla* are, it is hoped, evident from the material in the preceding chapter, and my purpose here is not to discuss them comprehensively, but rather to consider some of the implications of treating *Heimskringla* as a literary text.

It is possible and, I would argue, valid to cut *Heimskringla* free from its moorings and read it as an independent text without reference to the events, or accounts of events, on which it is based. To do so allows the writing to speak directly and freshly as story, to excite and move. The tale of Þóroddr Snorrason and Arnljótr gellini (*Ólhelg* 141), for example, offers a setting which is humble but romantic, a hero who is a glamorous scoundrel, and action of varied tempo which culminates in a visitation by a man-eating trollwoman; we might be reminded of *Beowulf*. The scenes on the eve of the battle of Stiklarstaðir, vivid, vigorous but touched by moments of tenderness and the pathos of foreboding, share something of the heroic dignity of Shakespeare's Agincourt.

However, to read *Heimskringla* in isolation from its sources limits recognition of its particular qualities. It makes value-judgements—both favourable and unfavourable—shaky and the detection of themes or tendencies in the material suspect. Indeed, the narrative can in places appear so unselfconsciously 'right' that there seems little to say about it until alternative options of style and content are laid bare by comparing parallel accounts. To take account of the work's position as the culmination of a long tradition, with all the benefits and constraints that implies, therefore seems the most fruitful approach, and fortunately it is one that, despite its difficulties, has found favour with some scholars of great learning and patience (see Further reading, pp. 144–6 below, esp. section 4).

Seen in the light of its sources, the achievement of *Heimskringla* is impressive. It combines many of the best attributes of the synoptic histories of Norwegian kings and of the individual biographies, covering a vast canvas with reasonable coherence. Much that is trivial, implausible or irrelevant is omitted, and the remaining materials are shaped into a saga-cycle which has a kind of unity. Within the cycle, individual sagas, sequences of chapters and single chapters often form satisfying narrative structures. Episodes of history are brought to life through graphic scene-setting and portrayal of action, and there is rich use of terse and tough direct speech, which is often well-turned without being obtrusively literary. There is an impartiality and breadth of vision which surpass most of its sources. Further, the usually lucid and measured narrative is undoubtedly one of the pleasures of reading *Heimskringla*;

and since few of the *Íslendingasögur* can be proved to pre-date *Heimskringla*, Snorri may have had a significant rôle in the evolution of Icelandic saga style.

This said, one feature of great importance remains: *Heimskringla*'s variety. It is to some extent a miscellany, its maker almost as much an editor as an author. It incorporates quite large chunks from other works more or less verbatim, e.g. from *Ágrip*, *Hryggjarstykki* and from miracle collections. This makes in certain places for stylistic shocks of the sort described in the section on variety in Chapter Five. In a wider sense too the work is uneven. The writing in *Heimskringla* is often at its most 'literary' when the source materials are fairly abundant and have already been shaped and polished to a high degree. This applies to much of *Óláfs saga helga*—something of a special case since it was written first of the *Heimskringla* sagas and probably before the idea of the whole saga-cycle was conceived—and to the sagas flanking it. Elsewhere, though, the materials were in literary terms unpromising and Snorri's version remains relatively uninspiring. For *Ynglinga saga* Snorri had, as far as we know, only very summary sources—mainly the poems *Ynglingatal* and *Háleygjatal*. There is some excellent story-telling in it, but much of the saga is sketchy, life after life in the centre of the saga is told according to the same formula, and there is virtually no direct speech (nine words, in fact). By contrast, the last four sagas of *Heimskringla* are packed with action so dense and complex that they make tortuous reading. There are few great heroes or grand causes or events, little dramatisation of scenes, little sense of pause or climax to relieve the monotonous round of move and counter-move between the various claimants to the throne. The problem here is to do with reality—a prolonged state of civil war—but also to do with the sources. Being so close in time to Snorri's own, these reigns were known in considerable detail. The happenings within them had not been sifted and glamorised by process of time and tradition and Snorri apparently had not the inclination to work them over much either.

This patchwork character of *Heimskringla* should not be exaggerated—the last four sagas only take up one-eighth of the whole work—but it is marked enough to have led some nineteenth-century scholars to suggest that Snorri did not write the closing sagas at all; and more recently Ole Widding has written about *Heimskringla* as a compilation (1976), while Lars Lönnroth has seen Snorri not as an author but as a patron of literature and centre of a circle of scribes (1965, 14; see p. 19 above).

The lack of homogeneity is there for all to see, but what we make of it is a subjective matter; we may condemn it as a flaw or praise it as interesting variety, or we may of course decline to judge in any direction. We may be forced into a position of critical double standards, in which we enjoy and praise the parts where, according to our modern taste, there is literary interest, then have to find excuses for the rest, resorting to what we take to be a more thirteenth-century viewpoint and maintaining that Snorri had no intention of writing great literature but only of representing the past. I think again that this kind of inconsistency has its own validity, provided that we are conscious of it. In any case, we, like Snorri, have to be practical. If all the reigns of kings from Haraldr hárfagri onwards had been worked over in the same way as Óláfr helgi's fifteen-year reign, the whole work would be about five thousand pages long, instead of the modest 640 pages it occupies in the one-volume edition of Finnur Jónsson's text.

A further consideration in approaching *Heimskringla* as literature concerns the appreciation of individual passages, for it often happens that the best bits are from identifiable sources. To take a single small example: at the close of the battle of Hjǫrungavágr in *ÓlTrygg* 41 we see the Jomsviking Búi grievously wounded and facing defeat, his ship boarded by the Norwegians. He slices an enemy in two, grabs his two chests of gold in his arms and shouts aloud 'Overboard all Búi's men' (*fyrir borð allir Búa liðar*). It is a stirring moment, but if we feel inclined to congratulate anyone it should be Oddr Snorrason (p. 62) or the author of *Jómsvíkinga saga* (ch. 33), or even Búi himself, but not Snorri. Similarly, there is much in the superb scenes at Óláfr Tryggvason's last battle at Svǫlð which is traceable to sources (see *Heimskringla* 1941-51, I, cxxix-cxxx). This may come as a disappointment to us, though it should cease to be a problem if we can free ourselves from post-Romantic notions about literary authorship and do not insist on originality as a criterion of literary worth.

However rigorous the comparisons drawn between *Heimskringla* and its sources and analogues, there is still room for personal taste in our response to Snorri's alterations—both particular ones and their general direction. This may again be illustrated from the Jomsvikings' battle at Hjǫrungavágr in *Heimskringla* (*ÓlTrygg* 41), compared with the version in *Jómsvíkinga saga*. We may be relieved that the injuries to Búi's face are not detailed with quite the horrific precision of *Jómsvíkinga saga* ch. 33, but slightly regretful that Snorri had the good taste to suppress Búi's quip, as his teeth spill out of his shattered jaw, that 'the Danish girl on

Borgundarholm [Bornholm] won't be so keen to kiss me now.' We may be pleased that Snorri streamlines the post-battle executions of the Jomsvikings, eliminating much that is gross or grotesque as well as some general heroics (*Jómsvíkinga saga* chs 36–37), but feel that his rendering of Vagn Ákason's attack on Eiríkr jarl's ship lacks the panache of *Jómsvíkinga saga*, where Vagn and Áslákr hólmskalli sweep down the ship, cutting swathes through the warriors on both sides until Áslákr's advance is dramatically arrested by Vígfúss Víga-Glúmsson (ch. 31). The 'we' here is of course an authorial one, referring only to the present writer, and everyone must judge for him- or herself.

Many of the attributes revealed by the comparative method and summarised above render *Heimskringla* more plausible as history and more interesting as literature. But what, in the end, is the nature of the combination? Throughout much of the work we find a reasonably happy meeting of history and literature, learning and art, information and entertainment. We may feel that the writing in *Heimskringla* is most successful where historically important events are vividly dramatised, for example the brilliant picture of the prelude to the battle of Stamford Bridge (*HSig* 87–91). But the two do not always marry well. Some of the best-told stories contain the least history—the tale of Þórarinn Nefjólfsson's ugly feet in *Ólhelg* 85, for example—and sometimes fidelity to sources takes second place to the desire for a streamlined and lively narrative. On the other hand, Snorri's historical discernment and emotional restraint have sometimes suppressed colourful episodes whose loss some may lament. The touching account of the death of the hound Vígi, heart-broken at the fall of his master Óláfr Tryggvason (Oddr Snorrason p. 240) is lacking, as is the tale preserved in *Flateyjarbók* III 240 in which the skald Sigvatr delicately induces Óláfr Haraldsson to accept the loan of his warm cloak. (See Guðbrandur Vigfússon 1878, lxxxiii–lxxxv for complaints about the 'dull skeleton-like abridgement' which is, in his view, the extant *Heimskringla*.) Snorri's duty to historical tradition can, moreover, produce ungainly and annalistic chapters like *Mberf* 11, or ones where the interests of imparting information are so dominant that the literary temperature drops below zero—as in *ÓlTrygg* 94, which is nothing but a list of names of the crew of Ormr inn langi. Whole tracts of the work, indeed, would fail to meet the qualifications commonly required of literature—criteria such as non-paraphrasability, the indivisibility of form and content, or heightened use of language.

CONCLUSION

Like many or most medieval texts, *Heimskringla* defies attempts to impose modern categories on it. The boundaries between fact and fiction, utilitarian and imaginative writing, history and literature are always difficult to draw, and certainly lay differently in Snorri's time. We may search *Heimskringla*, as all sagas, for many kinds of information—historical, linguistic, literary, ideological, anthopological and so on—or, in a less analytical way, we may simply be fascinated both by the world it depicts and the civilisation that produced it. We recognise what we may take as universals in human behaviour, while at the same time revelling in the differences.

Snorri never, either in the Prologue or the body of *Heimskringla*, states his overall aims and intentions. Nor is there any evidence that he was working for a patron or that he had any single persuasive purpose in mind. His intentions must therefore be extrapolated from the Prologue, from the way that he is used by his immediate successors as a historical authority, and from the *Heimskringla* sagas themselves, especially their kinship with other kings' sagas and their treatment of sources. In the end everything—or nearly everything—points to the probability that Snorri's first duty was to historical tradition as laid out in his sources. His writing is not too far distant from the desiderata of a modern historian: fidelity to sources, coupled with recognition of their limitations, and awareness of the danger of personal bias. Reconstruction of events by the operation of creative imagination on source-materials is common to all historical writing, and the particular, almost dramatised, form that this often takes in *Heimskringla* is standard for the Middle Ages. Whether Snorri more specifically intended to write an *origo gentis*, tracing the origins of a nation which ultimately was the same as his own (Sverrir Tómasson 1988, 288–89), is a question worth further investigation.

If *Heimskringla*'s roots in history are not kept in view the work as a whole will appear uneven and frequently dull. If we treat it primarily as a literary text, it is our choice, not Snorri's, and we must take the rough with the smooth. However, the interests of information-giving and entertainment are by no means necessarily at odds. Indeed, they fuse with unusually happy effect in the literature of medieval Iceland, and Snorri, like all the best saga-writers, happened to be a penetrating observer of human behaviour and a superb story-teller, who could recreate the past in vividly realised scenes. *Heimskringla* is neither a novel nor a modern textbook of history, but it has much of the appeal of both.

FURTHER READING

This guide supplements the specific references given in the main text of the book by citing more or less extended discussions of matters relevant to *Heimskringla*. The list is highly selective, with a slight bias towards more recent publications and ones written in English, although few of the most essential works fulfil both criteria. Items are referred to in the short form (full details being given in the Bibliography) and arranged according to the chapter divisions of this book. Some 'staples' whose coverage embraces more than one major area should, however, be mentioned at the outset, and chief among these are Nordal 1920 and the introductions to the three volumes of Bjarni Aðalbjarnarson's edition of *Heimskringla*. In English there are few general works on *Heimskringla* and its author, except for the introductions to English translations (see Chapter Three), the papers collected in *Parergon* 15 (1976), and Ciklamini 1978. The publication of Sverre Bagge's *Society and Politics in Snorri Stuluson's Heimskringla* by the University of California Press is expected late in 1991. Essential information on a wide range of medieval Scandinavian topics (including literary ones) is found in *Kulturhistorisk leksikon for nordisk middelalder* (1956-78) and in the *Encyclopedia of Scandinavia in the Middle Ages* (forthcoming from Garland). Translations into English are listed in Fry 1981. Further bibliography on *Heimskringla* is available in Halldór Hermannsson 1910 and 1937 and Raabe 1930, and on the kings' sagas generally in Andersson 1985, which, together with the other essays and bibliographies in Clover and Lindow 1985, provides a wide-ranging survey of saga studies. The *Bibliography of Old Norse-Icelandic Studies* (Copenhagen 1963–) provides regular updates for all relevant topics.

ONE: AUTHORSHIP

Evidence for Snorri's authorship: Jakob Benediktsson 1955; Lönnroth 1964, 78–97; Louis-Jensen 1977, 43–61; Berger 1979; Ólafur Halldórsson 1979, 113–27. Nature of authorship in medieval writings (especially sagas): Lönnroth 1964, 78–97 and 1965, 11–15; Steblin-Kamenskij 1973; Hermann Pálsson 1973; Hallberg 1974; Sverrir Tómasson 1988, 180–89.

Further Reading

TWO: SNORRI AND THE AGE OF THE STURLUNGS

General history of medieval Iceland: Jón Jóhannesson 1974; Hastrup 1985; Byock 1988. The Age of the Sturlungs: *Sturlunga saga* 1946, introduction and appendices (Jón Jóhannesson); Einar Ól. Sveinsson 1953; *Sturlunga saga*, 1970–74 translation, introduction (Thomas). Christianity in medieval Iceland: Turville-Petre 1942, introduction; Foote 1974. Norwegian history during Snorri's lifetime: Larsen 1948; Derry 1957; Helle 1974. Snorri's life: *Heimskringla*, 1893–1905 translation, IV xvii–liv; Paasche 1922a; Gunnarr Benediktsson 1957; Simon 1976.

THREE: THE TEXT

Manuscripts: Stefán Karlsson 1976; Louis-Jensen 1977, 16–43. Early editions and translations: Louis-Jensen 1977, 43–61; Sverrir Tómasson 1988, 375–77. Relations between *Separate* and *Heimskringla* versions of *Óláfs saga helga*: Nordal 1914. Prologues (of *Heimskringla* and other medieval Icelandic works): Wessén 1928–29; Sverrir Tómasson 1975 and 1988, 374–83 *et passim*.

FOUR: SOURCES

Snorri's sources and his use of them: Storm 1873, esp. parts II and IV; *Heimskringla* 1893–1901 (sources and analogues listed before each chapter); Schreiner 1927; Finnur Jónsson 1934; *Heimskringla*, 1951 translation, introduction (Foote). Literary history of medieval Iceland, and specific works: Turville-Petre 1953; Jónas Kristjánsson 1988. Development of the kings' sagas: Berntsen 1923; Bjarni Aðalbjarnarson 1937; Beyschlag 1950; Ellehøj 1965; Andersson 1985. Skaldic verse: Turville-Petre 1976; Frank 1978; Peters 1978. Folktale: Ciklamini 1979. (Most of the studies listed under Five involve comparison with sources.)

FIVE: STYLE AND STRUCTURE

Saga-style and its development: Springer 1939; Hallberg 1962a; Mundal 1977; Amory 1978; Jónas Kristjánsson 1981, 1985, and 1988 esp. pp. 149–51, 212–14. Style and Narrative Art in *Heimskringla*: Paasche 1916; Lie 1937; Finnbogi Guðmundsson 1951; Hallberg 1962b and 1968; Finnbogi Guðmundsson 1976; Rieger 1976; Sogge 1976; Andersson 1977; Bjarni Guðnason 1979; Blackall 1981, 144–98;

Ciklamini 1981; Knirk 1981. Themes and opinions: Koht 1914 and 1921; Paasche 1922b; Sandvik 1955; Koht 1954–56; Gunnar Benediktsson 1957, ch. 8; Gurevich 1971; Lönnroth 1976; Martin 1976.

SIX: FROM HISTORY TO LITERATURE?

Definitions of literature: Eagleton 1983, Introduction. Approaches to history: Elton 1967. Relations of history and literature: White 1978. Norwegian history in the period covered by *Heimskringla*: Andersen 1977. Historicity of *Heimskringla* and other sagas: L. Weibull 1911; Koht 1914 and 1921; Dahl 1959, esp. ch. 8; Mundal 1977 and 1987. Narrative: Miller 1974; Kermode 1979; White 1984. Medieval historiography (general): Smalley 1974; Hay 1977; Ray 1985; (Icelandic): Boyer 1984; Sverrir Tómasson 1988, 189–94, 245–60 *et passim*. The concept of truth in medieval Icelandic writing: Steblin-Kamenskij 1973, ch. 2 and reviews by Hermann Pálsson (1973) and Hallberg (1974). Genre in saga literature: Lönnroth 1965; Sverrir Tómasson 1988, 73–80; Tucker 1989, 3–4. Weighting of historical and aesthetic priorities in *Heimskringla*: Kuhn 1976; Blackall 1981, 144–98.

BIBLIOGRAPHY

NOTE. Abbreviations of frequently cited periodicals, series and volumes of studies are incorporated; those which apply to items in both sections are entered in section I.

Icelandic authors, except those with hereditary surnames, are entered under their first names.

Individual skaldic poems are not listed separately in section I, but can be traced through the index of *Skjaldedigtning*.

I. PRIMARY SOURCES: EDITIONS AND TRANSLATIONS

Adam of Bremen. *Gesta Hammaburgensis Ecclesiæ Pontificum*. 1917. Ed. Bernhard Schmeidler. Monumenta Germaniae Historica, Scriptores Rerum Germanicarum 2. Hannover and Leipzig.

Ágrip af Nóregskonunga sǫgum. Fagrskinna–Nóregs konunga tal. 1984. Ed. Bjarni Einarsson. ÍF 29.

Biskupa sögur I–II. 1858–78. [Ed. Guðbrandur Vigfússon and Jón Sigurðsson.] Copenhagen.

BA = Bibliotheca Arnamagnæana. Copenhagen.

Danakonunga sǫgur : Skjǫldunga saga. Knýtlinga saga. Ágrip af sǫgu Danakonunga. 1982. Ed. Bjarni Guðnason. ÍF 35.

Diplomatarium Islandicum I: *834–1264*. 1857–76. Ed. Jón Sigurðsson. Copenhagen.

EA = Editiones Arnamagnæanæ. Copenhagen.

Egils saga. 1933. Ed. Sigurður Nordal. ÍF 2.

Fagrskinna: see *Ágrip*.

Flateyjarbok [sic] I–III. 1860–68. [Ed. Guðbrandur Vigfússon and C. R. Unger.] Oslo.

Færeyinga saga. 1987. Ed. Ólafur Halldórsson. Stofnun Árna Magnússonar á Íslandi, Rit 30. Reykjavík.

Gamal Norsk Homiliebok. Cod. AM 619 4°. 1931. Ed. Gustav Indrebø. Oslo. Repr. 1966.

Geoffrey of Monmouth. *The History of the Kings of Britain*. 1966. Trans. Lewis Thorpe. Harmondsworth.

Guðmundar sögur biskups I: *Guðmundar saga A*. 1983. Ed. Stefán Karlsson. EA, B 6 [= the 'Oldest saga' printed in *Biskupa sögur* I 407–558; future volumes to include the saga printed in *Biskupa sögur* I 559–618, and the saga by Abbot Arngrímr, *Biskupa sögur* II 1–184. See also *Prestssaga* below.]

Hákonar saga Hákonarsonar. 1977. Ed. Marina Mundt. Oslo.

Hákonar saga Ívarssonar. 1952. Ed. Jón Helgason and Jakob Benediktsson. Samfund 62.

Heimskringla edr Noregs Konunga-Sögor I–III. 1777–83. Ed. G. Schöning and Th. Thorlacius. Copenhagen.

Heimskringla eller Noregs Kongesagaer. 1868. Ed. C. R. Unger. Oslo.

Heimskringla I–IV. 1893–1901. Ed. Finnur Jónsson. Samfund 23. [Vol. IV is interpretation of verses.]

Heimskringla. 1911. Ed. Finnur Jónsson. Copenhagen. Reprinted 1925 and 1966.

Heimskringla I–III. 1941–51. Ed. Bjarni Aðalbjarnarson. ÍF 26–28. [This is the edition used throughout the present work.]

[Heimskringla translation, c. 1551:] Laurents Hanssøns Sagaoversættelse. 1898. Ed. Gustav Storm. Skrifter 1898 no. 1 (published 1899).

[Heimskringla translation, 1594:] Mattis Størssøn. Den Norske Krønike. 1962. Ed. Mikjel Sørlie. Oslo, Bergen.

[Heimskringla translation, c. 1599:] Samlede Skrifter af Peder Claussøn Friis. 1881. Ed. Gustav Storm. Oslo.

The Heimskringla, or, Chronicle of the Kings of Norway I–III. 1844. Trans. Samuel Laing. London. [See below for 1951 and 1964 revisions.]

[Heimskringla:] 1865. Trans. Mrs. Joseph J. Reed. The Adventures of Olaf Tryggveson. London.

[Heimskringla:] 1893–1905. The Stories of the Kings of Norway called the Round World (Heimskringla) I–IV. Trans. William Morris and Eiríkr Magnússon. London.

Heimskringla or the Lives of the Norse Kings by Snorre Sturlason. 1932. Trans. Erling Monsen and A.H. Smith. Cambridge.

[Heimskringla:] 1951 revision, further revised 1961. Snorri Sturluson, Heimskringla. Part Two: Sagas of the Norse Kings. Trans. Samuel Laing, revised Peter Foote. London.

[Heimskringla:] 1964 revision. Snorri Sturluson, Heimskringla. Part One: The Olaf Sagas I–II. Trans. Samuel Laing, revised Jacqueline Simpson. London.

Heimskringla, History of the Kings of Norway, by Snorri Sturluson. 1964. Trans. Lee M. Hollander. Austin. Repr. 1977.

[Heimskringla:] King Harald's saga. 1966. Trans. Magnus Magnusson and Hermann Pálsson. Harmondsworth.

Historia Norvegiæ: in Monumenta Historica Norvegiæ, 69–124.

Bibliography

[Icelandic Annals:] *Islandske Annaler indtil 1578*. 1888. Ed. Gustav Storm. Oslo.

ÍF = Íslenzk fornrit, Reykjavík.

Íslendinga saga: in *Sturlunga saga* 1946, I 229–534.

Íslendingabók. Landnámabók. 1968. Ed. Jakob Benediktsson. ÍF 1.

Jómsvíkinga saga / The Saga of the Jomsvikings. 1962. Trans. N. F. Blake. London.

Knýtlinga saga: see *Danakonunga sögur*.

Kristnisaga etc. 1905. Ed. B. Kahle. Altnordische Saga-Bibliothek 11. Halle.

Laxdœla saga. 1934. Ed. Einar Ól. Sveinsson. ÍF V.

[*Legendary Saga of Óláfr helgi* :] *Ólafs saga hins helga. Die "Legendarische Saga" über Olaf den Heiligen*. 1982. Ed. and trans. Anne Heinrichs *et al*. Heidelberg.

Magnúss saga skemmri, Magnúss saga lengri: see *Orkneyinga saga* 1965, 309-83.

Monumenta Historica Norvegiæ. 1880. Ed. Gustav Storm. Oslo.

Morkinskinna. 1932. Ed. Finnur Jónsson. Samfund 53.

Norwegian Homily Book: see *Gamal Norsk Homiliebok*.

Oddr Snorrason. *Saga Óláfs Tryggvasonar*. 1932. Ed. Finnur Jónsson. Copenhagen.

Óláfs saga Tryggvasonar in mesta I–II. 1958–61. Ed. Ólafur Halldórsson. EA, A 1–2.

[*Oldest saga of Óláfr helgi*:] *Otte Brudstykker af den ældste Saga om Olav den Hellige*. 1893. Ed. Gustav Storm. Oslo.

Orkneyinga saga. 1965. Ed. Finnbogi Guðmundsson. ÍF 34.

Passio et Miracula Sancti Olavi. 1881. Ed. Frederick Metcalfe. Oxford.

Prestssaga Guðmundar góða: in *Sturlunga saga* 1946, I 116–159.

Samfund = Samfund til Udgivelse af Gammel Nordisk Litteratur, Copenhagen.

Saxo Grammaticus. *The History of the Danes*. 1979. I English Text. Trans. Peter Fisher, ed. Hilda Ellis Davidson. Cambridge.

[*Separate Saga of Óláfr helgi*:] *Saga Ólafs konungs ens helga*. 1853. Ed. P. A. Munch and C. R. Unger. Oslo.

[*Separate Saga of Óláfr helgi*:] *Saga Óláfs konungs hins helga. Den Store Saga om Olav den Hellige* I–II. 1941. Ed. Oscar Albert Johnsen and Jón Helgason. Oslo. [This is the edition used throughout the present work.]

Skjaldedigtning = Den norsk-islandske Skjaldedigtning. 1912–15. Ed.

Finnur Jónsson. A I–II Tekst efter Håndskrifterne, B I–II Rettet Tekst. Copenhagen. Repr. 1967–73.

Skjǫldunga saga: see *Danakonunga sǫgur*.

Skrifter = Skrifter udgivne af Videnskabsselskabet i Christiania / Skrifter utgitt av det Norske Videnskaps-Akademie i Oslo. II. Historisk-Filosofisk Klasse.

[*Snorra Edda*:] *Edda Snorra Sturlusonar*. 1931. Ed. Finnur Jónsson. Copenhagen.

Sturlu saga: in *Sturlunga saga* 1946, I 61–114.

Sturlunga saga I–II. 1946. Ed. Jón Jóhannesson, Magnús Finnbogason and Kristján Eldjárn. Reykjavík.

Sturlunga saga I–II. 1970–74. Trans. Julia H. McGrew. I *The Saga of Hvamm-Sturla and The Saga of the Icelanders*, with introduction by R. George Thomas. II *Shorter Sagas of the Icelanders* (with R. George Thomas). New York.

Sverris saga. 1920. Ed. Gustav Indrebø. Oslo.

Theodrici Monachi, *Historia de Antiquitate Regum Norwagiensium*: in *Monumenta Historica Norvegiæ*, 1–68.

Vatnsdœla saga. Hallfreðar saga. Kormáks saga. 1939. Ed. Einar Ól. Sveinsson. ÍF 8.

Willelmi Malmesbiriensis Monachi de Gestis Regum Anglorum Libri Quinque I–II. 1887–89. Ed. William Stubbs. Rolls Series. London.

Worm, Ole: *Ole Worm's Correspondence with Icelanders*. 1948. Ed. Jakob Benediktsson. BA 7.

Yngvars saga víðfǫrla. 1912. Ed. Emil Olson. Samfund 39.

Þórðar saga hreðu. 1959. Ed. Jóhannes Halldórsson in *Kjalnesinga saga*, ÍF 14, 161–226.

Þórðar saga kakala: in *Sturlunga saga* 1946, II 1–86.

Ættartölur: in *Sturlunga saga* 1946, I 51–56.

II. SECONDARY LITERATURE
(Includes editions to which reference is made for introductory material rather than text.)

Allen, Richard F. 1971. *Fire and Iron. Critical Approaches to Njáls saga*. Pittsburgh.

Almqvist, Bo. 1965. *Norrön niddiktning I: Nid mot furstar*. Stockholm.

Almqvist, Bo. 1975. *The Uglier Foot*. Folklore Studies Pamphlets 1. Dublin.

Amory, Fredric. 1978. 'Saga Style in some Kings' Sagas, and Early Medieval Latin Narrative', *APS* 32, 67–86.

Andersen, Per Sveaas. 1977. *Samlingen av Norge og kristningen av landet*. Bergen.

Andersson, Theodore M. 1977. 'The Conversion of Norway according to Oddr Snorrason and Snorri Sturluson', *MScan* 10, 83–95.

Andersson, Theodore M. 1985. 'Kings' Sagas (*Konungasögur*)'. In Clover and Lindow, 197–238.

ANF = *Arkiv för nordisk filologi*.

APS = *Acta Philologica Scandinavica*.

Arngrímur Jónsson. 1609. *Crymogaea*. Hamburg. Ed. Jakob Benediktsson, *Arngrimi Jonae Opera* II, Copenhagen 1951. BA 10.

Berger, Alan. 1979. '*Heimskringla* and the Compilations'. Unpublished paper given at the Fourth International Saga Conference, Munich.

Berntsen, Toralf. 1923. *Fra sagn til saga: Studier i kongesagaen*. Oslo.

Beyschlag, Siegfried. 1950. *Konungasögur: Untersuchungen zur Königssaga bis Snorri*. BA 8.

Beyschlag, Siegfried. 1956. 'Snorri Sturluson: Heidnisches Erbe und christliches Mittelalter im Geschichtsdenken Altislands', *Sæculum* 7, 310–20.

Beyschlag, Siegfried. 1966. 'Snorris Bild des 12. Jahrhunderts in Norwegen'. In *Festschrift Walter Baetke*, ed. Kurt Rudoph et al., Weimar; 59–67.

Bjarni Aðalbjarnarson. 1937. *Om de norske kongers sagaer*. Skrifter 1936, no. 4.

Bjarni Einarsson. 1975. *Litterære forudsætninger for Egils saga*. Stofnun Árna Magnússonar á Íslandi, Rit 8. Reykjavík.

Bjarni Guðnason. 1963. *Um Skjöldungasögu*. Reykjavík.

Bjarni Guðnason. 1978. *Fyrsta sagan*. Studia Islandica 37.

Bjarni Guðnason. 1979. 'Frásagnarlist Snorra Sturlusonar'. In *Snorri: Átta Alda Minning*, 139–59.

Blackall, S. E. 1981. 'A Stylistic Study of the Sagas of Sturla Þórðarson and their Relationship to some other Thirteenth Century Icelandic Historical and Literary Sagas'. Unpublished Oxford D. Phil. thesis.

Blöndal, Sigfús. 1978. *The Varangians of Byzantium*. Trans. and revised Benedikt S. Benedikz. Cambridge.

Boesen, J.E. 1879. *Snorre Sturlesøn. Et nordisk tidsbillede fra det 13de hundredår*. Copenhagen.

Boyer, Régis. 1984. 'L'Historiographie médiévale islandaise'. In *La Chronique et l'Histoire au Moyen Âge*, ed. Daniel Poirion. Paris; 123–36.

Bugge, Alexander. 1909. 'Den islandske sagas oprindelse og

troværdighed', *Nordisk Tidskrift för vetenskap, konst och industri, utgifven af Letterstedtska Föreningen,* 407–19. Reprinted in Mundal 1977, 103–14.

Byock, Jesse L. 1988. *Medieval Iceland. Society, Sagas and Power.* Berkeley.

Carlyle, Thomas. 1875. *The Early Kings of Norway.* [Published with 'An Essay on the Portraits of John Knox', 1882.] London.

Ciklamini, Marlene. 1975. '*Ynglinga saga*: Its Function and its Appeal', *MScan* 8, 86–99.

Ciklamini, Marlene. 1978. *Snorri Sturluson.* Boston.

Ciklamini, Marlene. 1979. 'The Folktale in *Heimskringla* (*Hálfdanar saga svarta–Hákonar saga góða*)', *Folklore* 90, 204–16.

Ciklamini, Marlene. 1981. 'A Portrait of a Politician: Erlingr skakki in *Heimskringla* and in *Fagrskinna*', *Euphorion* 75, 275–87.

Clover, Carol J. 1974. 'Scene in Saga Composition', *ANF* 89, 57–83.

Clover, Carol J. 1982. *The Medieval Saga.* Ithaca and London.

Clover, Carol J. 1985. 'Icelandic Family Sagas (*Íslendingasögur*)'. In Clover and Lindow, 239–315.

Clover, Carol J. and John Lindow (eds). 1985. *Old Norse-Icelandic Literature. A Critical Guide.* Islandica 45. Ithaca and London.

Clunies Ross, Margaret. 1978. 'The Myth of Gefjon and Gylfi and its Function in *Snorra Edda* and *Heimskringla*', *ANF* 93, 149–65.

Clunies Ross, Margaret. 1987. *Skáldskaparmál: Snorri Sturluson's Ars Poetica and Medieval Theories of Language.* Odense.

Dahl, Ottar. 1959. *Norsk historieforskning i 19. og 20. århundre.* Oslo.

Derry, T. K. 1957. *A Short History of Norway.* London.

Eagleton, Terry. 1983. *Literary Theory. An Introduction.* Oxford.

Einar Ól. Sveinsson. 1937. *Sagnaritun Oddaverja.* Studia Islandica 1.

Einar Ól. Sveinsson. 1937–38. 'The Icelandic Family Sagas and the Period in which their Authors Lived', *APS* 12, 71–90.

Einar Ól. Sveinsson. 1953. *The Age of the Sturlungs. Icelandic Civilization in the Thirteenth Century.* Trans. Jóhann S. Hannesson. Islandica 36. Ithaca. Repr. New York, 1966.

Einar Ól. Sveinsson. 1976. 'Landvættasagan'. In *Minjar og Menntir*, 117–29.

Ellehøj, Svend. 1958. 'The Location of the Fall of Olaf Tryggvason'. In *Þriðji Víkingafundur / The Third Viking Congress, Reykjavík 1956.* Ed. Kristján Eldjárn. Reykjavík; 63–73.

Ellehøj, Svend. 1965. *Studier over den ældste norrøne historieskrivning.* BA 26.

Elton, G. R. 1967. *The Practice of History*. Sydney.
Evans, David A. H. 1981. 'King Agni: Myth, History or Legend?' In *Speculum Norroenum*, 89–105.
Faulkes, Anthony. 1978–9. 'Descent from the Gods', *MScan* 11 (published 1982), 92–125.
Finnbogi Guðmundsson. 1951. 'Hvernig lýsir Snorri Sturluson orðfæri manna?' In *Á góðu dægri. Afmæliskveðja til Sigurðar Nordals*. Reykjavík; 58–75.
Finnbogi Guðmnndsson. 1976. 'Um gamansemi Snorra í Óláfs sögu helga í Heimskringlu'. In *Minjar og Menntir*, 145–51.
Finnur Jónsson. 1923. *Den Oldnorske og Oldislandske Litteraturs Historie* II. 2nd edition. Copenhagen.
Finnur Jónsson. 1934. 'Til belysning af Snorri Sturlusons behandling af hans kilder', *ANF* 50, 181–96.
Fleischhauer, Wolfgang. 1938. *Kalf Arnason. Die Berührungen zwischen Heldenlied und Königssaga*. Cologne.
Fleischman, Suzanne. 1983. 'On the Representation of History and Fiction in the Middle Ages', *History and Theory* 23, 278–310.
Foote, Peter. 1965. *On the Saga of the Faroe Islanders. An Inaugural Lecture*. London.
Foote, Peter. 1974. 'Secular Attitudes in Early Iceland', *MScan* 7, 32–44.
Frank, Roberta. 1978. *Old Norse Court Poetry. The Dróttkvætt Stanza*. Islandica 42. Ithaca and London.
Frankis, John. 1976. 'An Old English Source for the Guðbrandsdal Episode in *Óláfs saga helga*'. Unpublished paper given at the Third International Saga Conference, Oslo.
Fry, Donald K. 1981. *Norse Sagas translated into English. A Bibliography*. New York.
Guðbrandur Vigfússon, ed. 1878. *Sturlunga saga* I–II. Oxford.
Gunnar Benediktsson. 1957. *Snorri Skáld í Reykholti*. Reykjavík.
Gunnes, Erik. 1976. *Rikssamling og Kristning, 800–1177. Norges Historie* 2. Oslo.
Gurevich, A. Ya. 1971. 'Saga and History. The "Historical Conception" of Snorri Sturluson', *MScan* 4, 42–53.
Hallan, Nils. 1972. 'Snorri fólgsnarjarl', *Skírnir* 146, 159–76.
Hallberg, Peter. 1962a. *The Icelandic Saga*. Trans. Paul Schach. Lincoln, Nebraska.
Hallberg, Peter. 1962b. *Snorri Sturluson och Egils saga Skallagrímssonar*. Studia Islandica 20.

Hallberg, Peter. 1968. *Stilsignalement och författerskap i norrön sagalitteratur.* Nordistica Gothoburgensia 3. Göteborg.

Hallberg, Peter. 1974. 'The Syncretic Saga Mind', *MScan* 7, 102–17. [Review article on Steblin-Kamenskij 1973.]

Hallberg, Peter. 1978. 'Direct Speech and Dialogue in Three Versions of Óláfs Saga Helga', *ANF* 93, 116–37.

Halldór Hermannsson. 1910. *Bibliography of the Sagas of the Kings of Norway.* Islandica 3. Ithaca.

Halldór Hermannsson. 1937. *The Sagas of the Kings and the Mythical-Heroic Sagas: Two Bibliographical Supplements.* Islandica 26. Ithaca.

Hastrup, Kirsten. 1985. *Culture and History in Medieval Iceland: An Anthropological Analysis of Structure and Change.* Oxford.

Hay, Denys. 1977. *Annalists and Historians.* London.

Heinrichs, Anne. 1976. 'Episoden als Strukturelemente in der Legendarischen Saga und ihre Varianten in anderen Olafssagas'. Unpublished paper given at the Third International Saga Conference, Oslo.

Helle, Knut. 1974. *Norge blir en Stat, 1130–1319.* Bergen.

Hermann Pálsson. 1973. Review of Steblin-Kamenskij 1973. *MScan* 6, 215–21.

Hjärne, Erland. 1952. 'Svethiud', *Namn och Bygd* 40, 91–183.

Hofmann, Dietrich. 1978–79. 'Sagaprosa als Partner von Skaldenstrophen', *MScan* 11 (published 1982), 68–81.

Holm-Olsen, Ludvig. 1980. 'Snorri Sturluson og Norðmenn', *Andvari*, Nýr flokkur 22, 25–37.

Holtsmark, Anne. 1938. 'Om de Norske Kongers Sagaer' [critique of Bjarni Aðalbjarnarson 1937], *Edda* 38, 145–64.

Jakob Benediktsson. 1955. 'Hvar var Snorri nefndur höfundur Heimskringlu?' *Skírnir* 129, 118–27.

Janzén, Assar. 1966. Review of *Heimskringla* translations of 1964 (Hollander and Laing revised Simpson). *Scandinavian Studies* 38, 251–59.

Jochens, Jenny M. 1987. 'The Female Inciter in the Kings' Sagas', *ANF* 102, 100–19.

Jón Jóhannesson. 1974. *A History of the Old Icelandic Commonwealth.* Trans. Haraldur Bessason. Manitoba.

Jónas Kristjánsson. 1976. 'The Legendary Saga'. In *Minjar og Menntir*, 281–93.

Jónas Kristjánsson. 1981. 'Learned Style or Saga Style?' In *Speculum Norroenum*, 260–92.

Jónas Kristjánsson. 1985. 'Sagas and Saints' Lives'. In *The Sixth International Saga Conference, Workshop Papers*. Copenhagen (Det Arnamagnæanske Institut), 551–71.

Jónas Kristjánsson. 1988. *Eddas and Sagas*. Trans. Peter Foote. Reykjavík.

Jones, Gwyn. 1968. *The Legendary History of Olaf Tryggvason*. 22nd W. P. Ker Memorial Lecture. Glasgow.

Kalinke, Marianne E. 1984. 'Sigurðar saga Jórsalafara: The Fictionalization of Fact in *Morkinskinna*', *Scandinavian Studies* 56, 152–67.

Kermode, Frank. 1979. 'What Precisely are the Facts?' In his *The Genesis of Secrecy: On the Interpretation of Narrative*. Cambridge, Mass., 101–23.

KLNM = *Kulturhistorisk leksikon for nordisk middelalder* 1–22. 1956-78. Copenhagen.

Knirk, James E. 1981. *Oratory in the Kings' Sagas*. Oslo.

Koht, Halvdan. 1914. 'Sagaernes opfatning av vår gamle historie', *Historisk Tidsskrift* [Norwegian], Series 5, 2, 379–96; repr. in Koht 1921, 76–91 and Mundal 1977, 127–37.

Koht, Halvdan. 1921. *Innhogg og utsyn i norsk historie*. Oslo.

Koht, Halvdan. 1931. *The Old Norse Sagas*. London.

Koht, Halvdan. 1954–6. 'Tendens i Heimskringla?' *Historisk Tidsskrift* [Norwegian] 37, 366–68.

Kossuth, Karen C. 1980. 'The Linguistic Basis of Saga Structure', *ANF* 95, 126–41.

Krag, Claus. 1989. 'Norge som odel i Harald Hårfagres ætt', *Historisk Tidsskrift* [Norwegian] 68, 288–302.

Krag, Claus. 1991. *Ynglingatal og Ynglingesaga*. Oslo.

Kuhn, Hans. 1976. 'Narrative Structure and Historicity in *Heimskringla*', *Parergon* 15, 30–42.

Larsen, Karen. 1948. *A History of Norway*. Princeton.

Lie, Hallvard. 1937. *Studier i Heimskringlas stil: Dialogene og talene*. Skrifter 1936, no. 5.

Lie, Hallvard. 1961. 'Heimskringla'. *KLNM* VI, cols. 299–302.

Liestøl, Knut. 1930. *The Origin of the Icelandic Family Sagas*. Oslo.

Lönnroth, Lars. 1964. *Tesen om de två kulturerna*. Scripta Islandica 15. Uppsala (published 1965).

Lönnroth, Lars. 1965. *European Sources of Icelandic Saga-Writing. An Essay based on Previous Studies*. Stockholm.

Lönnroth, Lars. 1976. 'Ideology and Structure in *Heimskringla*', *Parergon* 15, 16–29.
Louis-Jensen, Jonna. 1970. '"Syvende og ottende brudstykke". Fragmentet AM 325 IV a 4to.' In *Opuscula* IV. BA 30; 31–60.
Louis-Jensen, Jonna. 1977. *Kongesagastudier. Kompilationen Hulda-Hrokkinskinna.* BA 32.
Madelung, Margaret Arent. 1972. 'Snorri Sturluson and *Laxdœla*'. In *Saga og Språk: Studies in Language and Literature*, ed. John M. Weinstock. Austin; 45–92.
Madelung, A. Margaret Arent. 1973. 'Snorri Sturluson's Mirror of the Thirteenth Century'. Unpublished paper given at the Second International Saga Conference, Reykjavík.
Magerøy, Hallvard. 1976. 'Ynglingasaga'. *KLNM* XX, cols. 360–62.
Mâle, Émile. 1925. *L'Art Religieux du XIIIe siècle en France*. Paris.
Martin, John Stanley. 1976. 'Some Aspects of Snorri Sturluson's View of Kingship', *Parergon* 15, 43–54.
Maurer, Konrad. 1867. *Ueber die Ausdrücke: altnordische, altnorwegische und isländische Sprache*. Abhandlungen der königlich bayerischen Akademie der Wissenschaften XI, 2. Munich; 457–706.
Miller, J. Hillis. 1974. 'Narrative and History', *English Literary History* 41, 455–73.
Minjar og Menntir. 1976. *Afmælisrit helgað Kristjáni Eldjárn*. Ed. Guðni Kolbeinsson et al. Reykjavík.
Moberg, Ove. 1987. 'Snorre Sturlasson, Knut den store och Olav den hellige', *Saga och Sed*, 53–80.
Moe, Moltke. 1926. 'Eventyrlige sagn i vor ældre historie'. In his *Samlede Skrifter*, ed. Knut Liestøl, Oslo, II 85–210.
MScan = *Mediaeval Scandinavia*.
Munch, P. A. 1852–63. *Det norske Folks Historie* I–VIII. Oslo.
Mundal, Else. 1977. *Sagadebatt*. Oslo.
Mundal, Else. 1987. 'Refleksjonar kring historie, sanning og dikting. Metodiske problem ved å bruke sagalitteraturen som historiske kjelder', *Acta Jutlandica* 63, 15–25.
Njarðvík, Njörður P. 1979. '800-Year Anniversary of Snorri Sturluson: Creator of Documentary Fiction', *Atlantica and Iceland Review* 17: 4, 34–9.
Nordal, Sigurður. 1914. *Om Olaf den helliges saga*. Copenhagen.
Nordal, Sigurður. 1920. *Snorri Sturluson*. Reykjavík. Repr. 1973.
Nordal, Sigurður. 1941a. 'Gunnhildur konungamóðir', *Samtíð og saga* 1, 135–55.

Nordal, Sigurður. 1941b. 'Snorri Sturluson. Nokkurar hugleiðingar á 700. ártíð hans', Skírnir 115, 5–33.
Ólafur Halldórsson. 1979. 'Sagnaritun Snorra Sturlusonar'. In Snorri: Átta alda minning, 113–38.
Ordbog over det norrøne prosasprog: Registre / A Dictionary of Old Norse Prose: Indices. 1989. Copenhagen.
Paasche, Fredrik. 1916. 'Heimskringlas Olavssaga. Komposition – Stil – Karaktertegning', Edda 6, 365–83.
Paasche, Fredrik. 1922a. Snorre Sturlason og Sturlungerne. Oslo.
Paasche, Fredrik. 1922b. 'Tendens og syn i kongesagaen', Edda 17, 1–17.
Parergon = Parergon, Bulletin of the Australian and New Zealand Association for Medieval and Renaissance Studies.
Peters, Pamela. 1978. 'Skaldic Verses as a Historical Source', Parergon 22, 29–37.
Raabe, Gustav E. 1930. Snorre Sturlason. Fortegnelser over hans Kongesagaer og Edda. Oslo.
Ray, Roger. 1985. 'Historiography, Western European.' In Dictionary of the Middle Ages, New York, 6, 258–65.
Rieger, Gerd Enno. 1976. 'Sukzessionsemphase in der Heimskringla'. Unpublished paper given at the Third International Saga Conference, Oslo.
Saltnessand, Erik. 1963. 'Svolder eller Nesjar?' Historisk Tidsskrift [Norwegian] 42, 232–34.
Sandvik, Gudmund. 1955. Hovding og Konge i Heimskringla. Oslo.
Schreiner, Johan. 1927. Tradisjon og saga om Olav den hellige. Skrifter 1926, no. 1.
Scott, Forrest S. 1953–57. 'Valþjófr jarl: an English earl in Icelandic sources', Saga-Book 14, 78–94.
Seip, Didrik Arup. 1954. 'Snorre Sturlason og Tønsberg-tradisjon i Heimskringla'. In his Nye Studier i Norsk Språkhistorie. Oslo; 153–61.
Simon, John. 1976. 'Snorri Sturluson: his life and times', Parergon 15, 3–16.
Smalley, Beryl. 1974. Historians in the Middle Ages. London.
Snorrahátíð 1947–8. 1950. Gefið út af tilhlutan Snorranefndar. Reykjavík.
Snorri: Átta Alda Minning. 1979. [Ed. Gunnar Karlsson and Helgi Þorláksson.] Reykjavík.

Sogge, Ingebjørg. 1976. *Vegar til eit Bilete. Snorre Sturlason og Tore Hund.* Trondheim.

Sólveig Hauksdóttir. 1974. 'Snorri Sturluson og konungsvaldið', *Mímir* 21, 5–11.

Sørensen, Preben Meulengracht. 1977. *Saga og Samfund.* Copenhagen.

Speculum Norroenum. Norse Studies in Memory of Gabriel Turville-Petre. 1981. Ed. Ursula Dronke et al. Odense.

Spiegel, Gabrielle M. 1975. 'Political Utility in Medieval Historiography: a Sketch', *History and Theory* 14, 314–25.

Springer, Otto. 1939. 'The Style of the Old Icelandic Family Sagas', *Journal of English and Germanic Philology* 38, 107–28.

Steblin-Kamenskij, M. I. 1973. *The Saga Mind.* Trans. Kenneth H. Ober. Odense.

Stefán Karlsson. 1976. 'Kringum Kringlu', *Landsbókasafn Íslands. Árbók,* 5–25.

Storm, Gustav. 1873. *Snorre Sturlassöns Historieskrivning. En Kritisk Undersögelse.* Copenhagen.

Storm, Gustav. 1883. 'Har Haandskrifter af "Heimskringla" angivet Snorre Sturlassøn som Kongesagaernes Forfatter?', *ANF* 1, 47–61.

Studia Islandica = Studia Islandica / Íslenzk Fræði. Reykjavík.

Sverrir Tómasson. 1975. 'Tækileg vitni'. In *Afmælisrit Björns Sigfússonar* [ed. Björn Teitsson et al.]. Reykjavík; 251–87.

Sverrir Tómasson. 1988. *Formálar íslenskra sagnaritara á miðöldum.* Stofnun Árna Magnússonar á Íslandi, Rit 33. Reykjavík.

Tucker, John. 1989. 'Introduction: Sagas of the Icelanders'. In *Sagas of the Icelanders, A Book of Essays,* ed. John Tucker. New York and London.

Turville-Petre, G. 1937–45, 'The first three hands of *Reykjaholts máldagi* ', *Saga-Book* 12, 195–204.

Turville-Petre, G. and E. S. Olszewska (trans.). 1942. *The Life of Gudmund the Good, Bishop of Holar.* London.

Turville-Petre, G. 1953. *Origins of Icelandic Literature.* Oxford.

Turville-Petre, E.O.G. 1976. *Scaldic Poetry.* Oxford.

Vésteinn Ólason. 1988. 'Planer om en utgave av *Heimskringla*'. In *Tekstkritisk Teori og Praksis,* ed. Bjarne Fidjestøl et al. Oslo; 130–37.

Weber, Gerd Wolfgang. 1987. 'Intellegere historiam. Typological perspectives of Nordic prehistory (in Snorri, Saxo, Widukind and others)', *Acta Jutlandica* 63, 95–141.

Weibull, Curt. 1964. 'Snorris Skildring av Sveriges Samhälls- och Författningsförhållanden. Torgny Lagman'. In his *Källkritik och*

Historia. Stockholm; 241–47.
Weibull, Lauritz. 1911. *Kritiska undersökninger i nordens historia omkring år 1000.* Lund.
Wessén, Elias. 1928–9. 'Om Snorres Prologus till Heimskringla och till den särskilda Olovssagan', *APS* 3, 52–62.
Wessén, Elias (ed.). 1952. *Snorri Sturluson. Ynglingasaga.* Nordisk Filologi A 6. Stockholm.
Wessén, Elias. 1964. 'Lagman och lagsaga', *Nordisk Tidskrift för Vetenskap, Konst och Industri utgiven av Letterstedtska Föreningen* 40, 73–92.
Whaley, Diana. 1987. 'The Miracles of S. Olaf in Snorri Sturluson's Heimskringla'. In *Proceedings of the Tenth Viking Congress,* ed. James E. Knirk. Oslo; 325–42.
White, Hayden V. 1975. 'Historicism, History and the Figurative Imagination', *History and Theory* 14, Beiheft: Essays on Historicism, 48–67.
White, Hayden. 1978. 'The Historical Text as Literary Artifact'. In his *Tropics of Discourse. Essays in Cultural Criticism.* Baltimore and London; 81–100.
White, Hayden. 1984. 'The Question of Narrative in Contemporary Historical Theory', *History and Theory* 23, 1–33.
Widding, Ole. 1976. 'Heimskringla som Kompilationsarbejde'. Unpublished paper given at the Third International Saga Conference, Oslo.

INDEX

Acta Sancti Olavi 66
Adam, bishop 24
Adam of Bremen 117
Aðalráðr, English king 53
Ágrip 64, 65, 67, 70, 74, 75, 80, 81, 90, 117, 118, 120, 122, 132, 140
Álfhildr 93
Álfr Alreksson, Swedish king 116
Álptanes 23
Alrekr Agnason, Swedish king 133
Andrés skjaldarband 24
Andvaka 33
Anglo-Saxon Chronicle 116
Ari Þorgilsson 14, 17, 30, 41, 55, 56, 58, 65, 69, 74, 75, 77, 78, 84, 114, 120, 126, 135, 137
Arnbjǫrn, priest 37
Arnfinnr Þjófsson 36
Arngrímr Brandsson, abbot 29
Arngrímur Jónsson 14, 73
Árni Magnússon 43, 62
Árni Magnússon óreiða 34, 36, 37
Arnljótr gellini 108, 139
Arnórr jarlaskáld 76, 82, 91
Arnórr Tumason 30
Ásbirningar 22, 34
Ásbjǫrn af Meðalhúsum 95, 100
Ásbjǫrn Selsbani 103, 107, 132
Ásgarðr 81
Ásgeir Jónsson 43, 44, 62
Áskell Magnússon 33
Áslákr hólmskalli 142
Ásta Guðbrandsdóttir 52, 94
Ástríðr Óláfsdóttir Svíakonungs 40, 61

Baden, G. L. 114
Barthes, Roland 127
Bede 18
Bergen 32
Berger, Alan 16-17
Bergliot 11
Bergljót Hákonardóttir jarls 95, 96
Berntsen, Toralf 79-80
Bersastaðir 9, 35, 37

Bersi inn auðgi 29
Bersǫglisvísur 76
Bjarkamál 98
Bjarmaland 24
Bjarnar saga Hítdœlakappa 75
Bjarni Aðalbjarnarson 41, 44, 47-8
Bjarni Guðnason 71
Bjǫrn stallari 103
Bjǫrn Þorvaldsson 33, 34
Bjørnson, Bjørnstjerne 12
Bókn 119
Borg 29, 30, 31, 38
Borgarfjǫrðr 9, 23, 30, 35
Borgundarholm 142
Breta sǫgur 128
Bugge, Alexander 80
Búi digri 84-5, 132, 141
Bull, Edvard 114
Búrizláfr (Boleslav), Wendish king 117

Carlyle, Thomas 12, 112, 138
Cicero 129
Constantinople 98
Crymogaea 14
Cuthbert, saint, life of 18

Dagr Hringsson 103
Dala-Guðbrandr 64, 85, 104, 116
Dalir 23
Dansa-Bergr 32
Dares Phrygius 128

Edda, Elder 63, 81-2
Edda, Snorra see Snorra Edda
Egill Skalla-Grímsson 38
Egils saga 10, 16, 26, 75, 114, 136
Einarr skálaglamm 76
Einarr Skúlason 38, 121-2
Einarr þambarskelfir 86, 95, 101, 109, 118
Einarr Þveræingr Eyjólfsson 40, 64, 96, 123
Eindriði Einarsson 101
Eiríkr Agnason, Swedish king 133

Index

Eiríkr blóðøx Haraldsson, king 54, 68, 104, 108, 110, 117, 122
Eiríkr jarl Hákonarson 52, 85, 142
Eiríkr Knútsson, Swedish king 33
Eiríkr Magnússon 50, 54
Eiríkr Oddsson 15, 65, 70, 78, 92, 120
Eiríksflokkr 117
Eiríksmál 121
Elgar, Edward 12
Emundr lǫgmaðr 88
Erlingr Eiríksson, king 54, 108
Erlingr Skjálgsson 67, 103, 119
Eyjafjǫrðr 9, 23
Eyjólfr, friend of Snorri 32
Eymundar þáttr 46
Eyrbyggja saga 29, 38, 75
Eysteinn Erlendsson, archbishop 26, 66
Eysteinn Magnússon, king 80, 101, 104, 109
Eyvellingagoðorð 30
Eyvindarstaðir 37
Eyvindr kinnrifa 100
Eyvindr skáldaspillir 55, 76, 108, 122, 123
Eyvindr úrarhorn 103

Faeroes 73
Fagrskinna 14, 17, 64, 69, 71, 72, 74, 75, 76, 85, 94, 95, 97, 99, 100, 103, 117, 118, 122, 124, 131, 132, 137
Finnr Árnason 82, 95, 101
Finnr Skoptason 88
Finnur Jónsson 47-8
First Grammatical Treatise 73
Fitjar 104
Flateyjarbók 13, 18, 45, 46, 67, 71, 73, 78, 84, 85, 137, 142
Fljótshlíð 34
Florence of Worcester 118
Flæmingjaland 53
Foote, Peter 50
Forminterra 90
Fóstbrœðra saga 46
Foster, Paul 12
Frakkland 38

Frigg 132
Friis, Peder Claussøn 14, 49, 58
Fræði 125
Fýrisvellir 87, 105
Færeyinga saga 10, 40, 46, 72, 73, 97

Gamal norsk Homiliebok (= Norwegian Homily Book) 66, 90, 131
Garðar 53, 94
Gautland (see also Västergötland) 33, 103
Gefjun 15, 120
Geisli 38, 46, 121
Geoffrey of Monmouth 128
Ghengiz Khan 24
Gizurr Hallsson 18, 38
Gizurr Þorvaldsson 29, 34, 35, 36, 37
Glúmr Geirason 122
Glymdrápa 122
Glælognskviða 76
Gormr inn gamli, Danish king 117
Grégoríús Dagsson 88, 98
Gregory VII 25
Gregory the Great 81
Grettis saga 75
Grieg, Edvard 11
Grímsey 24, 25, 124
Guðbrandsdalr (Gudbrandsdal) 79, 81
Guðbrandur Vigfússon 14, 16
Guðmundar saga (see also Prestssaga) 26, 34
Guðmundr Arason, bishop 20, 24, 25, 26, 29, 30, 32, 40, 76
Guðmundr inn ríki 38
Guðný Bǫðvarsdóttir 29, 30
Guðríðr Guthormsdóttir 78
Gunnhildr konungamóðir 108, 117
Gunnlaugr Leifsson 18, 68
Gunnlaugr ormstunga 38
Guthormr sindri 122
Gylfi 15
Gǫngu-Hrólfr 53, 93

Hafrsfjǫrðr 122
Hákonarmál 76, 121
Hákonar saga góða 61, 76, 93, 102, 110, 122

Hákonar saga Hákonarsonar 20, 28, 32, 33, 37, 46
Hákonar saga herðibreiðs 77, 88, 94, 98
Hákonar saga Ívarssonar 68, 120
Hákon góði Aðalsteinsfóstri Haraldsson, king 68, 100, 101, 104, 109–10, 122
Hákon Hákonarson, king 27–8, 29, 32, 33, 36, 37, 46, 47, 71, 76, 100
Hákon jarl galinn 32, 33, 76
Hákon jarl Sigurðarson 14, 40, 52, 89, 100, 101, 107, 120
Háleygjatal 55, 56, 121, 140
Hálfdan svarti Guðrøðarson, king 68, 72, 80, 105, 110
Hálfdanar saga svarta 52, 105, 110, 116
Hallbera Snorradóttir 30, 34, 35, 36, 37
Hallberg, Peter 16
Halldórr ókristni 117
Halldórr skvaldri 102
Halldórr Snorrason 38, 79, 93
Hallfreðar saga 10, 85
Hallfreðr vandræðaskáld Óttarsson 75
Hallfríðr Þorgilsdóttir 30
Hallr Koðránsbani 98
Hallveig Ormsdóttir 32, 33–4, 40
Hanssøn, Laurents 14, 49, 57, 58
Haraldr blátǫnn Gormsson, Danish king 14, 63, 117, 125
Haraldr gilli Magnússon, king 43, 53, 71, 95, 97, 109
Haraldr gráfeldr Eiríksson, king 14, 54, 108
Haraldr Guðinason, English king 96, 97, 106, 116, 133
Haraldr hárfagri Hálfdanarson, king 19, 26, 40, 52, 55, 56, 68, 70, 80, 90, 99, 100, 102, 107, 109–10, 111, 121, 125, 141
Haraldr jarl Maddaðarson 38
Haraldr Sigurðarson, king 38, 59, 68, 71, 76, 78, 79, 80, 86, 90–1, 93, 95, 96, 97, 101, 102, 106, 108, 109, 115, 116, 118, 119, 123, 133, 137

Haraldskvæði 122
Haralds saga gráfeldar 54, 60, 109, 116
Haralds saga hárfagra 53, 78, 80, 90, 92, 93, 100, 102, 107, 110, 116, 122, 126
Haralds saga Sigurðarsonar 43, 58, 88, 89, 90–1, 93, 95, 96, 97, 98, 101, 106, 108, 115, 118, 122, 123, 142
Haraldssona saga 71, 77, 92
Hárekr ór Þjóttu 79, 88
Hastings (Helsingjaport) 96, 122
Háttatal 9, 33, 76
Haugesund 38
Haukdœlir 22, 28, 33, 34
Hauksbók 74, 81
Hávarðr hǫggvandi 89
Heiðarvíga saga 75
Hekla 24
Helga Sturludóttir 29
Helganes 116
Helsingjaland 102
Henry of Huntingdon 128
Herburt 32
Herdís Bersadóttir 29, 30, 34
Hermann Pálsson 51
Historia Norvegiæ 70, 117, 118
Hítará 31
Hjalti Skeggjason 103
Hjǫrungavágr 84, 85, 120, 124, 132, 141
Hlaðir, jarls of 52, 73, 99
Hlýrskógsheiðr 53, 124, 130
Hólar 22, 24, 25, 30, 74, 76
Hollander, Lee M. 51
Hrafn á Eyri, sons of 23
Hrafnkels saga 130, 136
Hringr Dagsson, king in Heiðmǫrk 133
Hróa þáttr 46
Hrólfr kraki 35, 73
Hryggjarstykki 65, 66, 68, 70–1, 72, 120, 140
Hrœrekr Dagsson, king in Heiðmǫrk 95, 96, 100, 123, 133
Hulda-Hrokkinskinna 16, 44, 46, 48, 76
Hulð 99, 110

Index 163

Húnavatnsþing 30
Hungrvaka 18, 19, 74, 79
Hvammr 29, 30, 35
Hvamm-Sturla see Sturla Þórðarson

Ibsen, Henrik 12
Icelandic annals (see also *Islandske Annaler*) 20, 24, 29
Ingi Bárðarson, king 27, 32
Ingi Haraldsson, king 70, 88
Ingibjǫrg Snorradóttir 30, 34, 35
Ingibjǫrg Þorgeirsdóttir 29
Ingigerðr Óláfsdóttir Svíakonungs 40, 97, 103
Ingunar-Freyr 56
Islandske Annaler (see also *Icelandic annals*) 14, 24, 37
Ísleifr, bishop 14
Íslendingabók 17, 69, 74, 75, 84, 113
Íslendinga saga 13, 18, 19, 20, 23, 26, 28, 29, 30, 31, 32, 33, 34, 35, 36, 37
Ívarr af Útvíkum 24

Jakob Benediktsson 14
Jamtaland 102, 109
Járn-Skeggi 107
Jessen, E. 114
Jómsvíkinga drápa 132
Jómsvíkinga saga 63, 64, 68, 73, 84, 85, 124, 133, 141, 142
Jomsvikings 84, 85, 86, 132, 141, 142
Jón Árnason 102–3
Jón Eggertsson 43
Jón Loptsson 18, 25, 29, 31, 33, 38, 39, 69, 79
Jón murtr Snorrason 30, 33, 34, 35
Jón sterkr 32
Jón Þórðarson 46
Jón Ǫgmundarson, bishop 74
Jónas Jónsson frá Hriflu 10
Jǫrmunrekkr 82
Kálfr Árnason 48, 53, 86, 97, 109, 132

Kálfr Arnfinnsson 48
Karl Jónsson 68

Karli í Langey 107
Kekaumenos 116
Ketill Þorsteinsson, bishop 18
King Olaf 12
Klœngr Bjarnarson 34, 37
Knútr inn ríki Sveinsson, king of Denmark and England 53, 65, 67, 87–8, 93, 100, 106, 109, 110, 118, 119
Knýtlinga saga 13, 14, 47
Koht, Halvdan 99
Kolbeinn Sigvatsson 36
Kolbeinn ungi Arnórsson 34, 35, 36, 37
Kolskeggr auðgi 34
Konungahella 79
Kormáks saga 75
Kristín Nikulássdóttir 33, 76
Kristni saga 68, 74
Kristni þáttr 64, 67

Laing, Samuel 49–50, 112
Landkjenning 11
Landnámabók 18, 26, 67
Laxdœla saga 26, 75, 110, 136
Legendary Saga of Óláfr helgi 64, 67, 74, 81, 85, 86, 94, 98, 118, 120, 123, 131
Lífssaga Óláfs helga see Styrmir Kárason
Logos nuthetikos 116
Longfellow, Henry 12
Loptr Pálsson 33
Louis-Jensen, Jonna 44
Lucan 128
Lundarmannagoðorð 30
Lǫgrinn (= Mälaren) 120

Magnús allsherjargoði 31
Magnús berfœttr Óláfsson, king 13, 38, 68, 79, 88, 96, 99, 109, 125
Magnús blindi Sigurðarson, king 71
Magnús Einarsson, bishop 79
Magnús Erlingsson, king 14, 27, 38, 46
Magnús góði Óláfsson, king 46, 53, 68, 82, 93, 94, 97, 101, 110, 116, 118, 124, 130, 131

Magnús lagabœtir Hákonarson, king 27, 46
Magnús of Orkney, saint, saga of 46
Magnús Pálsson 30, 32
Magnús Þórhallsson 46
Magnúss saga berfœtts 96, 98, 102, 104, 109, 125, 142
Magnúss saga blinda ok Haralds gilla 43, 71, 88, 93, 94, 97
Magnúss saga Erlingssonar 38, 59, 111
Magnúss saga góða 13, 53, 66, 76, 88, 93, 96, 97, 108, 110, 111, 116, 124, 131
Magnúss saga lengri 13
Magnúss saga skemmri 13
Magnusson, Magnus 51
Magnússona saga 66, 80, 90, 92, 98, 104, 109, 110, 122
Máni, skald 32
Maríu saga 19
Markús Sigvatsson 36
Markús Skeggjason 38
Maurer, Konrad 15, 16
Melr 31
Miðfjǫrðr 31
Monsen, Erling 50
Morkinskinna 10, 41, 45, 46, 49, 63, 64, 65, 71, 72, 74, 75, 76, 79, 88, 91–2, 95, 97–8, 99, 101, 103, 109, 120, 131, 137
Morris, William 11, 50, 51
Mortensen, Jens 49
Mýramenn 29
Mälaren (= Lǫgrinn) 120

Nesjar 118
Nesjavísur 121
Niðaróss (see also Trondheim) 25, 26, 36, 66
Niebelung(s) 81, 118
Nikulás Árnason, bishop 27
Niz 64, 97
Njála, Njáls saga 39, 75, 96, 113, 115, 136
Nordal, Sigurður 54–5
Nóregs konungatal 38–9, 69

Norwegian Homily Book (= *Gamal norsk Homiliebok*) 66, 90

Oddaverjar 18, 22, 23, 28, 33, 74
Oddi 23, 29, 38, 39
Oddr Snorrason 18, 41, 64, 68, 74, 85, 89, 103, 117, 118, 133, 137, 141, 142
Oddverja annáll 14
Óðinn 73, 132
Óláfr digri / helgi Haraldsson (St Óláfr) 7, 8, 16, 18, 38, 40, 42, 46, 48, 50, 52, 53, 55, 56, 64, 66, 67, 68, 70, 71, 74, 75, 76, 78, 79, 81, 89, 90, 92, 93, 94, 95, 96, 97, 100, 102, 103, 105, 106, 107–8, 109, 110, 111, 116, 118, 119, 120, 121, 123, 124, 125, 131, 132, 135, 137, 141
Óláfr Eiríksson Svíakonnngr 97, 102, 103, 118, 124, 125
Óláfr hvítaskáld Þórðarson 18, 19, 36, 39, 47, 76
Óláfr kyrri Haraldsson, king 59, 76, 101, 109
Óláfr trételgja Ingjaldsson, king 79
Óláfr Tryggvason, king 13, 16, 46, 52, 66, 68, 74, 75, 80, 81, 87, 89, 104, 107, 108, 109, 110, 111, 117, 118, 120, 131, 133, 135, 141, 142
Óláfs saga helga 16, 40, 42, 44, 48, 52, 53, 54, 55, 56, 59, 61, 64, 66, 67, 68, 72, 73, 76, 78, 86, 88, 89, 90, 92, 93, 94, 95, 97, 98, 100, 102, 103, 104, 105, 106, 107, 108, 109, 111, 116, 118, 119, 120, 121, 123, 124, 125, 131, 132, 133, 139, 140, 142
Óláfs saga kyrra 59–60, 76
Óláfs saga Tryggvasonar 11, 12, 45, 49, 61, 63, 64, 66, 73, 74, 76, 77, 80, 81, 85, 86, 87, 89, 91, 92, 93, 94, 100, 104, 105, 107, 108, 109, 110, 111, 116, 121, 123, 124, 125, 132, 133, 136, 141
Óláfs saga Tryggvasonar in mesta 13, 16, 46, 68, 73

Index

Ólafur Halldórsson 14
Olav, Crown Prince of Norway 10
Olav Trygvason 11
Olavus (= Óláfr Haraldsson) 66
Oldest saga of Óláfr helgi 41, 67, 75, 106, 124, 137
Orkney 38, 54
Orkneyinga saga 10, 13, 40, 46, 63, 65, 72–3
Ormr Bjarnarson 34
Ormr inn langi 64, 87, 109, 142
Ormr Jónsson 33, 39
Órœkja Snorrason 23, 30, 34, 35, 36, 37
Oslo 24, 118–19
Ótta (= Otto II of Saxony) 125
Óttarr svarti 56

Paasche, Fredrik 99
Páll Jónsson, bishop 25, 33, 38, 39
Passio et Miracula beati Olaui 66
Pedersen, Christiern 14
Peringskiöld, Johan 47, 57
Pétr Skúlason 36
Prestssaga Guðmundar góða 32

Ragnhildr Sigurðardóttir 110
Randvér 81
Rang rivers 39
Rauðr inn rammi 87, 105
Rauðúlfs þáttr 45
Ré 72
Reed, Mrs Joseph 11
Rekstefja 46
Reykdœla saga 75
Reykjaholt 10, 13, 20, 23, 30, 32, 35, 37
Reykjaholtsmáldagi 20, 32
Reykjanes 31
Rome 26, 38
Rómverja saga 128
Rouen, jarls of 116
Rúgmann, Jón 49
Rǫgnvaldr jarl Úlfsson 95, 103

Sallust 128
Sauðafell 23, 36

Saxo Grammaticus 65, 115, 128, 130, 132
Schjøtt, Steinar 10
Schöning, Gerhard 47, 49, 58
Scilly Isles 81
Sefsurð 64
Seip, D. A. 78–9
Sel-Þórir 103
Separate Saga of Óláfr helgi 7, 8, 13, 14, 18, 19, 33, 41, 42, 43, 44, 45, 46, 47, 48, 49, 52–5, 56, 57, 59, 60, 61, 62, 67, 69, 78, 85, 114, 123, 124, 131
Sibjørnus 12
Sicily 96–7, 102, 106, 123
Sigríðr Skjálgsdóttir 107, 116
Sigríðr stórráða Tóstadóttir 81, 116, 117, 118, 136
Sigurd Jorsalfar 11–12
Sigurðr, bishop 96, 100, 105
Sigurðr Fáfnisbani 118
Sigurðr Hákonarson Hlaðajarl 54
Sigurðr hjǫrtr Helgason. king in Hringaríki 65, 77
Sigurðr Jórsalafari Magnússon, king 15, 64, 80, 98, 99, 101, 102, 104, 110, 125
Sigurðr, Norwegian supporter of Snorri 32
Sigurðr Ribbungakonungr 24
Sigurðr slembidjákn / slembir (?)Magnússon 71, 93–4
Sigurðr sýr Hálfdanarson 52, 89, 95, 96, 109
Sigurðr tafsi Eindriðason, archbishop 26
Sigvatr Sturluson 23, 25, 26, 29, 30, 32, 35, 36,
Sigvatr Þórðarson 56, 66, 76, 94–5, 97, 102, 120, 121, 122, 124, 142
Simpson, Jacqueline 50
Skagafjǫrðr 9, 22, 30, 36
Skálaholt 22, 23, 24, 25, 38, 39, 74, 79
Skerfsurð 64
Skjǫldr 73, 120
Skjǫldunga saga 65, 73

Skopti Ǫgmundarson 96
Skúli jarl Bárðarson 27, 28, 29, 32, 33, 36, 76
Smith, A. H. 50
Snorra Edda / Prose Edda 10, 14, 24, 33, 56, 76, 82, 86, 125, 132
Snorralaug 34
Snorri goði 29, 38, 79
Snorrungagoðorð 29, 30, 35
Snæfellsnes 23
Snæfríðr Svásadóttir 80, 90
Solveig Ormsdóttir 33, 34, 36, 40
Sparfwenfelt 43
Stafaholt 34
Stamford Bridge (Stanforðabryggjur) 49, 64, 91, 101, 142
Steigar-Þórir Þórðarson 78, 102
Steingrímur Pálsson 47
Steinn Skaptason 124
Stiklarstaðir 53, 64, 66, 72, 75, 95, 98, 101, 103, 108, 120, 123, 139
Storm, Gustav 10
Stúfr blindi 91
Sturla Bárðarson 32, 35
Sturla Sigvatsson 13, 18, 23, 25, 26, 34, 35, 36
Sturla Þórðarson 18, 20, 30, 31, 32, 33, 34, 36, 39, 46, 74, 76, 113
Sturla Þórðarson (Hvamm-Sturla) 21, 22, 29
Sturlu saga 21, 29, 40
Sturlunga saga 20, 21, 24, 25, 29, 31, 39, 135
Sturlungar 9, 21, 22, 23, 35–6, 79
Styrbjarnar þáttr 46
Styrmir Kárason 18, 19, 32, 36, 39, 45, 67–8, 137
Størssøn, Mattis 14, 49
Suðrvík 53
Sveinn Álfífuson, Danish king 96
Sveinn jarl Hákonarson 52
Sveinn tjúguskegg Haraldsson, Danish king 53, 106, 117, 118
Sveinn Úlfsson, Danish king 97, 109
Sverrir Sigurðsson 17, 27, 32, 66, 68, 69, 76, 100, 114, 125
Sverris saga 10, 46, 66, 68, 96
Svignaskarð 31

Svínafell 23
Svínfellingar 22
Svǫlð 13, 59, 85, 86, 101, 114, 117, 118, 120, 125, 141
Sæmundr Loptsson 29
Sæmundr Sigfússon 18, 38, 69, 72, 114
Sørensen, studiosus 12

Tafl-Bergr 32
Theodoricus 65, 66, 69–70, 132
Thorlacius, Skúli 47
Times Literary Supplement 11
Tómass saga erkibiskups 46
Torfæus (Þormóður Torfason) 43
Tósti Guðinason 82, 96, 106, 109
Trójumanna saga 128
Trondheim (see also Niðaróss) 25, 32, 38, 66, 72
Trøndelag 79
Tumi Sigvatsson 24
Túnsberg (Tønsberg) 32, 78–9

Úlfr jarl 105
Úlfr stallari 86
Úlfreksfjǫrðr 96
Ulster 13, 98
Unger, C. R. 47, 49, 50, 54
Upplǫnd 52, 76, 90, 103, 119
Uppsala 79, 81
Útfarardrápa 102

Vagn Ákason 110, 142
Valdimarr Knútsson 14
Valland 53
Valþjófr, jarl in England 122
Varangians (see also Væringjar) 97
Vatnsfirðingar 22
Vatnsfjǫrðr 35
Vellekla 76, 123
Vermaland (Värmland) 79
Vestfirðir 23, 35
Viðey 32
Víðidalr 31
Víðimýrr 31
Víðkunnr Jónsson 103
Vigdís Sturludóttir 29
Vigeland, Gustav 12

Vígfúss Víga-Glúmsson 124, 142
Vígi 142
Vík 78, 131
Víkingarvísur 102
Vilhjálmr, conqueror of England 93, 116
Vincent of Beauvais 17
Vænir (= Vänern) 73
Væringjar / Varangians 78, 97
Vänern (= Vænir) 73
Västergötland (see also Gautland) 37, 79

Weibull, Lauritz 117-18
William of Malmesbury 128, 130, 134
William of Sabina, cardinal 27, 28
Worm, Ole 14, 49, 57

Ynglinga saga 43, 52, 57, 58, 62, 63, 64, 65, 73, 74, 87, 88, 91, 92, 99, 104, 105, 110, 116, 120, 132, 133, 140
Ynglingar 56, 99, 110
Ynglingatal 55, 56, 121, 140
Yngvars saga víðfǫrla 18
Yngvi Alreksson, Swedish king 116
Yngvi-Freyr 56
York 96, 122

Þingeyrar 25, 68
Þingvǫllr 22, 79
Þjóðólfr inn Hvinverski 55, 65, 133
Þóra Skagadóttir 107
Þórarinn loftunga 66, 76
Þórarinn Nefjólfsson 54, 64, 80, 88, 142
Þorbjǫrn hornklofi 122
Þórdís Snorradóttir 30, 34
Þórðar saga hreðu 13
Þórðar saga kakala 32, 37
Þórðr Bǫðvarsson í Gǫrðum 30

Þórðr kakali Sigvatsson 37
Þórðr krókr Sigvatsson 36
Þórðr Sturluson 23, 29, 34, 35
Þórðr Þorvaldsson 23
Þorfinnr hausakljúfr 77
Þorfinnr Sigurðarson, jarl of Orkney 76
Þorgeirr af Kvistsstǫðum 103
Þorgils saga skarða 37
Þorgils Snorrason 78
Þorgnýr lǫgmaðr 40, 95, 124
Þórir, archbishop 26
Þórir hundr 67, 78, 79, 95, 96, 100, 107, 131, 132
Þorkell inn hávi 53
Þorkell leira 110
Þorkell Skallason 122
Þorlákr Rúnólfsson, bishop 18
Þorlákr Þórhallsson, bishop and saint 25, 74
Þorleifr í Gǫrðum 36
Þorleifr spaki 116
Þorljótr frá Bretalœk 31
Þormóðr Kolbrúnarskáld 98
Þormóður Torfason (= Torfæus) 43
Þóroddr Snorrason 97, 139
Þórr 107
Þórsnessþing 35
Þorsteinn Ívarsson 30
Þorvaldr Vatnsfirðingr Snorrason 23, 34, 35
Þorviðr stammi 95
Þrándheimr 107
Þyri Haraldsdóttir 89, 94, 117, 118

Ælfric 81
Æsir 125
Æskil (= Áskell) 33

Qnundr Óláfsson Swedish king 67
Ǫrlygsstaðir 23, 36